941.081
ELD
13641 ✓

7802

VICTORIAN IMPERIALISM

VICTORIAN IMPERIALISM

C C Eldridge

HODDER & STOUGHTON
London Sydney Auckland Toronto

British Library Cataloguing in Publication Data

Eldridge, C C
    Victorian Imperialism
    1. Imperialism 2. Great Britain – Foreign relations –
    1837–1901 3. Great Britain – Foreign relations
    1901–1910
I. Title
321'.03'0941 JV1017

ISBN 0–340–20504–0
    0–340–20505–9 Pbk

ISBN 0 340 20504 0 Boards
ISBN 0 340 20505 9 Paperback

Printed and bound in Great Britain for Hodder and Stoughton Educational,
a division of Hodder and Stoughton Ltd, Mill Road, Dunton Green, Sevenoaks, Kent,
by Morrison and Gibb Ltd, London and Edinburgh

Acknowledgments

The author and publishers wish to thank the National Trust and the Macmillan Company of London and Basingstoke for permission to include verses from Rudyard Kipling's 'The White Man's Burden' and 'Recessional' (from *The Definitive Edition of Rudyard Kipling's Verse*).

For permission to reproduce the illustrations, thanks are due to the Mansell Collection (illustrations pp 1, 6–7, 16); Mary Evans Picture Library (pp 2–3, 8, 9, 11, 15); Radio Times Hulton Picture Library (pp 4, 11, 14); the India Office Library (p 5); National Film Board of Canada (pp 8–9); Anne Horton (p 10); Weidenfeld and Nicholson (p 11); Popperfoto (pp 12–13).

The author also wishes to thank Professor W. D. McIntyre, Dr. M. E. Chamberlain and Professor M. R. D. Foot for their helpful comments on the text. Mr. C. I. Lewis kindly drew the maps and Mrs. Inez Crowdy typed the manuscript with her usual speed and precision. My wife read the proofs, compiled the index and, in her professional capacity as a librarian, assisted me in many ways too numerous to list. I was also fortunate in obtaining financial assistance from the Pantyfedwen Fund of Saint David's University College.

Finally, I would like to record my appreciation of the help and encouragement received from Mr. R. Ben Jones, Mr. H. S. Foster, Mr. A. Raven, and the staff of Hodder and Stoughton.

Contents

Maps

Part I
The Framework of Victorian Expansion

[1] Imperialism: A Definition

Today, 'imperialism' is a term of abuse. It is a word much used in the forum of the United Nations. It is frequently heard on the lips of Soviet and Chinese Communist leaders as well as in the speeches of Asian, African and Latin American politicians. It is a term applied to the former policies of the once-great colonial powers and to the remnants of those empires which still exist today. It is also used to vilify present-day American policy in South-East Asia, the Caribbean and South America. Indeed, in many parts of the world it has become a convenient, multi-purpose, anti-Western slogan. And like all such polemical terms, with great emotional overtones, it is a word difficult to define; the *Oxford English Dictionary*'s definition differs greatly in tone and emphasis from that of the *Soviet Dictionary of Foreign Words*. It is a word which tends to confuse rather than to clarify but nevertheless it remains a part of the international vocabulary.

Imperialism entered the English language in the 1840s, and has always possessed rather unpleasant connotations. It was first used to criticise the ambitions of Prince Louis Napoleon in France and the demands of the *partie impérialiste* who called for a revival of the glories of the Napoleonic era. When Louis Napoleon came to power in 1852 and took the title Napoleon III, it was feared that the French would embark on an aggressive policy overseas. This is what 'imperialism' meant then.

In January 1868, the British journal *Spectator* tried to put a different gloss on the word. It referred to 'Imperialism in its best sense', which signified 'the consciousness that is sometimes a binding duty to perform highly irksome and offensive tasks'. The writer was referring to the defence of Canada, the government of Ireland and a general obligation to take colonial responsibilities seriously and to give good government to other races. This definition did not gain much popularity, however, largely because it was eclipsed in the 1870s by the notoriety imperialism achieved as a slogan condemning Disraeli's empire and foreign policies.

The title 'Empress of India', for example, was described by *The Times* as 'threatening the Crown with the degradation of a tawdry Imperialism'. And after Disraeli's brinkmanship in the Russo-Turkish war, Robert Lowe, in an October 1878 issue of the *Fortnightly Review*, thundered:

> What does *Imperialism* mean? It means the assertion of absolute force over others . . . if we can conquer our adversary in open fight, and impose our own conditions at the bayonet's point, then, as Dryden sings, 'these are imperial arts and worthy thee'.

To Lowe, a policy of imperialism was fraught with dangerous delusions of power.

In the same year the Earl of Carnarvon, who had just resigned from Disraeli's Cabinet, lectured in Edinburgh on 'a true and a false brand of imperialism'. He dreamed of the day when the colonies of British settlement would become 'a great English-speaking community, united together in a peaceful confederation, too powerful to be molested by any nation, and too powerful and too generous, I hope, to molest any weaker State'. As for the colonies of the dependent empire:

> There we have races struggling to emerge into civilisation, to whom emancipation from servitude is but the foretaste of the far higher law of liberty and progress to which they may yet attain; and vast populations like those of India sitting like children in the shadow of doubt and poverty and sorrow, yet looking up to us for guidance and for help. To them it is our part to give wise laws, good government, and a well ordered finance, which is the foundation of good things in human communities; it is ours to supply them with a system where the humblest may enjoy freedom from oppression and wrong equally with the greatest; where the light of religion and morality can penetrate into the darkest dwelling places. This is the real fulfilment of our duties; this, again, I say, is the true strength and meaning of imperialism.

But Carnarvon's effort to rescue the term from the mud-slinging campaigns of 1877–8 was not entirely successful. In the 1880 General Election, 'imperialism' became a prominent anti-Disraeli slogan.

By the end of the century, when the age of the New Imperialism was coming to an end, there were two clear attitudes on the subject. For some, like Milner, Curzon and Joseph Chamberlain, imperialism and empire represented the 'white man's burden', an imperial mission, an obligation to spread Western civilisation, European technology and the Christian gospel. To others, however, imperialism meant wars, bloodshed, exploitation and a sordid search for profits. J. A. Hobson, in his book *Imperialism, A Study* (1902), argued that it was the outcome of the need for new outlets for capital investment. Some of Hobson's ideas were later adapted by Lenin, and imperialism, as the 'highest stage of capitalism', was absorbed into the Marxist creed. Since then imperialism has had a new career and has been used as a general term of abuse by the leaders of former colonies and the critics of the West.

Imperialism is, then, a word which should be used with extreme caution. It lacks precise meaning and an agreed definition. It meant different things at different times. One writer in *Punch* in 1878 fumed:

> Imperialism! Hang the word! It buzzes in my noddle
> Like bumble-bees in clover time. The talk on't's
> mostly twaddle;
> Yet one would like to fix the thing, as farmers nail
> up vermin;
> Lots o' big words collapse, like blobs, if their sense you
> once determine.

Lord Rosebery, the Liberal Prime Minister, later defined it as a 'greater pride in Empire'. Perhaps this is the simplest and most neutral of all the definitions. It is the sense in which it will be used in this book. Imperialism, in fact, has become an 'umbrella-word' which covers not only the events which led to the establishment of imperial dominion, but the motives behind those events and the theories which have been based on them. It is with these three aspects of British imperialism in the Victorian age — events, motives and theories — that this book is concerned.

[2] Economics, Foreign Policy and Domestic Politics

It is, of course, impossible to treat the British empire as something static. In reality, the empire was a loose association consisting of a series of bilateral relationships between a strong European power and a host of weaker units. It never constituted a self-contained area and was never seen in such isolation by contemporaries. If anything, the needs of colonies were regarded as subordinate to the interests of Great Britain. The colonies, in most cases, were remote and their situation and problems were unfamiliar. The Victorians always maintained that they had the interests of colonists and subject peoples at heart. That the 'moral betterment' of the colonies always seemed to coincide with the interests of Great Britain, must have been doubly gratifying.

The economic background to the Victorian empire is of great importance. In the first half of the nineteenth century, British industrialists and investors concentrated on the home market, the development of communications and of industry. The lead given by early industrialisation was capitalised on to the full. For a time Great Britain virtually had a monopoly of the new techniques of production. British goods, machinery and know-how were in high demand. Thus Great Britain began to find the Old Colonial System of protected trade and shipping monopolies restrictive and began to preach a policy of international free trade. This led to the boom of the mid-nineteenth century when Great Britain became known as the 'workshop of the world'. By the early 1870s, however, the British industrial and commercial lead was under attack. When the 'Great Depression' ended in 1896 Great Britain's economy, if not stagnating, was certainly seen to be expanding at a slower rate than those of her continental and New World competitors. These developments provided the background for the reversion to 'neo-mercantilist' techniques of territorial expansion towards the end of the century when tariff barriers began to rise and British traders were gradually being squeezed out of Europe. Overseas markets — especially in underdeveloped countries — then assumed a new importance.

Thus the empire continued to be affected by Great Britain's economic position. But the needs of British trade and investment were but one factor in British imperial policy. Empire possessed a momentum of its own. Strategic needs assumed an increasingly important role and the activities of humanitarians, missionaries and, above all, British governors and officials on the spot were also important. Economics, therefore, formed but one important thread in a more general political context. British governments rarely intervened in the internal politics of Great Britain's trading partners and even more rarely came to the assistance of individual trading enterprises or investors. Even the gunboat diplomacy of Palmerston had more to do with prestige than with the hope of economic gain.

Foreign policy was another factor which influenced British policy towards the empire. The years of the 'workshop of the world' were also the years of the *Pax Britannica* when the Royal Navy ruled the waves and Great Britain (mainly through the absence of rivals) acted as a self-appointed policeman. The defence of the empire, and in particular of India, certainly came to be an overriding concern of Salisbury at the end of the century. But, once again, the British national interest took precedence over the parochial interests of colonies.

Finally, a point concerning domestic politics needs to be stressed. The influence of political preconceptions and party interest can be traced in the Victorian handling of imperial affairs from the time of the Canadian Rebellions in 1837 to the conduct of the Boer War in 1901. It did matter which party and which men were in power. The outlooks of the Liberal and Conservative leaders, Gladstone and Disraeli, were certainly very different. It is doubtful, for example, whether Great Britain would have acquired shares in the Suez Canal Company in 1875 if Disraeli had not been Prime Minister. The problems which dominated internal politics are also of importance. The divisions between Radical, Whig and moderate in Gladstone's Cabinet of 1882 affected not only reform of the franchise and the government of Ireland, but also developments in the Transvaal and Egypt. The completely unorganised, not to say chaotic, manner in which Great Britain came to occupy the latter country was largely the result of Cabinet squabbles and Liberal party dissensions. In such circumstances an objective appraisal of imperial questions was frequently lacking in Great Britain.

Thus the nineteenth-century British empire cannot be studied in a vacuum. It was very much a part of the Victorian age and its history must be interpreted in the light of the economic situation, the international scene and the domestic politics of the period. These provide an essential background to any understanding of Victorian imperialism.

[3] The Debate

Much of the early writing on Victorian Imperialism was done by theorists who had a preconceived concept to air or an idea to put across. Consequently in the now vast mountain of accumulated literature there are numerous statements of doubtful validity and generalisations which, on closer analysis, are found to be poorly documented, exaggerated or untrue. Before the Second World War a framework of British imperial history in the nineteenth century (which, for convenience, may be labelled the 'accepted hypothesis') seemed to be well established. Subsequent historical investigation, however, has demolished much of the old orthodoxy. Unfortunately no generally acceptable framework has been found to replace it. Historians are still burrowing in the archives and until the essential sub-structure has been reconstructed, our understanding of the Victorian empire must remain incomplete.

The accepted hypothesis

For nearly fifty years historians of British colonial policy in the nine-teenth century accepted a framework of ideas which, in many instances, closely followed the analyses that were made by contemporaries. Following in the footsteps of J. A. Froude and J. R. Seeley, imperial historians in the early twentieth century adopted the legalistic approach to empire evident in the pioneering study of H. E. Egerton, *A Short History of British Colonial Policy* (1897). The approach was endorsed by other leading authorities in the field, including A. P. Newton, Sir Charles Lucas and A. B. Keith. Their conception of a Victorian age neatly divided into a period of 'anti-imperialism' before 1870, followed by an age of belligerent expansion, became the orthodox interpretation of nineteenth-century British imperial history. New editions of the works by Egerton and Newton continued to be printed after the Second World War, and this pattern of British imperial development was embodied in most standard text-books on the British empire written before the late 1950s.

According to this interpretation, the early decades of the nineteenth century were the years when the lessons of the American War of Independence and the ideas Adam Smith put forward in his *Wealth of Nations* were gradually absorbed by British economists and politicians. As a result mercantilism died a lingering death. Colonies then became a burden. Not only did their possession add nothing to the British economy, but the cost of government and protection made them a drain on the British exchequer. Hence the period 1840–70 was dubbed the 'Little England' era or the 'Age of Separatism', when most leading statesmen apparently contemplated the impending break-up of the empire with feelings ranging from resignation to pleasure.

The 1860s were singled out as the decade when separatist ideas and the doctrines of the Manchester School reached their peak. Indeed, the years 1868–70 have been called 'the climax of anti-imperialism' when Gladstone, with Earl Granville at the Colonial Office, attempted to begin the dismemberment of the empire during his first ministry. But Granville's colonial policy precipitated such an outcry that the policy had to be abandoned. Even Disraeli, who had previously shown little interest in the empire, made a notable speech in its defence at the Crystal Palace in 1872. And as Great Britain's position in the world, both commercially and politically, seemed less secure with the Germany of Bismarck dominating the Continent, empire began to assume a new importance. The increasing industrialisation of continental competitors, the lack of raw materials and the need for new markets forced Great Britain to join the notorious scramble for colonies. The late Victorians indulged in an orgy of territorial expansion, and, supported by philanthropists, missionaries and merchants alike, British ministers took their share of the remaining 'unoccupied' regions of Africa and the Pacific — thus creating an empire larger than the world had ever seen, on which the sun would never set. When Queen Victoria died the empire had reached its zenith. Such in outline is the traditional picture of the Victorian years.

The new view
It is only in the last two decades that this approach has been seriously challenged. In 1953, two Cambridge historians attacked the accepted interpretation and suggested that earlier writers had adopted an extremely blinkered approach to imperial history. John Gallagher and Ronald Robinson, in a now famous article in the *Economic History Review*, argued that for the purpose of economic analysis it was unreal to confine discussion to those colonies painted red on the map. The empire was not an historically comprehensible unit in itself and could not be cut out of its context in world politics and British economic expansion. The Victorians were interested in trade, not territory, and Gallagher and Robinson adopted the term 'informal empire' to describe the expansion of British commercial and financial power beyond the boundaries of political jurisdiction. They pointed out that British economic expansion overseas had been continuous in the nineteenth century but commercial penetration did not always require political domination. In fact, the costly extension of formal political control was always a last resort. The late Victorians were not more 'imperialist' than their predecessors simply because they were driven to annex more often. British policy always followed the dictum, 'trade with informal control if possible; trade with rule when necessary'. In the circumstances of mid-century, informal techniques of control often proved sufficient to attain these ends. Gallagher and Robinson concluded, therefore, that the process of expansion had reached its most valuable targets long before the exploitation of such marginal fields as tropical Africa. Here, the imperialists were merely scraping the bottom of the barrel. Thus, according to this view, the mid-Victorian period, far from being an age of stagnation and indifference, was the golden age of British expansion, beside which the later pegging out of claims in African jungle and bush pales into insignificance.

It was a novel and skilfully presented argument, and since 1953 the nature of Victorian imperialism has become a subject of intense controversy in scholastic circles. No part of the old orthodoxy has been safe from attack. It has been asserted that the period of the fall of the Old Colonial System witnessed the rise of a 'free trade imperialism'; the 'Little England' era has been dubbed a myth; and that most celebrated of centres, the Manchester School, has suffered the same fate. It now seems doubtful whether there ever was any period of 'anti-imperialism' in nineteenth-century England. And so the controversy which has never ceased to surround the actions and motives of the late Victorian imperialists has engulfed the early and mid-Victorians as well.

After two decades of intensive publication the framework for discussing British colonial policy in the Victorian age lies in shreds. It is not the purpose of this study to survey the history and individual development of that heterogeneous collection of colonies which together are termed the British empire. Instead, our intention is to re-examine the events, motives and theories behind Victorian imperialism, to discuss the interpretations currently being put forward and to indicate the lines along which some agreement is at last beginning to emerge. No grand hypothesis will be offered. Wherever possible the Victorians will be allowed to speak for themselves. Doubtless some myths will have penetrated these pages. Perhaps a new framework will soon be established. For the present, however, purely for convenience, this study has been divided into three chronological phases: early Victorian imperialism (1837–59), mid-Victorian imperialism (1859–80) and late Victorian imperialism (1880–1901). A discussion of the current controversy concerning the New Imperialism has been included and, to complete the picture and to put the end of the Victorian age into perspective, the passing of the *Pax Britannica* is covered in Part VI. But, first, we must begin with a brief survey of the empire in 1837.

Further Reading
Useful introductions to British imperial history in the nineteenth century are:
R. Hyam, *Britain's Imperial Century 1815–1914: A Study of Empire and Expansion*. Batsford (London, 1976).
W. D. McIntyre, *Colonies into Commonwealth*. Blandford, 3rd ed. (London, 1974).
G. S. Graham, *A Concise History of The British Empire*. Thames & Hudson (London, 1970).

D. Judd, *The Victorian Empire*. Weidenfeld and Nicolson (London, 1970).

C. E. Carrington, *The British Overseas: exploits of a nation of shopkeepers*. Cambridge University Press (Cambridge, 1950).

R. Koebner & H. D. Schmidt, *Imperialism: The Story and Significance of a Political Word, 1840–1960*. Cambridge University Press (Cambridge, 1964).

R. Hyam & G. Martin, *Reappraisals in British Imperial History*. Macmillan (London, 1975).

B. Porter, *The Lion's Share: A Short History of British Imperialism, 1850–1970*. Longmans (London, 1975).

For the economic and foreign policy background to the nineteenth-century empire, see:

E. J. Hobsbawm, *Industry and Empire*. Weidenfeld and Nicolson (London, 1968).

W. W. Rostow, *The British Economy of the Nineteenth Century*. Oxford University Press (London, 1948).

R. Tames, *Economy and Society in Nineteenth Century Britain*. Allen & Unwin (London, 1972).

D. C. M. Platt, *Finance, Trade and Politics in British Foreign Policy, 1815–1914*. Oxford University Press (London, 1968).

C. J. Bartlett, *Britain Pre-eminent: Studies in British World Influence in the Nineteenth Century*. Macmillan (London, 1969).

K. Bourne, *The Foreign Policy of Victorian England, 1830–1902*. Oxford University Press (London, 1970).

Part II
Early Victorian Imperialism

The first major problem encountered in a study of the Victorian empire concerns the nature and extent of early Victorian imperialism. When Queen Victoria came to the throne, the British empire was in a state of flux. The established economic and constitutional bases of empire were all under fire. The first half of the nineteenth century saw the removal of the commercial restrictions of the Old Colonial System and the victory of free-trade ideas. The first two decades of Victoria's reign also witnessed the introduction of internal self-government into British North America, Australia and New Zealand. These two innovations removed the strongest props of the eighteenth-century empire. How, then, did the early Victorians view their heritage? Did they regard the remnants of the mercantile empire as a burden and view its break-up with equanimity, or did 'imperialism' continue to play a role in the early Victorian scene? Indeed, what part could empire play in the approaching age of free trade? These are the questions we must consider first.

[4] The Victorian Inheritance

The empire the Victorians inherited was the product of over two hundred years of competition for overseas trade with Spain, Portugal, Holland and France. The great imperial wars, which characterised the eighteenth century, had finally come to an end in 1815. By that date the empires of most European rivals had virtually ceased to exist, leaving Great Britain's imperial position and naval supremacy unchallenged. By that date Great Britain had become the leading industrial nation of Europe. Thus as many parts of the world experienced the expansion of British commerce, finance and naval power, the age of the *Pax Britannica* dawned. But the early Victorians were not entirely enthusiastic about their inheritance: the confines of the mercantile empire were thought to be limiting, rather than assisting, the expansion of British trade.

The Old Colonial System had been based on the needs of an earlier age. According to the economic theories then current, a nation's power and military security were dependent upon the accumulation of wealth through a favourable balance of trade. Only through an excess of exports over imports could a surplus of precious metals be created to foster economic growth and raise revenue for war, thus permitting a strong nation-state first to achieve, and then to maintain, a dominant position in the world. Consequently, British merchants in the seventeenth century had sought to reduce Great Britain's dependence on foreign imports and to exclude foreign rivals from acting as middlemen in British trade. In this process colonies were valuable assets as sources of raw materials and as markets free from European interference. It seemed to make sense, therefore, to shape the economic resources of empire into a self-sufficient trading economy. It was in the interests both of British commerce and of national power.

To this end a series of Trade and Navigation Acts — beginning with the Trade Ordinance of 1651 and culminating in the Navigation Act of 1696 — were passed in an attempt to create a monopoly of export, import and transit in British and colonial goods. The aim was a closed market. The bulk of colonial exports, especially certain enumerated items, was sent to England and all colonial imports came from or via England. All trade was carried in British or colonial shipping. Thus Great Britain not only exploited colonial resources and controlled colonial export and import trade but also acted as middleman both for foreigners who wanted East Indies spices or colonial products and for colonists who wanted certain continental goods. However dubious the economic reasoning may have been, British merchants and industrialists certainly prospered and the system permitted Great Britain to reach the point of 'take-off' for the Industrial Revolution.

In practice, the letter of many of the acts of trade was enforced only intermittently and British parliamentary sovereignty was asserted infrequently. However, the capitulation of the French in Canada, the West Indies and West Africa at the end of the Seven Years' War in 1763 presented the British with a unique opportunity to make the Old Colonial System work — at a time when many infant North American industries, tied to a guaranteed British market, had won their way to viability and were eager to escape from the British commercial straitjacket. When the British also tried to recoup their war expenditure by indirect taxes, an open breach occurred. The central authority of the British Crown and Parliament was contested and conflict over the Revenue and Stamp Acts of 1764 and the Townshend duties of 1767 ensued. As violent incidents in the colonies met with an equally violent reaction on the part of the British government, the situation deteriorated until in 1776 the thirteen American colonies issued their famous Declaration of Independence.

The loss of the American colonies reinforced a tendency in Great Britain's overseas trade policy which had begun during the Seven Years' War: the so-called 'swing to the East'. The eastern trade routes to India and beyond to the elusive market of China, if nowhere near eclipsing Great Britain's transatlantic commercial interests, were beginning to exercise an increasing attraction. The East India Company, founded in 1600, had established a very successful trade in silks, spices, tea, coffee and Chinese porcelain. With the crumbling of the Mughal Empire, however, the Company had been obliged to exert some political control. This led to financial difficulties and in 1773 the British government was dragged into India to bail the East India Company out. The loss of the American colonies soon afterwards and Great Britain's accelerated industrial growth thus confirmed a tendency away from an empire based on the colonial staples of the North Atlantic. After 1783 Great Britain's colonial acquisitions tended to be trading and strategic bases. By 1815 the British empire had taken on a new shape. The Victorians, therefore, inherited not only the remnant of the mercantile empire based on the West Indies, North America and West Africa, but also the commercial network of the new eastern trade routes based on India and stretching as far as China.

What, then, was the physical shape of the empire in 1837? On the east coast of the North American continent were to be found the oldest British settlement on the island of Newfoundland, the British and French settlers of the two Canadas and the colonies of Nova Scotia, New Brunswick and Prince Edward Island. The Hudson's Bay Company, founded in 1670, operated a lucrative fur trade inland. To the south, in the Caribbean, were the British West Indian islands, some being old-established British colonies dating back to the seventeenth century, such as St Kitts, Barbados, Antigua and Jamaica, others being more recent acquisitions like the French sugar islands of Trinidad and Tobago. To the north of these islands were situated the Bahama Islands and Bermuda. Completing the colonies of the Atlantic trade routes

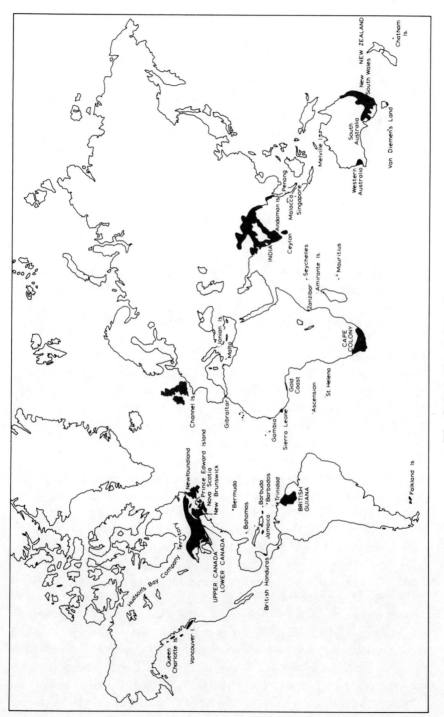

The British Empire in 1837

were the small, fever-ridden West African settlements of Sierra Leone, the Gambia and the isolated forts of the Gold Coast.

The eastern trade routes were based on India, the heart of the new empire and the centre of a commercial network covering the Indian Ocean and the South China Sea. The sea route to India was protected by the islands of Ascension, St Helena and Tristan da Cunha in the Atlantic Ocean and by the naval base at Cape Town. The Cape of Good Hope, which had been retained in 1815 at the cost of £6,000,000 compensation to the Dutch, was known as the 'tavern for India'. The final leg of the journey in the Indian Ocean was dominated by the British-held islands of Mauritius, the Seychelles and Ceylon.

The alternative route to India, involving an overland crossing of the isthmus of Suez, was also well protected. The British possessed fortified bases in the Mediterranean at Gibraltar and Malta and in the Ionian Islands off the western coast of Greece. The strategic base of Aden, dominating the Gulf of Aden, was subsequently acquired in 1839 as a sentry-box on the Red Sea approach to India.

The flourishing tea trade with China and the possibility of developing the Chinese market had led to an extension of this network of commercial bases and naval stations to the Far East. The East India Company had established a naval base on the island of Penang off the west coast of the Malay peninsula, and a mainland base at Province Wellesley. Stamford Raffles impetuously raised the company's flag at Singapore in 1819. Singapore, like Aden, soon became a pivot of empire and, being equidistant from Calcutta and Canton, became a focal point for British trade and defence. The route beyond Singapore was less well protected, but the early Victorians soon plugged this gap with the acquisition of Hong Kong in 1842 and the island of Labuan off the northern coast of Borneo in 1846. The chain of strategic ports running from the Red Sea to the China coast was then complete.

The periphery of the British empire lay in the South Pacific. James Cook had explored these waters in the late 1760s and 1770s. He had charted the main Pacific island groups, circumnavigated New Zealand and explored the unknown eastern coast of Australia. With the loss of convict contracts from the American colonies, land for a penal colony was sought. And so, in 1788, the first party of convicts arrived at the great harbour of Port Jackson, New South Wales, to begin a new life at Sydney. A prison settlement in Van Diemen's Land (known as Tasmania from 1853) was begun in 1803, the small isolated colony of Western Australia was founded in 1829, and the colony of South

Australia was established in 1836. By the beginning of Queen Victoria's reign, a British future had been assured for the Australian continent behind the protective shield of the Royal Navy.

In fact, by the early years of the nineteenth century the Royal Navy dominated all the sea routes of empire. There were, however, two weak spots in Great Britain's empire defence strategy: one was caused by Russia's Black Sea fleet, the other by the overland threat of the Russian empire to India. Victorian foreign policy became increasingly concerned with these two problems. For a large part of the century closure of the Dardanelles and the territorial integrity of Turkey were major concerns of British foreign secretaries. Both Palmerston and Disraeli regarded Constantinople as 'the Key to India'. Of equal concern was Russian expansion across central Asia in the direction of Afghanistan, the north-west frontier of India and Persia. Thus Russia came to replace France as the most dangerous enemy of the British empire in the nineteenth century.

This, then, was the empire the Victorians inherited. How was this heterogeneous collection of colonies, naval bases, islands, entrepôts and penal settlements governed? After the American War of Independence and the acquisitions of the French Revolutionary Wars, the colonies conformed, broadly speaking, to two types of constitutional government. In some of the older colonies in the West Indies and British North America locally elected colonial assemblies had survived, thus providing the colonists with some representation in local government. The government of the new post-1783 colonial possessions, largely non-British conquered colonies, was dictated autocratically from Whitehall. These two systems are known as representative government and the Crown colony system.

In the colonies with representative government, there usually existed a nominated legislative council and an elected assembly which approximated to the upper and lower houses of the British Parliament. The governor was assisted by an executive council of officials who performed the function of an advisory cabinet. Since the governor was a temporary incumbent, he generally relied heavily on these experienced local officials (who usually sat with other office-holders, prominent colonists and rich landowners on the legislative council). As they were appointed for life, these men formed a narrow governing class and were, in effect, largely responsible only to themselves. Consequently the representatives of the people in the lower house had little influence or power, apart from the right to vote taxes. The system has sometimes been dubbed 'irresponsible government' since the officials were in no way responsible to the elected representatives of the people. The assemblies tended to attract agitators and colonial demagogues and thus frequently became a virtually permanent opposition conducting assaults on the authority and independence of the executive. It was not a system which could be expected to last indefinitely.

In the Crown colonies there was not even a façade of democracy. Since most of the new colonies had been obtained by conquest and usually contained a mixture of peoples, there was no question of granting representative institutions. Instead the governor ruled under strict instructions from Whitehall. The inhabitants could retain their own languages, revenue systems and laws, but the conduct of administration was carried out, as far as possible, by orders-in-council without recourse to the British Parliament or to local opinion. A separate government department was created in London to supervise these colonies.

In 1801, colonial affairs were added to the responsibilities of the recently created Secretary of State for War who was henceforth known (until 1854 when the offices were divided) as the Secretary of State for War and the Colonies. After 1815, during Lord Bathurst's extraordinarily long secretaryship which lasted from 1812 to 1827, the colonies became the principal concern of the department. Aided by two capable Parliamentary Under-Secretaries, Henry Goulburn (1812–21) and R. J. Wilmot Horton (1821–8), Bathurst created a Colonial Office where none had existed before and the Secretary of State gradually assumed supervision of most matters affecting the colonies. In this way the business of the empire came to be conducted, under the guidance of the Secretary of State, a Parliamentary Under-Secretary and the civil servants in the Colonial Office, from a dark, damp and dilapidated house at the end of Downing Street.

By 1837, the administration of the office was undergoing a thorough overhaul instituted by the second head of the civil service, James Stephen, who was Permanent Under-Secretary from 1836 to 1847. Stephen, in fact, helped to create the modern civil service with its high standards of integrity and public spirit. For his pains this hard-working official was dubbed 'Mr Oversecretary' and 'Mr Mother Country'. Stephen had a bad press from his contemporaries. That he possessed great influence is undoubtedly true, but that was the natural result of his great industry, knowledge and ability. He was far from being a narrow-minded bureaucrat. Indeed, as the son of one of the most uncompromising Abolitionists who was a brother-in-law of Wilberforce, he was a champion of the coloured races in the empire and a friend to reform of colonial administration and policy. He certainly had his hands full in 1837: the Colonial Office was having to deal with the aftermath of the abolition of slavery in the West Indies, the Boer exodus from the Cape of Good Hope and, most serious of all, rebellions in the two Canadas.

[5] The Problems of the Empire in 1837

The abolition of slavery

In the first three decades of the nineteenth century, the question of slavery eclipsed all other purely colonial problems. During the secretary-ship of Bathurst, the Colonial Office had gradually come under the influence of the humanitarians. Thenceforth it was in the vanguard of the movement to abolish the status of the slave from the British empire.

Ever since the seventeenth century, millions of West African slaves had been transported across the Atlantic, often in horrifying conditions, to provide cheap labour for the plantations of the West Indies and American mainland. For over a century profits from sugar cultivation soared. Absentee landlords grew rich in England, the ports of Liverpool and Bristol flourished, and the trade provided, it has been suggested, some of the capital which prepared the way for the Industrial Revolution. By the beginning of the nineteenth century most of this trade in slaves had fallen into British hands. But this period also saw the Evangelical revival and the start of a campaign to abolish slavery throughout the world. It was to have a tremendous impact on parts of the British empire.

In 1787 a group of Evangelicals, aided by the Quakers and led by William Wilberforce, founded a Society for the Abolition of the Slave Trade. The efforts of this society (which soon found a focus in the 'Clapham Sect'), assisted by the newly-founded missionary societies — the Baptist Missionary Society (1792), the London Missionary Society (1795) and the Church Missionary Society (1799) — resulted in the termination of the British trade in slaves exactly twenty years later. Most European powers, except Spain and Portugal, had passed similar legislation by 1821. But the slave traffic did not stop. A new generation of philanthropists, therefore, led by Thomas Fowell Buxton MP, a wealthy brewer, campaigned for the abolition of slavery in the British empire. Success finally came after a slave revolt in Jamaica in 1831 in which some 500 slaves lost their lives. The British Prime Minister, Earl Grey, pushed through an Emancipation Act in 1833. Thus, on 1 August 1834 all slaves became free, although ex-slaves over six years old were required to continue working as 'apprentices' to their former masters for another six years. The Colonial Office was still dealing with the aftermath when Queen Victoria ascended the throne.

The major effects of abolition were felt in the West Indies. By the beginning of the nineteenth century the British West Indian islands were no longer the brightest jewels in the British Crown: sugar production was becoming less and less profitable. The growing number of absentee plantation owners had led to an increasing amount of capital leaving the islands and a deterioration in estate management. Jamaica, Barbados and the Leeward Islands found themselves faced with competition from the recently annexed colonies of Trinidad, Tobago and British Guiana, from the more efficiently organised French islands of Guadaloupe and Martinique and from Cuba and Brazil. Clearly the bottom was falling out of the British West Indian sugar market. Furthermore, after the British opened up a direct trade with the newly independent Latin American republics in the 1820s, the West Indies lost their value as entrepôts. When trade with the USA also rapidly expanded, their value as a market declined further. By the 1830s the islands were becoming something of a liability.

These facts have led one West Indian historian, Dr Eric Williams, the first prime minister of Trinidad and Tobago, to conclude that the waning of the sugar industry played a more important role in the abolition of slavery than the efforts of hypocritical philanthropists in Great Britain. In his stimulating study, *Capitalism and Slavery* (1944), Williams argued that once British West Indian sugar could no longer compete on economic terms, the British sponsored an international campaign against slavery in order to ruin their French and Spanish rivals and ensure that British East Indian sugar, not dependent on slave labour, captured the European market. It is a controversial thesis. Many East Indian merchants certainly voted for abolition in Parliament but the efforts of the philanthropists were also sincere and the revulsion against the slave trade in a staunchly religious age was genuine. One thing is certain, however: it dealt a severe blow to the existing West Indian economy. The planters now faced a labour shortage as well as capital deficiency and foreign competition. Indeed, a final shattering blow was dealt to sugar production in 1854 when, in the interests of free trade, Great Britain abandoned sugar protection. Thus within the first two decades of Queen Victoria's reign the British West Indies fast declined in economic importance and rapidly became a backwater of the British empire.

The Great Trek

Repercussions of the abolition of slavery were also felt in South Africa. The Dutch Boers, a Calvinistic people who practised a form of domestic slavery and justified their way of life by reference to the Old Testament, abhorred the measure. Ever since the Cape had been annexed in 1815, they had opposed the introduction of British laws. They disliked the autocratic rule from Cape Town, they objected to the humanitarian standards of the Colonial Office and they were alienated by the liberal impulses and the highly-coloured criticisms of the London Missionary Society. Thus the Boers became increasingly hostile to British rule as the British government allowed free non-Europeans to buy and sell land and to move freely about the country, and allowed slaves to give evidence against their owners in criminal cases. Here, the abolition of slavery was merely the climax in a long series of hated measures. As one Boer lady wrote, to accept that heathen slaves, 'Hottentots' and 'Kaffirs', could be placed 'on an equal footing with Christians' was 'contrary to the laws of God and the natural distinction of race and religion'.

Even more feared was the British attempt to hem the Boers in. To avoid a clash with the Africans on the eastern frontier of the Cape the British had created a neutral zone and established a line of British settlements. The government's attempt to make treaties with and protect the African chiefs on the northern frontier alarmed the Boers even more. Beset by the scourges of drought and cattle disease which demanded new grazing lands, by the farm-burning and the cattle-slaughter of the so-called 'Kaffir War' of 1834–5, and by the urgent need to provide 6,000-acre farms for the sons of large families, the Boers decided in 1835 to cross the Orange river and go beyond the frontiers of British rule. Thus began the Great Trek as the Boers undertook their epic march into the heartlands of the Tswana (Bechuana), the Basotho (Basuto), the Zulu, the Ndebele (Matabele) and the Swazi in pursuit of the *lekker lewe* (the sweet life). Some settled across the Orange river; some settled in Natal and established the first Afrikaner Republic at Pietermaritzburg; others trekked on across the Vaal to the Limpopo river. The exodus created new problems for the British government. Should the *voortrekkers* be abandoned and left to their own devices with the Africans or should British government, law and order pursue them? It was a crucial decision for the Victorian policy-makers and one about which they were unable to make up their minds.

The attention of Parliament, however, had been focused on the plight of 'aboriginal populations' within and on the frontiers of the empire. Largely influenced by the missionaries at the Cape, the philanthropists in the British Parliament secured the appointment of a Select Committee on Aborigines in 1835. The committee, which was chaired by Thomas Fowell Buxton, reported in the year Queen Victoria ascended the throne. Its recommendations could have been predicted: aborigines should be protected by the imperial government, British subjects beyond colonial frontiers should be made amenable to British law, and the law should be tempered for natives within British colonies. Territorial expansion and treaties were frowned upon. Instead missionaries should be encouraged to spread the gospel and bring social and political advancement to native peoples. That these objectives were not necessarily harmonious does not seem to have occurred to the committee, or to the Aborigines Protection Society which was formed in 1837 to promote the committee's ideals. For the present, however, attention was soon focused elsewhere, for within a few months of Victoria's succession to the throne, the Queen's English- and French-speaking subjects in the two Canadas were in open revolt.

The Canadian rebellions

Rebellion is really too strong a word for the small, easily quelled, armed uprisings of a few extremists which occurred in Upper and Lower Canada shortly before Christmas in 1837. Nevertheless, although their military significance was not great, the political repercussions were of far-reaching importance.

The unrest was largely the result of the complete break-down of the system of representative government in the two Canadas. In Upper Canada, deadlock over land development, clergy reserves (the reservation of land for supporting Anglican and Scottish Presbyterian clergy) and tariffs had been reached between the elected representatives of the people in the assembly and the narrow oligarchy at the top, the few Anglican upper-class families (dubbed the 'family compact') who comprised the executive and legislative councils. The Colonial Office, largely through the influence of Sir James Stephen, the Permanent

Under-Secretary, had urged the governor to pay closer attention to the wishes of the assembly. But an experiment appointing three members of the assembly to the executive council had broken down. As a result the council resigned and the assembly withheld the vote of supplies. A radical agitator, William Lyon Mackenzie, then gathered round him a few hundred discontented farmers and in early December 1837 attempted to capture Toronto. Within three days British troops had cleared the streets of the city and the rebels had fled to the USA. As an armed insurrection Mackenzie's rising was a ludicrous failure.

In Lower Canada the unrest was more serious: political frustration and constitutional grievances were complicated by a conflict of nationality. Here, a similar bigoted governing group and privileged social class existed, but this time the English-speaking minority in Montreal and Quebec, known as the *'chateau clique'*, was confronted by a French majority in the assembly led by the pugnacious Louis-Joseph Papineau. Demands for reform in the system of government were being used as a cover for nationalist designs.

Once again the Colonial Office was prepared to see reforms introduced. The Roman Catholic Bishop of Quebec was given a seat on the executive council, Papineau himself was offered a place, and similar offers were made to other French Canadians. The British government would not, however, concede an elected upper house or assembly control of finance. That would be to hand the reins of government to the French. The result, once again, was the assembly's refusal to vote supplies and its subsequent dismissal by the governor. Thereupon 'Sons of Liberty' societies were formed and a republic was proclaimed. Violence and bloodshed ensued and British troops were called in to defeat the rebels. By mid-December the brawls were over and Papineau had fled to the United States. The rebellion was yet another military farce.

The Whig government now had to deal with the aftermath of the risings. Serious attention was given to constitutional reform. Since 1829 requests had been pouring into the Colonial Office from British North American colonists for one reform in particular: that the governor's executive council should be made 'responsible' to the elected assembly. Robert Baldwin, an influential Canadian politician, had urged the Secretary of State in 1836 to put 'the Executive Council permanently upon the footing of a local Provincial Cabinet and apply to such provincial Cabinets both with respect to their appointment to, and continuation in, office the same principles as those which are acted upon by His Majesty with respect to the Imperial Cabinet'. Government by a cabinet possessing the confidence of the lower house, instead of an executive council that was remote from the assembly and rarely changed in membership, was clearly the general demand. However, Baldwin and his allies were not at this stage seeking rule by majority party. They still expected the governor to exercise a personal discretion in appointing and removing his advisors so as to keep them in harmony with the assembly.

In the Maritime Provinces some progress was made in this direction. In 1837, after the assembly of New Brunswick had promised a fixed revenue to maintain the government, the Lieutenant-Governor was instructed to change his executive council so that it could command the confidence of the assembly. The Lieutenant-Governor of Nova Scotia received a similar instruction. Thus the Colonial Office had already conceded that in New Brunswick and Nova Scotia the executive council might become an embryo cabinet and the governor could alter its composition to conform with the political situation. In these circumstances, one influential Nova Scotian journalist, Joseph Howe, called the 1837 rebellions the 'maddest rebellions on record'.

The revolts did, however, serve to convince the Whig ministers that gradual reform was not enough. The Prime Minister, Lord Melbourne, decided to send a 'strong man' with extensive powers as Captain-General, High Commissioner and Governor-in-Chief, to sort out the situation. For this purpose he selected a wealthy former Cabinet minister of radical convictions, the first Earl of Durham. It was a neat way of getting rid of a difficult colleague and at the same time pacifying certain of the more radical members of his Cabinet. However, Durham, not the most cooperative or pleasant of men, was reluctant to go. He delayed his departure for several months making lavish preparations for his progress through the Canadas. The High Commissionership was to be to the greater glory of the Earl of Durham.

To assist him in his task, this haughty, sensitive and extremely irritable nobleman selected three men: Charles Buller, the outspoken critic of the Colonial Office who later created the image of 'Mr Mother Country'; Edward Gibbon Wakefield, a specialist in colonial immigration, who had a well-deserved reputation for trickery and deceit and had already been jailed once for inducing an immensely rich school-girl to marry him at Gretna Green; and, as his legal adviser, Thomas Turton, whose private life had also been clouded by a domestic scandal involving his wife's sister. None of these appointments, all of which caused a great deal of outraged public comment, met with the Melbourne government's approval. Wakefield eventually had to journey to Canada in a private capacity.

The Durham mission arrived in Canada at the end of May 1838. The new High Commissioner, dressed in a brilliant uniform and mounted on a magnificent white charger, made a spectacular entry into Montreal on 29 May. A month later, to celebrate the young queen's coronation day, he announced a general amnesty for the hundreds of rebels under arrest with the exception of eight ringleaders who were to be banished to Bermuda. In all, Durham spent five months in British North America. He left suddenly on 1 November after the Melbourne government, under attack in Parliament, had been obliged to disallow the Bermuda ordinance. In exiling the eight rebels Durham had exceeded his authority as High Commissioner. To the proud nobleman it was a snub not to be endured. He resigned immediately but decided, as a private citizen, to submit his report on the situation in Canada for the benefit of the government which had (allegedly) treated him so badly. He died, eithteen months after completing his report, at the early age of forty-eight. His name has lived on, however, in the pages of most books on imperial history.

[6] Lord Durham's Report

The Durham Report was published in February 1839. It must have made rather dull reading at the time — 'a politician's re-hash of recent Canadian history' — and it makes duller reading today. Nevertheless it is worth examining in some detail as high praise has been lavished on it and great claims have been made for it.

Durham claimed to have found two objectionable features in the British North American system: the 'conflict of races' and a defective form of government. On the first point he wrote:

> I expected to find a contest between a government and a people: I found two nations warring in the bosom of a single state: I found a struggle not of principles but of races; and I perceived that it would be idle to attempt any amelioration of laws or institutions until we could first succeed in terminating the deadly animosity that now separates the inhabitants of Lower Canada into the hostile divisions of French and English.

The solution was the union of Upper and Lower Canada into a single province. Durham had no doubt that Anglo-Saxon society was more dynamic and progressive than its French counterpart. Canada, therefore, ought to be anglicised, English language and laws gradually adopted and representation by population instituted. In this way the French majority in Lower Canada would be swamped in the new province and only then would the French abandon 'their vain hopes of nationality'. This part of the report certainly reflected the anti-French bias of the High Commissioner's confidential advisers.

The second great defect Durham detected was in the working of representative government. He summed up its consequences in a telling paragraph:

> A governor, arriving in a colony in which he almost invariably has had no previous acquaintance with the state of parties or the character of individuals is compelled to throw himself almost entirely upon those whom he finds placed in the position of his official advisers. His first acts must necessarily be performed and his first appointments made at their suggestion. And as these first acts and appointments give a character to his policy, he is generally brought thereby into immediate collision with the other parties in the country and thrown into more complete dependence upon the official party and its friends.

The resulting evil was 'this system of irresponsible government':

> It may fairly be said that the natural state of government in all these Colonies is that of collision between the executive and the representative body. In all of them the administration of public affairs is habitually confided to those who do not cooperate harmoniously with the popular branch of the legislature; and the government is constantly proposing measures which the majority of the Assembly reject and refusing its assent to bills which that body has passed.

Durham was merely stating the obvious. But once again he was confident as to the solution: concede what the Canadian leaders had been demanding and permit development along the lines of New Brunswick where the government had already 'been taken out of the hands of those who could not obtain the assent of the majority of the Assembly, and placed into the hands of those who possessed its confidence'. The members of the executive council should constitute a ministry possessing collective responsibility to the assembly. The governor, like the British sovereign, should retain a large, independent discretion in appointing, maintaining in office and, finally, in dismissing those advisers whom he no longer trusted or whose relations with the

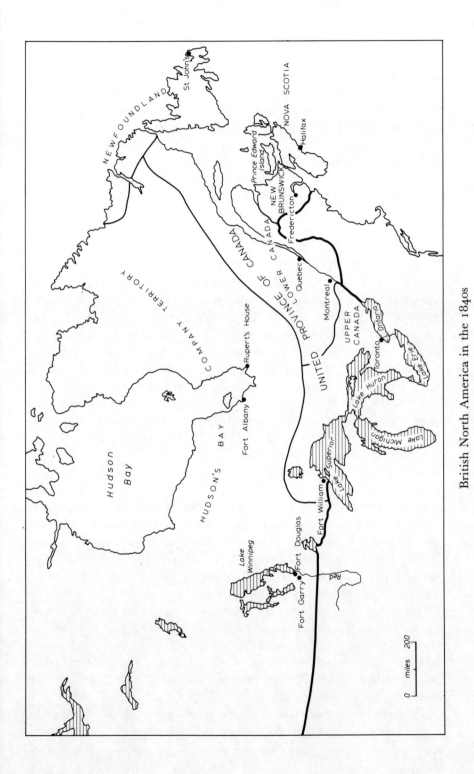

British North America in the 1840s

assembly were unsatisfactory — subject in the last resort to the ability of his new ministers to obtain from the assembly the measures and money needed for their policies. Thus by introducing a system of 'responsible' or 'municipal' government, and following through the principles of the British constitution, the basis of conflict would be removed. Clearly, Durham intended the united Canada to have the British cabinet system of 1839.

Obviously there was nothing original in all this. Local self-government had a long pedigree from the American revolution through Tom Paine and Charles James Fox to Jeremy Bentham. It had been demanded in the colonies by the Baldwin family and by Joseph Howe. It had been urged by Radicals at home such as J. A. Roebuck, Joseph Hume, Francis Place and Daniel O'Connell. What is interesting, however, is the operation of responsible government as Durham conceived it. Naturally, the colonial governor should not attempt to interfere in domestic affairs. He emphasised that the matters which concerned the British government were very few: principally the amendment of colonial constitutions, the conduct of foreign relations, the regulation of trade policy and the disposal of public lands. In all other matters the local government would be supreme.

The division between imperial and colonial matters was neat, the system was simple to introduce, and everything was crystal-clear — or so it appeared to the author. Durham, however, had not thought very deeply about the operation of his system. The powers withheld from the colonial government may have been few but they were important. The sale of public lands and tariffs were the most important sources of revenue for societies in which direct taxes were regarded with abhorrence. Yet the imperial government was to retain control of these matters. Would this division of affairs be acquiesced in for long? Would not some internal matters also affect foreign affairs and commercial policy? And what was to prevent an assembly coercing a governor by withholding supplies when it came to the reserved areas? Durham's ideas were deceptively simple. In fact, although Durham's championing of the principle of self-government was striking, the system he advocated was basically impracticable. His version of responsible government with its formal areas of imperial control would have prevented the growth of any strong popular government and any large measure of self-government.

Durham's recommendations were not well received. A self-governing dependency was thought to be a contradiction in terms. It is true the

new Colonial Secretary, Lord John Russell, agreed to the union of the
two Canadas, but union had been advocated long before Durham
came on the scene. And when it came about in 1840 it was not accompanied by the constitutional changes Durham had recommended.
Indeed it took on an entirely different form. Whereas Durham had
urged representation by population in the central parliament, so as to
swamp the French voters, equal representation was awarded to the
former provinces. Thus the French Canadian national character, far
from being stamped out, has survived into the 1970s. Russell also urged
the new Governor-General of the United Provinces to avoid saying
anything which might countenance 'what is absurdly called responsible
government' which, of necessity, conflicted with imperial authority.
In a despatch dated 11 October 1839, he raised some of his objections
to the proposed system:

> Can the colonial council be the advisers of the Crown of England?
> Evidently not, for the Crown has other advisers, for the same functions,
> and with superior authority.
> It may happen, therefore, that the Governor receives at one and the
> same time instructions from the Queen, and advice from his executive
> council totally at variance with each other. If he is to obey his instruc-
> tions from England, the parallel of constitutional responsibility entirely
> fails; if, on the other hand, he is to follow the advice of his council he is
> no longer a subordinate officer, but an independent sovereign . . . there
> are some cases of internal government in which the honour of the
> Crown or the faith of Parliament, or the safety of the state, are so
> seriously involved, that it would not be possible for Her Majesty to
> delegate her authority to a ministry in a colony.

Russell refused to endorse Durham's theories. The British government,
however, had no wish to retain a system of government 'which opinion
condemns'. The governor was urged, therefore, to restore harmony
between the executive and legislative branches: 'the executive should
be carried on in such a way that their measures should be agreeable
and acceptable to the representatives of the people'.

Unlike Durham, Russell was not prepared to lay down any definite
division of responsibilities:

> While I have thus cautioned you against any declaration from which
> dangerous consequences might hereafter flow, and instructed you as to
> the general line of your conduct, it may be said that I have not drawn
> any specific line beyond which the power of the Governor on the one
> hand, and the privileges of the Assembly on the other, ought not to
> extend. But this must be the case in any mixed government. . . . The

Governor must only oppose the wishes of the Assembly where the honour of the Crown, or the interests of the empire are deeply concerned; and the Assembly must be ready to modify some of its measures for the sake of harmony, and from a reverent attachment to the authority of Great Britain.

To assist this objective Russell announced a few days later that office-holders in the colonies were no longer to have permanent tenure. Officials could be removed when a new governor took office or when public policy required a change. Thus the way for a type of cabinet government was opened up. In future a governor could act, virtually, as his own 'prime minister' selecting (and changing) his advisers so as to ensure that they always had the confidence of the assembly. Where this experiment would end, only experience and time could determine. Future relations would be dictated not by any doctrinaire report but by practical politics. Russell's compromise may have been less visionary and more cautious than the view of the dogmatic Durhamites, but it was more practical and perhaps better suited to an age when not only the structure of empire but the very purpose and future of colonies were being debated afresh.

[7] The Rise of Free Trade

The colonial agitation against the centralised system of government was paralleled in the mother country by an attack on the economic system of the eighteenth-century empire. Now that England had achieved an early lead in industrialisation, high protection no longer worked to her advantage. In a world where British manufactures were in great demand and British traders could undercut their continental rivals, the confines of a monopolistic economic system were found to be constrictive. Relieved of the restrictions of the mercantile system, Great Britain would soon become, it was asserted, not simply an imperial metropolis, but the commercial fountainhead of a far-flung economy. From the 1820s reality and theory combined to cause the demise of the Old Colonial System and the victory of free trade.

The theory behind the mercantile system had come under attack at the end of the seventeenth century, but the most effective arguments against the system were marshalled in 1776 by a Glasgow professor, Adam Smith, in a two-volume work entitled *An Inquiry into the Nature and Causes of the Wealth of Nations.* In this book Smith examined the whole structure of the mercantile system and concluded that the traditional idea of the balance of trade was fallacious. The purpose of foreign trade was not simply the accumulation of precious metals and had nothing to do with the possession of territory. The wealth derived from overseas trade came from the actual exchange of goods:

> Between whatever places foreign trade is carried out they all of them derive two distinct benefits from it. It carries out that surplus part of the produce of their land and labour for which there is no demand among them, and brings back in return for it something else for which there is a demand. It gives a value to their superfluities by exchanging them for something else, which may satisfy a part of their wants and increase their enjoyments.

According to Smith's analysis, Great Britain's restrictions on imports in an effort to maintain a surplus balance of trade had caused the British to produce goods at home which could be bought much more cheaply abroad. As a result foreign countries suffered a loss of income and could not afford to purchase British exports. Thus the attempt to achieve imperial self-sufficiency hampered the natural flow of trade, depressed the standard of living at home, and, in the end, handicapped the growth of national strength. Smith did not deny the advantages of an exclusive colonial trade: under a British monopoly certain indispensable overseas products could be obtained more cheaply than by foreign rivals. But even here he argued that if colonial commerce were opened up, the price of colonial exports would probably fall to the benefit of all. Whichever way you looked at it, Smith concluded: 'under the present system of management Great Britain derives nothing but loss from the dominion which she assumes over her colonies'. The mercantile system benefited the merchants alone.

Similar ideas were expressed by the controversial pamphleteer, Josiah Tucker, and also by other economists including David Ricardo, James Mill and J. R. McCulloch. All these men condemned the restrictions of the colonial system and, as Radicals, regarded the existing system of colonial government as oppressive. In 1793 Jeremy Bentham, the Utilitarian philosopher, called upon the French National Convention to emancipate their colonies. Reduced armaments and 'the emancipation of the distant dependencies of each state' were the twin bases of Bentham's plan for 'universal and perpetual peace'. Indeed, after the 1840s the Manchester School of economists welded the Benthamite ideas of individual liberty, limited government, free

trade and international peace into a moral law. By this date British
manufacturers had no use for the protective tariffs and navigation laws
of the Old Colonial System. The whole world was to be their oyster
during the years of the mid-Victorian boom.

But the mercantile system did not die overnight. Not until the
1820s did the free-trade movement as a conscious effort begin. Before
that date certain inroads on the system had been made, it is true: free
ports where no customs duties were levied had been established in the
Caribbean; the trade monopoly of the East India Company had been
abolished in 1813; small American ships had been permitted to trade
with the West Indies; and Singapore became a free port in 1819. But
more than anything else the opening up of the South American trade
after the successful independence movements and the threat of punitive
tariffs against British vessels if reciprocity were not granted, led
William Huskisson, President of the Board of Trade between 1823 and
1827, to place legislation before Parliament permitting freer trade. The
reforms allowed foreign countries to trade direct with British colonies,
lowered customs duties on many items and offered a reciprocal reduction of shipping regulations to foreign nations. It was a compromise between monopoly and free trade permitting international
reciprocity limited by imperial preferences. Great Britain guarded
herself by duties on the import of certain foreign goods, and customs
duties remained sufficiently high to enable Canadian lumber, West
Indian and Mauritian sugar and Canadian wheat to be admitted to
the British market at a lower price.

Moderate though the changes were, a severe blow had been given to
the mercantile system. Nevertheless tradition and the influence of
vested interests remained uppermost. By the 1840s, however, the influential manufacturers of the factory age and the ambitious merchants
who were at the head of a new class in British society were making
strident demands for the abolition of all trade restrictions. They
demanded the right to buy food staples and raw materials in the
cheapest market and to sell manufactured goods in the dearest market.
The struggle came to a head over the duties on foreign grain. The
campaign of the Anti-Corn Law League and the Irish potato famine
in 1845 finally convinced Sir Robert Peel in 1846 that it was necessary
to repeal the Corn Laws. Within a few years the mercantile system
had been dismantled. The Navigation Acts were abolished in 1849 and
shortly afterwards imperial preference for sugar, coffee and timber
disappeared. In 1853, Disraeli remarked that nothing remained of

protection but 'rags and tatters'. By 1860 the movement had reached its climax with Cobden's treaty with France and the removal of customs duties on all but forty-eight items. Free Trade ideas had triumphed.

It was inevitable that, as the Old Colonial System disappeared from sight, people should begin asking questions about the purpose of empire in an age of free trade. The editors of the *Edinburgh Review* in April 1851 noted that in the past colonies had been valued as markets and sources of supply. They were

> the principal and the surest channels for that commerce which we felt to be the life-blood of the nation . . . we compelled them to trade with us exclusively, to take from us exclusively all the articles with which we could supply them; and to send us exclusively all the produce of their soil . . . our colonies were *customers who could not escape us*, and vendors who could sell to us alone.

Now, however, the situation had completely changed:

> The very object for which we founded, governed, defended and cherished them has been abandoned; why then should we any longer incur the cost of their maintenance?

To an economy-minded nation of shopkeepers, the expensive paternalism of empire seemed to create too many debit entries in the ledgers of the workshop of the world. It was against this background that the early Victorians rejected one of the basic assumptions underlying the Durham Report. In Durham's system the existence of favourable trade laws had been one of the basic links between responsibly governed colonies and the mother country. The coming of free trade destroyed all that. Indeed, most historians have argued that the subsequent political settlement was largely facilitated, even dictated, by the pragmatic acceptance of this new economic system. Certainly the coming of free trade reduced the need for strict imperial supervision of colonial laws and administration. And colonies became correspondingly resentful of restrictions on their rights to self government once Britain had given up the commercial system, the benefits of which allegedly justified their subordination. But British ministers continued to think control of colonial commercial policy essential: every part of the empire had to adopt free trade policies. Thus the triumph of free trade did not imply freedom of fiscal policy for the colonies. Instead responsible government was introduced for completely different reasons — entirely dependent on changed circumstances both in Great Britain and the colonies.

[8] The Quiet Revolution

Lord Durham, of course, had advocated his version of limited self-government in 1839. The difficulties of operating the sophisticated British Cabinet system in small, politically inexperienced colonial assemblies, most of which did not even possess easily identifiable political parties, do not seem to have worried him. Russell's belief that under Durham's system the position of the governor would soon become intolerable and his decided opinion on the impossibility of separating internal and imperial business were well-founded. There was indeed a certain illogicality in awarding internal self-government and yet retaining control of such things as the disposal of public lands; in granting self-government and yet continuing to dictate to the colonies what was good for them. Durham was too optimistic in these matters. He was correct, however, in asserting that only by the grant of some form of internal self-government could Great Britain continue 'governing' the North American colonies. Within a few years British politicians were forced to concede this point.

Durham, however, had not invented responsible government. And there were other paths to self-government. In the event the British government gradually surrendered to pressures from the colonies. Parliamentary or party government was indeed established. But it would be a mistake to believe, as many historians have suggested, that Durham's Report was the guiding star pointing the way to 'dominion status' and the modern Commonwealth relationship. Colonial devolution occurred in the 1840s and 1850s in a completely unplanned fashion. The result was very different from what Lord Durham had envisaged and involved a complete *volte face* on the part of British politicians.

The introduction of responsible government
Lord John Russell's instructions to Charles Poulett Thomson, the first Governor-General of united Canada, have already been outlined. Thomson (created Lord Sydenham in 1840) was to act as head of the executive, drawing his advisers from the moderates of the various political factions. The new governor (who was killed in a riding accident in 1841) had a temporary personal success in the manipulation of a non-partisan administration. His successor, Sir Charles Bagot, however, was obliged to reform his ministry to include a French Canadian from Canada East, Louis Lafontaine (a reported follower of Papineau), and from Canada West, the radical leader, Robert Baldwin.

Shortly before he died, Bagot explained: 'whether the doctrine of responsible government is openly acknowledged, or is even tacitly acquiesced in, *virtually it exists*'. The Secretary of State, Lord Stanley, was furious and Bagot's replacement as Governor-General in 1843, Sir Charles Metcalfe, was sent out with instructions to stand firm. Metcalfe did his best and as a result found himself at loggerheads with the reformers. In the Colonial Office, Sir James Stephen concluded:

> Canada appears to have shaken off, or laid aside, the colonial relation to this country, and to have become in everything but name, a distinct state. . . . There are this moment, in Canada, almost as many Europeans as there were in the United States when they declared their independence — a very pregnant fact.

Once again the government of Canada was breaking down and the colonial connection was strained to breaking-point.

The dilemma was quickly resolved with the return of the Whigs to power in 1846. Cabinet government was immediately conceded by the third Earl Grey, the Colonial Secretary in the new Russell administration. Grey, a decided critic of Durham's ideas, bowed to the inevitable. But why did this *volte face* come about? In part the situation in Canada was responsible: the Canadian reformers had become totally dissatisfied with the system introduced by Sydenham in 1841 and as a result Baldwin and his allies demanded government by parties responsible to the assembly, with the governor-general's discretion in appointing and removing ministers reduced to a minimum. In turn the British response to this demand was influenced by changes in British constitutional practice during the previous few years, for it was during this period that the monarch's loss of power in the Commons and in the country was finally recognised, so that the choice of the party (or coalition) to hold office was no longer regarded as the personal prerogative of the sovereign. After Peel's motion of want of confidence in Melbourne's government in 1841, the essential principle of responsible government (that the will of the Commons must prevail in appointing and removing ministers) came to be regarded as generally binding. Government by ministers commanding a majority in the Commons meant government by party. Thus when Grey was faced with the demands of the Canadian reformers in 1846 his views had undergone a marked change since 1839.

The problem Grey now pondered was this: if party government, as it had recently evolved at home, were not inconsistent with monarchy

or the stability of the realm, why should not the Queen's representative
in a self-governing colony also be served by parties — be guided by a
local party rather than a party in Britain? What would Great Britain
lose by entrusting the administration of a politically mature colony to
members commanding a majority in a locally-elected house, instead of
to executive councillors chosen and appointed by the British Crown?
Were there not political advantages to be gained from containing within
each colony every political question on which the mother country did
not reasonably need to have the final word, and by reducing the
constitutional difficulty of colonial subordination to a list of reserved
imperial powers? To Grey the advantages were numerous and the
course to adopt seemed obvious. Thus in 1846 he informed a rather
surprised Sir John Harvey, Lieutenant-Governor of Nova Scotia, that
all future governments should be dependent on the 'wishes of the people
themselves'. Consequently, after a general election in August 1847,
Nova Scotia came, in January 1848, to possess the first fully responsible
ministry in the British empire. At the same time Grey instructed Sir
Edmund Head, Lieutenant-Governor of New Brunswick, to turn his
executive council into a cabinet. The coalition government continued
in power, however, and responsible government was not seen to come
into operation in New Brunswick until after an election in 1854.

Inevitably, it was in Canada that events attracted most attention. To
inaugurate the new policy, Grey appointed, in August 1846, a former
Governor of Jamaica, the eighth Earl of Elgin. Elgin called a general
election at the end of 1847 and the first responsible ministry was formed
in Canada under Baldwin and Lafontaine in March 1848. From then on
in matters of local administration Elgin followed the advice of his
ministers. He even accepted the controversial Rebellion Losses Bill
which permitted compensation to former rebels for damage to property,
and other losses, suffered through the activities of loyalist volunteers
or British troops in 1837. Despite the ensuing riots, during which an
angry mob in Montreal bombarded the Governor-General in his state
coach with stones and rotten eggs and burned down the Parliament
buildings, and despite heated criticism in the British press, the Act was
not disallowed. The Whig government supported Elgin's decision. It
was the first, and one of the most notable, victories for internal self-
government.

Thus it was left to two of Durham's relatives to introduce responsible
government into Canada. Grey was Durham's brother-in-law and
Elgin had married Durham's eldest daughter three months after his

appointment. But there the coincidence ends. Political ideas are not usually adopted through marriage connections and neither man's conception of responsible government was the same as Durham's. A division between imperial and colonial business was deliberately avoided, as Russell had earlier instructed, and problems were left to solve themselves by good sense and mutual understanding. In his early correspondence with his new wife (who apparently revered the dead even more than Queen Victoria) Elgin may have made some flattering references to his late father-in-law's ideas but in later life he usually referred to responsible government as 'my system'. Indeed, in his pragmatic conduct of affairs in Canada, he was more influential in evolving a pattern of self-government than the dead earl. His claims to be the father of responsible government stand far higher than those of Durham and even of Earl Grey. Elgin's idea of informal influence over a ministry triumphed over, and was in marked contrast to, their conception of formal imperial reservations. In this respect Elgin proved himself to be a far-sighted statesman. He even managed to conciliate the Canadians and retain their loyalty at the time when, to Canadian chagrin, Great Britain embraced free trade. After a notable speech in the House of Commons by Lord John Russell, he informed Grey in March 1850:

> I have never been able to comprehend why, elastic as our constitutional system is, we should not be able, now more especially when we have ceased to control the trade of our colonies, to render the links which bind them to the British Crown at least as lasting as those which unite the component parts of the union. . . . One thing is, however, indispensable to the success of this or any other system of Colonial Government. You must renounce the habit of telling the Colonies that the Colonial is a provisional existence. You must allow them to believe that, without severing the bonds which unite them to Great Britain, they may attain the degree of perfection, and of social and political development, to which organized communities of free men have a right to aspire.

Earl Grey was in whole-hearted agreement. Thus by 1850 a new solution to the age-old problem of the relationship between mother country and colony seemed to have been stumbled on: the grant, within certain limits, of internal self-government to politically advanced colonies. What this system would amount to in the end, only the future could reveal.

Grey, however, had his own ideas about the progress and extent of

responsible government. In his view, self-government was a privilege
and not a right. It had to be earned after a period of training in
municipal government graduating by stages to a share in power. It
must involve not only the acceptance of responsibility for administration
and local defence but also the cost. The British government should,
however, retain control of commercial policy, the disposal of public
lands and 'native policy'. Earl Grey's later years in office, therefore,
when he attempted to stem the tide of colonial advance, were less happy.
Having been a pioneer in the initial grant of self-government to Nova
Scotia, Canada, New Brunswick and Prince Edward Island (where the
parliamentary system was reluctantly conceded in 1851), Grey then set
his face against its extension. Above all, he was unfortunate enough to
make a stand on that least defensible of issues, the convict system. Grey
retired from active politics in 1852, a bitter and disillusioned man.

Grey's greatest shortcoming, however, was an inability to realise that
the opposition his policies encountered in various parts of the empire
was the mark of a growing political maturity. One member of the
Colonial Office, Sir Frederic Rogers, later recalled:

> Lord Grey was possessed with the idea that it was practicable to give
> representative institutions, and then to stop without giving responsible
> government — something like the English Constitution under Elizabeth
> and the Stuarts. He did not understand either the vigorous independ-
> ence of an Anglo-Saxon community or the weakness of an executive
> which represents a democracy.

Grey's theories suffered a similar fate to Durham's: events took their
own course and left his theories behind. Gladstone showed greater
understanding in a speech reported in *Hansard* for April 1851:

> It was taken for granted by many of our statesmen that that doctrine
> was correct which taught that the best system of colonial policy was to
> deal with the colony as with an infant. First, it was to have long clothes,
> and then short clothes; it was to be taught to walk; and the hope of
> freedom was only at intervals to be held out to it. This, he maintained,
> was a great practical fallacy, and, moreover, the most mischievous
> fallacy. They must found their colonies in freedom if they would have
> them really free.

After Grey's resignation, the barriers against the rapid advance of
responsible government came down and an administrative revolution
quietly spread through the Australian colonies and New Zealand. In

most of these colonies political parties were not yet sufficiently developed for the Cabinet system. Responsible government was not always demanded. In some cases, however, colonies had it thrust upon them.

Australia and New Zealand

Within five years of Grey's departure from the Colonial Office, responsible government had been introduced into all the Australian colonies with the exception of Western Australia. It was a startling reversal of former policy. By the 1850s, however, the Australian colonies had made great strides in development under the impact of the gold rushes, and political development now accompanied economic growth. Despite unpromising beginnings as a penal colony, by 1828 free immigrants outnumbered their less desirable predecessors. Immigration was further encouraged by state assistance in 1831 and by the publicity attached to the ideas of Edward Gibbon Wakefield, a member of Durham's mission to Canada in 1838.

Wakefield's schemes have a special place in British imperial history. Writing from the cells of Newgate Prison, he contended, in his diplomatically named and purely imaginary *A Letter from Sydney* (1829), that if land were sold in Australia at a 'sufficient price' — high enough to prevent impoverished new arrivals from purchasing land but low enough for them to aspire to land ownership after a few years — there would never be any shortage of employment or manpower. Such an arrangement would assist a concentration of settlement, rather than the dispersal of population, and also help to create a balanced society. The profits of land sales and land taxes could then be used to finance immigration. It was a brilliant theory, but Wakefield's system was never given a full trial. A policy which prevented easy acquisition of land was bound to be unpopular in the colonies and immediately gave settlers a political grievance against imperial control of unoccupied public or 'waste' lands.

Land was the most important commodity in Australia. Wool was the basis of early Australian economic growth and the many 'squatters' who grazed sheep over enormous expanses began to grow rich. Behind the sheep flocked immigrants and capital investment. A profitable export trade was established and by 1859 Australian wool exports, valued at £40,000,000 per annum, provided half the raw wool imported by Great Britain. By this time Australia had experienced a second and greater burst of immigration when gold was discovered near Bathurst, in New South Wales, in 1851. The subsequent stampede was comparable to the Californian gold rush of three years earlier. The diggings eventually came to centre on the rich and extensive goldfield from Ballarat to Bendigo in the newly-created colony of Victoria. The population soared from 77,000 at the colony's foundation in 1850 to 250,000 within a decade. Few fortunes were made but the growth of population accelerated economic, social and political developments, especially the rise of Melbourne.

New South Wales, the oldest and most advanced of the Australian colonies, led the fight to wrest the 'privilege' of self-government from the mother country's grasp. In 1842, a colonial legislative council and elected district councils at the local government level had been established by the New South Wales Government Act. But as this advance was accompanied by an unpopular measure raising the price of land to a 'sufficient price' (in an attempt to try Wakefield's theory) of £1 per acre, general dissatisfaction set in and larger powers were demanded. Additional protests about the restricted franchise and high property qualifications came from squatters who leased or held their lands by licence and were thus excluded from the political influence which their economic importance undoubtedly warranted. Still more demands were heard from the Port Philip District (later Victoria), 600 miles distant from the seat of government, where the cry was for the establishment of a separate colony.

Earl Grey did not believe that the Australian colonies possessed sufficient political experience or population to warrant the introduction of responsible government. To quell the constitutional clamour he suggested instead a federation of the colonies under one governor-in-chief. The suggestion was not acceptable to the colonists. When the colony of Victoria was established, therefore, Grey simply permitted, in the Australian Colonies Government Act of 1850, the introduction of limited representative government into Victoria, South Australia and Van Diemen's Land, thus placing these colonies on a par with New South Wales. The power to levy customs duties, amend their constitutions and change the voting qualifications of electors was granted, but responsible government was withheld. This did not worry the Australian colonists too much. The example of the Rebellion Losses Act of 1849 in Canada had been sufficient to convince the conservative members of the legislative councils that the system of responsible government was open to alarming excesses.

Nevertheless the legislative council of New South Wales, which had gained no benefits from the 1850 Act, continued to lead the campaign for greater self-government. In a 'Declaration, Protest and Remonstrance' in 1851, it demanded an end to imperial control of taxation, land policy and revenue, a dilution of the Crown veto and a constitution 'similar in outline to that of Canada' (not a reference to responsible government but to bi-cameralism and increased powers of self-government, including control of patronage and plenary powers of legislation in all colonial matters). The campaign was stepped up in 1852, the year Earl Grey gave up the seals of office. His successor, the Tory baronet Sir John Pakington, upheld Grey's views on almost every point of principle but admitted that 'it has become more urgently necessary than heretofore to place full powers of self-government in the hands of a people thus advanced in wealth and prosperity'. He then proceeded, in a despatch of December 1852, to concede all the demands of the legislative council. He also confirmed the end of transportation to Van Diemen's Land and requested the colonies of New South Wales, Victoria and South Australia to submit draft constitutions. He suggested a bicameral system with an elected assembly and a nominated upper chamber.

The colonists set to work. They were still in the process of drawing up new constitutions when a further directive was sent from London in August 1853. Pakington had been succeeded in December 1852 by the fifth Duke of Newcastle whose views were more progressive. Newcastle instructed that the upper houses need not be nominated, that Van Diemen's Land should also have a new constitution and that all the new constitutions should contain provision for responsible government:

> All will agree as to the extreme difficulty of withholding political privileges from bodies of men to whom maxims now prevailing in British domestic policy afford so strong a right to claim them, and of keeping our fellow-subjects in Australia on a different political footing from those to whom these rights have been fully conceded in America.

Newcastle insisted that although

> public expectation is as yet but little excited on the subject of Responsible Government, it is very desirable that we should prepare ourselves to regard its introduction as a change which cannot be long delayed, and for which the way should be smoothed as far as possible by the removal of unnecessary impediments . . . the change should take place before the occurrence of any of those reactions of temporary adversity which cannot but be anticipated as probable after a period of such unparalleled advance.

Thus the legislative council of New South Wales, which was in the midst of drafting a constitution providing for self-government without a ministerial system based on party government, was obliged to scrap its plans. The conservatives received a further blow when the imperial government struck out the elaborate safeguards against constitutional change contained in the two-thirds majority clauses of their draft. In fact, the new constitutions which came into force in 1856–7 were remarkably democratic in character. The South Australian constitution, for example, provided for manhood suffrage in elections to the lower house, a secret ballot, triennial parliaments, and the separation of church and state. To one of the Law Officers, Sir Frederic Rogers, the new constitutions were 'little less than a legislative Declaration of Independence by the Australian colonies'.

The first ministries formed under the new system were short-lived and unstable but faction politics soon began to emerge. When Queensland was separated from New South Wales in 1859, responsible government was in operation there within three years.

Thus it was the Colonial Office which took the decisive steps in extending responsible government to the eastern colonies of Australia. In New Zealand, 1,200 miles to the east, however, the story was rather different. The colonists demanded responsible government; the Colonial Office did not raise the slightest objection.

New Zealand had been annexed in 1840 after some 2,000 settlers had established themselves there over a period of twenty years, and a New Zealand Company had been formed by Wakefield, Durham and Molesworth to arrange the 'systematic colonisation' of the islands. The activities of the company were frowned upon by the Church Missionary Society which had friends in high places — Lord Glenelg and Sir James Stephen in the Colonial Office. On 6 February 1840 the Treaty of Waitangi was signed with about 180 chiefs who, in return for British protection, surrendered their rights of sovereignty to the Crown and were then guaranteed full possession of their lands. It was agreed that the Crown should have the sole right to purchase any lands the Maori chiefs were prepared to sell. The government's desire to protect the Maoris and the colonists' desire for land soon came into conflict. Prior to the Crown's intervention the settlers were prepared to ride roughshod over the complex system of land tenure and acquired land wherever they could, sometimes paying for it with blankets or cheap jewellery. Relations between Maori and settler rapidly deteriorated.

It was in this situation that Earl Grey announced in 1846 that he was prepared to give representative institutions to the settlers under a complex system of municipal, provincial and general government. The Governor of New Zealand, Sir George Grey, protested that the moment was not opportune and to the fury of the colonists Earl Grey retreated. Thus the New Zealand Government Act was suspended for five years in 1848. When the General Assembly finally met in 1854, however, Edward Gibbon Wakefield, who had emigrated to New Zealand in 1853 and had been elected to the House of Representatives, demanded responsible government for the centre. (The system had been inaugurated in the provinces of Canterbury and Wellington in 1853.) The acting governor, Colonel Wynward, immediately appointed three members of the assembly to his executive council pending approval from London. The Colonial Secretary, Sir George Grey (yet another Colonial Secretary and yet another Sir George Grey) acceded. Thus the concession was achieved without a battle. It was left to the new governor, Thomas Gore Browne, who summoned the first responsible ministry in 1856, to reserve the conduct of Maori affairs to the British Crown. The Maoris could not be left at the mercy of the settlers. Thus the New Zealanders achieved responsible government without full responsibility. The governor retained control of Maori policy but remained dependent on the assembly for funds. It was a situation which was accepted at the time and remained in operation for some years. But it was a burdensome situation. It was one of the many loose ends left by the spectacular but completely unplanned grant of responsible government.

The growth of responsible government

In less than twenty years after the suppression of the Canadian rebellions in 1837 the early Victorians had arrived at a whole-hearted recognition of internal self-government, based on the comparatively recent British model of a ministry responsible to the elected legislature, as the panacea for discontent in the colonies of British settlement. It was one of the most important advances in British colonial policy in the nineteenth century. The system developed piecemeal and was defined as it was made. The Colonial Secretary, Sir George Grey, informed the New Zealanders: 'The system rests on no written law but on usage only'. The constitution was left flexible. The strength of self-government depended on the stability of the local political leadership and the creation of a reliable bureaucracy and administrative system. In colonies where the British political system of parties did not yet exist, and where local politicians were inexperienced or incompetent, the governor frequently retained a great deal of influence. Thus the system developed in different directions at a different pace in different places according to local conditions and the personalities involved.

Nevertheless within two decades Great Britain's relations with her colonies of settlement had been decisively and irreversibly transformed. Colonial devolution occurred in a haphazard and disordered fashion. The British government surrendered control as colonial pressure became too great. Inroads were even made on British control of the empire's commercial policy. Earl Grey had asserted in 1846 that the British government did not intend to abandon 'the right and authority which Parliament always possessed of regulating the general trade of the colonies and the mother country in the manner most conducive to the welfare and prosperity of the Empire'.

However, in 1854, the Canadians signed a Reciprocity Treaty with the United States whereby the natural products of the United States were admitted to Canada duty-free in return for reciprocal concessions. In 1859 the Canadians went even further: heavy import duties were placed on manufactured goods which could be produced in Canada. This time Newcastle, during his second term as Colonial Secretary from 1859 to 1864, did protest. As a good Peelite and keen free trader he regretted that 'the experience of England, which has fully proved the injurious effect of the protective system, and the advantage of low duties upon manufactures, both as regards trade and revenue, should be lost sight of, and that such an Act as the present should have passed'. The Canadian Finance Minister, A. T. Galt, was quick to take up the implied challenge and flatly denied that imperial interference with colonial tariffs levied for revenue purposes was consistent with self-government. He asserted:

> Self-government would be utterly annihilated if the views of the Imperial Government were to be preferred to those of the people of Canada. It is, therefore, the duty of the present Government distinctly to affirm the right of the Canadian Legislature to adjust the taxation of the people in the way they deem best, even if it should unfortunately happen to meet the disapproval of the Imperial Ministry. Her Majesty cannot be advised to disallow such acts, unless Her advisers are prepared to assume the administration of the affairs of the Colony irrespective of the views of its inhabitants.

Newcastle was forced to retreat, admitting that the principle of self-government must take precedence over free trade. After this confrontation, although colonial control of commercial policy was not admitted, it became practically impossible for the British government to force its trade policy on a colony against the wishes of the inhabitants. Clearly Canada was beginning to lead the way towards an even greater degree of independence.

By 1859, then, a new concept of empire was in the making. But the introduction of responsible government had left many loose ends and undefined spheres of responsibility — control of commercial policy, conduct of native affairs, colonial contributions to imperial defence and the limitations on colonial and imperial legislation. The division of powers and responsibilities had deliberately been left vague and these questions would have to be decided in the future. In the meantime, despite the set ideas of Durham, Wakefield and Molesworth, room had been made in the imperial system for colonial nationalism. Internal self-government had been granted to all the colonies that were thought fit for it. Each colony proceeded at its own pace along its own separate path.

This, then, was the achievement of the early Victorians. Why had responsible government been introduced? Partly to avoid another American revolution, partly through necessity as events gathered momentum and colonial pressures grew, partly at the desire of British politicians — in the light of recent changes in British constitutional practice. Was it an attempt to rid Great Britain of the useless remnant of the mercantile empire? The early Victorians may not have been imperialists in the sense of vigorous expansionists, and they may also have desired to be relieved of some of the financial burdens of colonial government, but whatever some contemporaries may have said, the maintenance of empire undoubtedly remained a basic feature of British policy. In fact, the triumph of free trade ideas helped to make colonies of settlement more attractive: as commercial partners and complements of the mother country in a free trade empire. Indeed from the 1840s a new idea of a great imperial destiny to plant British people and institutions overseas developed, based on the twin foundations of British emigration to, and investment in, the colonies of British settlement.

[9] Changing Theories of Imperialism

The rise of free trade, the spread of responsible government and the new concept of colonies of settlement transformed the empire. For many contemporaries, however, whereas mercantilism and colonies had gone hand in hand, there was no such obvious link between empire and free trade. Indeed, to Cobden and the economists of the Manchester School, who preached the gospel of free trade, laissez-faire and pacifism, the possession of colonies seemed not only an extravagant waste but positively harmful. The more extreme theorists in their midst therefore advocated the immediate dismemberment of the empire. The most brilliant literary exponent of this point of view was Goldwin Smith, the Regius Professor of Modern History at Oxford.

People who subscribed to such ideas have been dubbed 'separatists' or 'Little Englanders'. It was an attitude which won several converts, especially among those concerned with matters of the purse. In 1841 Sir George Cornewall Lewis, who later became Chancellor of the Exchequer, Home Secretary and Secretary of State for War, wrote in his *Essay on the Government of Dependencies*:

> If a dominant country understood the true nature of the advantages arising from the relation of supremacy and dependence to the related communities, it would voluntarily recognize the legal independence of such of its dependencies as were fit for independence; it would, by its political arrangements, study to prepare for independence those which were still unable to stand alone; and it would seek to promote colonization for the purpose of extending its trade rather than its empire, and without attempting to maintain the dependence of its colonies beyond the time when they need its protection.

In 1849, Earl Grey, the Colonial Secretary, reported to the Earl of Elgin, the Canadian Governor-General:

> Unfortunately there begins to prevail in the House of Commons and I am sorry to say in the highest quarters, an opinion (which I believe to be utterly erroneous) that we have no interest in preserving our colonies and ought therefore to make no sacrifice for that purpose. Peel, Graham and Gladstone, if they do not avow this opinion as openly as Cobden and his friends, yet betray very clearly that they entertain it, nor do I find some members of the cabinet free from it, so that I am powerless to do anything which involves expense — it is the existence of this feeling here which is to me by far the most serious cause of apprehension for the future.

What, then, was the attitude of the early Victorians to the continuing existence of empire? It is difficult to be exact as no political party or group can be placed in a watertight compartment. The views of those who regarded the empire with distaste and called for abandonment and those who viewed the future of the empire pessimistically, believing the colonies of settlement were destined for independence, have been well documented by historians. More recently, however, attention has been devoted to those writers and thinkers who felt that the survival of empire was essential to Great Britain's future well-being. John Stuart Mill, for example, in a pamphlet on *Systematic Colonization* (1847) argued, against the economic assessment of the Manchester School, that 'the alternatives of pecuniary loss and gain are not the only, or even the primary considerations of enlightened statesmen'. A few years later Thomas Carlyle expressed the same sentiment in his *Latter Day Pamphlets* (1850):

> Bad state of the ledger will demonstrate that your way of dealing with your colonies is absurd, and urgently in want of reform; but to demonstrate that the Empire itself must be dismembered to bring the ledger straight? O never.

In fact, a large body of opinion in support of empire continued to exist.

A new interest in empire was promoted in the early Victorian era by a group of propagandists known as the 'Colonial Reformers'. Like Cobden and the Manchester School these men were critics of the Trade and Navigation Acts and the system by which the colonies were governed. Unlike the Cobdenites, however, they actively supported the cause of empire. Several of these people have already been mentioned: Edward Gibbon Wakefield, Lord Durham, Charles Buller and Sir William Molesworth. They were influential in promoting certain schemes of emigration and land settlement, and in founding new settlements in South Australia and New Zealand and, above all, were foremost in the attack on the bureaucratic system of the Colonial Office. They were forceful exponents of responsible government and the ending of imperial expenditure on colonies. But they were not anti-empire in sentiment. They argued that colonial freedom and self-government were not incompatible with the existence of empire. Molesworth insisted in the House of Commons in 1838:

> Instead of wishing to separate from our colonies, or to avert the establishment of new ones, I would say distinguish between the evil and the good; remove the evil, but preserve the good; do not 'Emancipate your Colonies', but multiply them, and improve — reform your system of colonial government.

This was the constructive purpose of colonial reform.

To achieve this end the Colonial Reformers conducted a programme of ceaseless propaganda. They used whatever weapons came to hand

and were not above distorting the views of their critics, denigrating the achievements of their predecessors and generally attributing to themselves an importance and uniqueness they did not merit. Typical of their approach were Buller's abuse of James Stephen and Molesworth's description of the Colonial Office in another Commons debate in 1838:

> In the dark recesses of the Colonial Office, in those dens of peculation and plunder — it was there that the real and irresponsible rulers of the millions of inhabitants of our colonies were to be found. Men utterly unknown to fame, but for whom, he trusted, some time or other, a day of reckoning would come, when they would be dragged before the public and punished for their evil deeds. These were the men who, shielded by irresponsibility and hidden from the public gaze, continued the same system of misgovernment under every party which alternately presided over the destinies of the Empire.

In reality, the Colonial Reformers had as little understanding of the difficulties of colonial and imperial government as they had appreciation of the problems of squatting in Australia. They posed as experts on the empire: yet their land schemes proved utterly impracticable in Australia; South Australia went bankrupt under their tutelage; the New Zealand Company passed unmourned; finally, their ideas on limited self-government proved ill-conceived and, by the 1850s, the practical politicians had moved ahead of the theoreticians in the extension of responsible government. In fact, the Colonial Reformers possessed no great statesman among their number and few of their disciples reached high office. Molesworth alone held the seals of the Colonial Office for four months before his death in 1855. The Colonial Reformers were born propagandists, however, and the influence they exerted was largely the work of their leader, the abductor of heiresses and land speculator, Gibbon Wakefield.

Wakefield is usually remembered today for his advocacy of 'systematic colonisation' and for his role as a founder of settlements. His practical achievements have often been over-estimated. It cannot be denied, however, that he was a talented publicist and that his role was important in creating a new faith in colonies at a time when the old economic and political bases of empire were crumbling. Wakefield, in proposing his positive programmes of empire, put forward a series of economic arguments for creating new colonies, based upon the new economic science, of which the keystone was the necessity of empire to an industrial England. These views elicited a response from better-known writers and won over a number of critics of the Old Colonial System. As a result, in many economic circles, the old concept of empire based on colonial trade was replaced by a new emphasis on the importance to Great Britain of migration and colonial investment.

In the years after the Napoleonic Wars, Great Britain experienced periods of trade depression, chronic unemployment and social unrest. Talk of social revolution was in the air. Wakefield believed this situation to be the product of overpopulation and a glut of capital: the 'excess of capital above the means of profitable investment' was the cause of England's 'social ills'. Commercial crises, business failures and widespread misery were caused by a fall in profits brought about by too much capital seeking investment. In *A View of the Art of Colonization* (1849), he argued:

> If the continually increasing capital of Great Britain could be continually invested so as to yield high profits, the labourers' competition would cease because there would be ample employment at good wages. Trade of every kind would present an unlimited field of employment for classes above the common people; the professional field of employment would be equally large in proportion to the cultivators. . . . The one thing needed for all society is more room for the profitable employment of capital.

The result of the existing shortage of investment opportunities was that capital was lying idle and the economy was beginning to stagnate. This could only increase the distress in certain industrial districts of particular groups like the handloom weavers, extend the widespread pauperism in the English agricultural counties, and exacerbate the problem caused by evictions and clearances in Scotland and the general level of poverty in Ireland. In a country with a large working-class population this would inevitably encourage a 'wild vision of political and social change' and might lead to a confrontation between rich and poor. It was a gloomy prognosis.

Wakefield's remedy for avoiding the conflagration was simple: emigration and colonial investment. Emigration of Great Britain's 'redundant' population would ameliorate the prevalent distress and remove the threat to peace; colonial investment would keep up the rate of profit at home; colonisation of new lands would increase the supply of foodstuffs and raw materials and create additional markets for British manufactures. In fact, Wakefield with his surplus capital theory arrived at an analysis of Great Britain's economic and social ills remarkably similar to that of Marx. To save the capitalist system and avoid revolution in the old world, colonisation of the new was advocated.

Much of Wakefield's thesis was not new: fear of a declining rate of profit on the basis of diminishing returns was orthodox economics and Jeremy Bentham had discussed the 'emigration of capital' as a possible remedy for this in 1801; Robert Torrens had also suggested a well-regulated system of colonisation as 'a safety valve to the political machine' in 1817; and programmes of assisted emigration (denigrated by Buller as 'the shovelling out of paupers') had been undertaken during the years 1820–31 largely through the influence of Wakefield's antagonist, Robert Wilmot Horton. Ideas concerning a glut of capital and possible stagnation of the economy were, however, novel, and Wakefield's tireless repetition of these ideas provoked a fresh argument among economists.

Wakefield's ideas on the benefits of colonisation won grudging support from such respected economists as James Mill, Malthus, Nassau Senior and McCulloch and enthusiastic support from Torrens and Richard Whately. His most impressive convert was John Stuart Mill, who suggested that the cost of producing food would be reduced by opening up new territories. This would improve Great Britain's terms of trade, raise the rate of profit at home, broaden the British economy and increase domestic investment beyond its former level. Thus, Mill concluded in his *Principles of Political Economy* (1848):

> The exportation of capital is an agent of great efficacy in extending the field of employment for that which remains: and it may be said that up to a certain point the more capital we send away, the more we shall possess.

In fact, in flat contradiction of his father, he stated:

> There need be no hesitation in declaring that Colonisation, in the present state of the world, is the best affair of business in which the capital of an old and wealthy country can engage.

After this enthusiastic backing, colonial investment and emigration became important elements in the arguments in defence of colonial possessions.

By the end of the early Victorian age, therefore, there was clear disagreement among economists and political commentators about the value of empire. One school, commonly known as the Manchester School, attacked its existence; another influential section of opinion regarded empire as necessary to industrial England. Quotations from the speeches and selections from the writings of politicians, political economists, academics and others can be made to support either side of the argument. As such they are inconclusive and unreliable. An examination of the policy of the early Victorians should, therefore, be more revealing about their attitudes towards the empire.

[10] The Early Victorian Debate

A current of opinion indifferent to empire certainly existed throughout the nineteenth century. Its strength and influence waxed and waned but it never penetrated Victorian consciousness very deeply and never exerted a positive influence over British colonial policy. In the early Victorian years it was still at a comparatively early stage of growth. It grew somewhat larger with the victory of free-trade ideas. But separatists who demanded the immediate abandonment of colonies were few and never formed anything more than a vociferous minority. The Colonial Reformers, for example, were able to rally most critics of empire behind their call for the extension of self-government and the reduction of financial burdens. It was the system of government which was frequently the cause of criticism, not the existence of colonies *per se*. Even J. R. McCulloch, one of the most persistent critics of empire, acknowledged in 1840:

> We hope it will not be supposed, from anything now started, that we consider the foundations of colonial establishments as, generally speaking, inexpedient. . . . It is not to the establishment of colonies . . . but to the trammels that have been laid upon their industry, and the interference exercised by the mother country that we object.

It was the restrictive political ties and tariffs which caused most adverse comment.

The assertion has frequently been made that early Victorian politicians were not interested in the British empire. This would appear to be one of those myths which persist in the face of factual evidence to the contrary. Nevertheless, complaints of Colonial Reformers, who were always only too willing to explain the failure of their proposals to gain popular support by attributing to others a general lack of interest in the empire, and the statement by Lord Stanley that colonial affairs 'rarely came on' and when they did were 'debated before an audience which knows nothing about them and takes no interest in them', continue to be cited.

Many critics of colonial policy were indeed ill-formed. They were also often verbose and repetitive. A 2½-hour speech by Joseph Hume could be guaranteed to empty the chamber. But were all colonial debates unpopular, ill-attended and unimportant, as has so frequently been asserted? An examination of the pages of *Hansard* indicates a different state of affairs. Professor A. G. L. Shaw in an article entitled 'British Attitudes to the Colonies ca. 1820–1850' in the *Journal of British Studies* (1969), has published the following statistics: in the years 1830–40, when the question of slavery and affairs in the West Indies and Upper and Lower Canada loomed large in public discussion, there were on average about forty colonial debates each year; in the following decade when questions concerning Canada, Australia, the sugar duties and colonial emigration received most attention, there were about thirty colonial debates every year, covering on average some 8 per cent of the columns in each edition of *Hansard*. This is a fairly sizeable proportion when it is remembered that there were also several select committees appointed in this period as well as a constant stream of papers and correspondence on colonial subjects.

An analysis of parliamentary divisions during the life of the 1837 Parliament and its successor is also revealing. On average a larger number of members consistently voted in divisions on colonial, as opposed to non-colonial, matters and the proportion of 'colonial' divisions to the total number was, once again, about 7 per cent. Furthermore, many of these debates and divisions were extremely important and some were even crucial to the survival of the ministry. This artificially inflated the number voting in the division lobbies, it is true, but it also demonstrates the importance that could be attached to such matters. What is even more surprising is that in this period more attention was devoted to colonial affairs than to the conduct of foreign policy — and there has never been any complaint about Parliament's lack of interest in the latter. Indeed, the colonial debates in the early Victorian Parliaments are very informative, especially about the wide range of views held on colonial matters. What, then, can be deduced from the government's policy?

The British government's views on free trade have already been traced. It is worth remembering, however, what Huskisson, who instituted the first major steps towards free trade, had to say in 1828:

> England cannot afford to be little. She must be what she is, or nothing.
> . . . In every quarter of the globe we have planted the seeds of freedom,
> civilization and Christianity. To every quarter of the globe we have

carried the language, the free institutions, the system of laws, which prevail in this country; — in every quarter they are fructifying and making progress; and if it be said by some selfish calculator, that we have done all this at the expense of sacrifices which we ought not to have made, my answer is, — in spite of these sacrifices, we are still the first and happiest people in the old world; and, whilst this is our lot, let us rejoice rather in that rich harvest of glory which must belong to a nation that has laid the foundation of similar happiness and prosperity to other nations, kindred in blood, in habits, and in feelings to ourselves.

There was no suggestion here that Great Britain should abolish her empire. The empire of trade and strategy — the long chain of naval bases, dockyards, entrepôts and coaling stations across the world — continued to be vital to British commercial interests. Nobody suggested that India should be cut loose. And the colonies of British settlement continued to be attractive markets and suppliers of raw material. Theoretically, at least, they possessed advantages for British investors and emigration. It was also argued (before the Canadian tariff of 1859) that Great Britain could retain control of imperial trade. Buller insisted that 'of the fiscal policy of the different portions of your own empire, you can always make sure', and Lord John Russell informed Earl Grey in 1849:

> As to Colonial Reform, as it is called, I am much in favour of it, but not of Cobden's reform — which would be a dissolution of the connection. Even in his own narrow view I wonder he does not see that the imposition of a duty from 30 to 40 per cent on British manufactured goods from the Mississippi to the St. Lawrence would be a great blow to Manchester and Leeds. We must endeavour to make clear to our own minds what are the benefits which remain to us from the Colonial connection, free trade being taken for granted . . .

In 1850 Great Britain's trade with her empire accounted for some 30 per cent of British exports and about 23 per cent of her imports. British investors were also to turn to the colonies of settlement in the not too distant future, thus establishing a further economic stake in empire.

The attitude of successive British governments to the extension of responsible government has also been traced. In fact, the handing over of control of internal affairs gave additional life to the empire as most causes of friction were now removed. The din of indignation against Downing Street, stretching from the Cape to New Zealand, from bishop to potboy, which Salisbury had heard in 1852, gradually died away and was replaced by loyalty and affection. Stephen, writing in 1850

to his former superior, Earl Grey, declared that 'there is no longer a
man to be found who dissents from the opinion, which thirty-five
years ago no man ever assented to — the opinion that the intervention
of the British Government in the local affairs of a colony is an in-
convenience to be avoided by every concession and arrangement
which would not evidently induce some still greater mischief'. Unfortunately, in this rather haphazard process of colonial devolution,
colonial responsibilities, as opposed to powers, had not been clearly
delineated. It was left for the mid-Victorians to sort out the problem of
imperial defence and 'native policy'.

The imperial relationship for the future envisaged towards the end
of the 1850s was one of a federal character. Stephen, writing in 1850,
asserted that Great Britain had adopted the only right course towards
Canada:

> It was that of cheerfully relaxing, one after another, the bonds of
> authority, as soon as the colony itself clearly desired that relation — so
> substituting a federal for a colonial relation, the change being real, not
> nominal — no national pride wounded, or national greatness diminished,
> or national duty abandoned. It remains for the Canadians to cut the
> last cable which anchors them to us. But it is for them, not for us, to
> take that step, and to assume the consequent responsibility.

Few critics of the colonial system would have wished to go beyond this
statement. Even Sir George Cornewall Lewis who, it has been said,
provided the political arguments for separation in his *Essay on the
Government of Dependencies*, acknowledged:

> It is obvious to remark, that the dominant country ought not to
> abandon its authority over a dependency, unless the people of the
> dependency consent to the cession, and are capable of forming an
> independent community. It is bound morally, not to throw off a helpless
> dependency, although the possession of it should promise no advantage
> to itself.

Whatever might be the future of the settlement colonies, it is clear that
few thinkers formulated, few responsible politicians advocated, and no
British government followed, a policy of scuttle.

Perhaps the attitude of the British government was most clearly
explained in a speech by Lord John Russell introducing the Australian
Colonies Government Bill in 1850. The Prime Minister affirmed:

> I consider it to be our bounden duty to maintain the colonies which
> have been placed under our charge. I think we cannot get rid of the
> obligation and responsibility to govern those colonies for their benefit,

and I trust we may be the instrument of improving and civilising those portions of the world in which they are situated. In the next place, I say that there are many reasons why we should consider that our colonies form part of the strength of the empire. I think that, in peace as well as in war, it is a question of the utmost importance whether we should retain these supports of the imperial authority of this country, or whether we should be deprived of them.

Russell then proceeded to recite most of the reasons for retaining the empire that his predecessors had put forward: the civilising of distant portions of the world, responsibility for the welfare of 'native' races, the security offered by colonial ports to British shipping (especially in time of war), the inability of the colonies to defend themselves and the risk of annexation by foreign powers, the existence of fields for emigration and great potential markets for British trade. He argued that, in return for defending the colonies, colonial commercial policies should conform to that of the mother country. In all other respects the government's policy was one of self-government, self-reliance and reduced colonial expenditure. He concluded by looking into the future:

> I anticipate indeed with others that some of the colonies may so grow in population and wealth that they may say — 'Our strength is sufficient to enable us to be independent of England. The link is now become onerous to us — the time is come when we can, in amity and alliance with England, maintain our independence.' I do not think that that time is yet approaching. But let us make them as far as possible, fit to govern themselves — let us give them as far as we can, the capacity of ruling their own affairs — let them increase in wealth and population, and whatever may happen, we of this great empire shall have the consolation of saying that we have contributed to the happiness of the world.

This was the 'sting in the tail' that so much upset Lord Elgin in his correspondence with Earl Grey.

Quotations such as this, numerous references to the impossibility of defending Canada, and criticisms of British expenditure on the empire, were once the basis of a long-held view that these years witnessed an age of anti-imperialism. It is a view still to be found in certain quarters but one which is gradually disappearing from the textbooks. However, heavy criticism of a recent argument that the early Victorian age witnessed a period of economic aggression in areas beyond the colonies painted red on the map has led to a renewed assertion that not only was there little imperialist activity of any kind, but there was also a 'retreat from empire' or, at least, that it was a time when the idea of empire was at an unaccustomed discount. It is a view which deserves careful consideration.

It is true that the growth of colonial self-government involved a disengagement by the British from political control. It is true that during these years Great Britain refused to annex several new lands to the empire. It is also true that there was some abandonment or attempted abandonment of territory. But does this really add up to a 'retreat from empire'? The old concept of empire was certainly at a discount. The search for a new relationship was implicit in the introduction of responsible government. But the point has been made frequently enough that, in general, it was not the existence of colonies in themselves that was challenged but the system of their management. There was plenty of justification for empire both in theory and in practice, in the early Victorian age.

Most important of all, however, it should be emphasised that for the British the purpose of empire was normally to do with trade and not with dominion in itself. Rarely was there a simple lust for territory, and annexation, even in the late Victorian age, always remained a last resort. In general, the 'Second Empire' did not require new lands, and the Victorians, until the last quarter of the century, remained highly selective in the acquisition of new territory. In the early Victorian age British manufacturers and traders concentrated on the established markets in Europe, the United States, India and the colonies of settlement. Chances that Great Britain would be required to exert political control over existing markets or be called upon to extend her influence into unstable areas on the periphery of empire were, therefore, minimal. In the unstable commercial and financial climate of the time when short booms were followed by disastrous slumps and long periods of slow growth, when panics hit the British money market in 1825, 1837, 1847 and 1857 and were accompanied by a host of smaller, more localised crises, British overseas investors sought safe markets for their capital. Thus, certainly in the economic field, the situation was not ripe for conditions which frequently led to an extension of territory. In any case the British attitude always revolved round the simple question of expediency. For example, in the South Pacific, offers of cession from the Fiji Islands in 1855 and 1858 were declined. Annexation was not thought to be expedient and several alternative means of exerting influence were tried. These, however, failed and Great Britain finally annexed the islands from a mixture of motives in 1874. It was then thought to be in the British interest. Thus to cite refusals to annex as evidence that the idea of empire was at an unaccustomed discount is merely to state that eighteenth-century ideas of empire were no longer acceptable in the nineteenth century. Empire took on a new shape in the early Victorian age and was backed by a new set of ideas.

Was there, then, a 'retreat from empire' in these years? What about the abandonment of territory? When this is examined it does not amount to very much. The cession of the Indonesian islands of Java (1816) and Sumatra (1824), of the Bay Islands in the western Caribbean (ceded to the neighbouring Republic of Honduras in 1860) and, at a slightly later date, the cession of the Ionian Islands in the Mediterranean to Greece in 1864, may be cited. These latter islands — some so small that you have to search the map for them — were all ceded in the political or economic interests of Great Britain. They hardly support the thesis of a 'retreat from empire'. There was only one other area where a withdrawal of British power occurred. This was in South Africa and deserves separate consideration.

Following the Great Trek, the British government had passed an Act extending Cape laws to British subjects up to the line of 25° S (north of modern Pretoria). After further soul-searching Natal was annexed in 1843; three years later the area beyond the eastern frontier of the Cape up to the Great Kei river, known as British Kaffraria, was added to the British dominions; and in 1848 the Boer lands between the Orange and Vaal rivers became the Crown colony of the Orange River Sovereignty. But this extension of British government proved a costly and thankless task. In the 1850s the British government decided that the burden was too great. First, in 1852, any intention of controlling the Boers beyond the Vaal river was renounced in the Sand River Convention, and then, in 1854, the colony of the Orange River Sovereignty was emancipated by the Bloemfontein Convention and was renamed the Orange Free State. Here, indeed, were two acts of political abdication. But the accompanying expansion of territory which had preceded these events, the additions to the empire which were retained, and the small additions to territory which continued to be made in the 1860s cannot be ignored. Moreover, since it must be admitted that a kind of paramountcy was asserted over the whole subcontinent and that successive governments worked the convention policy to British advantage by controlling Boer access to the sea, the withdrawal of government did not amount to complete political abdication. A less costly policy was adopted to secure British ends. In fact, the whole history of British involvement in South

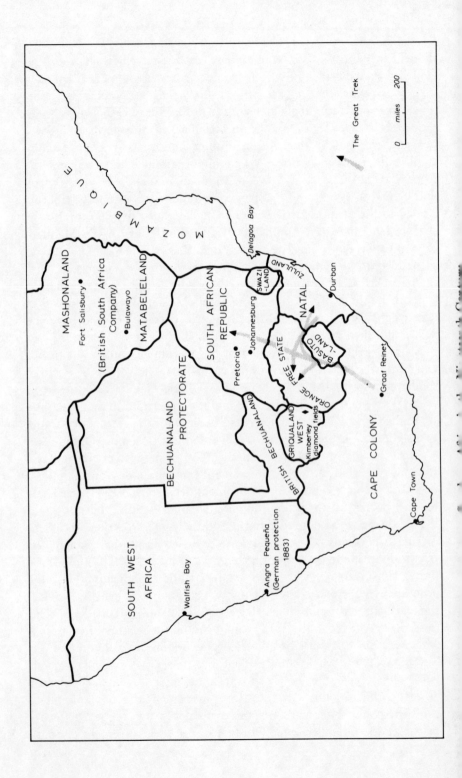

Africa reveals the most extraordinary amount of vacillation. After the convention policy was officially abandoned in 1877, it was reinstated in 1881. Thus the early Victorian age was no exception in seeing both expansion and contraction. The convention policy of 1852–4 merely emphasises that what was believed to be in the British interest was at the bottom of it all.

It was exactly the same elsewhere. It was in the British interest that free trade was adopted, and responsible government, in removing many of the financial burdens of empire and the sheer irksomeness of government at a distance, was equally to British advantage. But because conditions did not require extensions of territory, it does not mean that anti-empire sentiment had triumphed. The empire continued to exist and efficient use was made of it. Uncertainty as regards the future did not lead to a general policy of abandonment and, indeed, did not check the extension of the empire. Admittedly, outside India this was not very great. It amounted to the annexations of Aden, New Zealand, Hong Kong, Natal and Labuan. In India, however, during the years 1843–56, British control was asserted over Sind, the Punjab, Kashmir, Nagpur, Jhansi, Berar and Oudh. The second Burmese war resulted in the annexation of Lower Burma in 1852. These are extensions of British power which cannot be ignored. In fact, colonies continued to be valued for their wealth, prestige and potential commercial value. Even Canada, that most abused and expensive of possessions, remained a part of the empire and British money continued to be spent on Canadian defence in the 1850s and early 1860s. That Canada, the *bête noire* of the separatists, remained a part of the empire demonstrates how little influence over policy the idea of separation attained in the early Victorian age.

In the late 1850s a new interest in empire arose. Gold rushes took place in Australia in 1851, in British Columbia in 1858, and in New Zealand in 1861; and these, in turn, triggered off more primary and secondary industries. The colonial cry for railways diverted some British capital from the declining railway investment market of Europe. During the years 1855–80 a quarter of British overseas investment went into British colonies. India, Australia, New Zealand and Canada became heavy borrowers on the London money market and a new stake in empire was established. In fact, British overseas trade and investment policy, the growth of self-governing colonies, the empire of trade and strategy and British expansion in India were all different aspects of the early Victorian empire. It is difficult, and would probably be misleading, to force these components into a set pattern. India, in particular, defies categorisation. It illustrates a separate, and frequently contradictory, aspect of Victorian imperialism. And it is to India that we must now turn in order to complete our survey of the early Victorian empire.

[11] India from Company Rule to British Raj

Events in India during Queen Victoria's long reign reveal the complexity of Victorian imperialism. In many respects British policy towards India was the very antithesis of the idea of free trade, laissez-faire, responsible government and limited expansion promoted in other parts of the empire. Even the strongest advocates of free trade and laissez-faire became manipulators of tariffs and bureaucratic planners where India was concerned. Victorian expansion in the sub-continent was virtually over by the time the 'Age of Imperialism' dawned. India was, in every way, an empire in its own right.

The East India Company and its impact
In the seventeenth century, the East India Company had begun a profitable trade in silks, calicoes, spices and chinaware. It established important commercial bases in the three presidencies (trading stations under a president) at Bombay, Madras and Calcutta. The break-up of the Mughal empire after the death of Emperor Aurangzeb in 1707, however, disturbed trading conditions. British traders then gradually became more and more involved in internal upheavals and in restoring order and dispensing rough justice until, by Victorian times, the British had become responsible for the judicial, financial and diplomatic affairs of provinces comprising a million square miles and containing a population of over 100 million. In fact, the British eventually became responsible for the government, commerce and defence of the polygot dominion once ruled by the Muslim conquerors of Hindustan.

How did this state of affairs come about? In the mid-eighteenth century, amid the turmoil which accompanied Mughal decline and the power vacuum caused by rivalries among successor states — the Muslim-ruled Kingdoms of Mysore and Hyderabad in the south, the Hindu Maratha states in the centre, the independent provinces of Sind and the Punjab in the west, and Oudh, Bihar and Bengal in the east — the British and French traders found it necessary to seek Indian allies in order to protect their property and preserve their trade. The result was twofold. The European wars were fought out in India as well as the Americas and at the end of the Seven Years' War the French were excluded from India except for the purposes of trade. But the wars in India went on. The British now had enemies among the indigenous rulers who had been allies of the French and the power struggle continued until the East India Company emerged as victor in the early nineteenth century. The ruler of Bengal was defeated in 1757; Mysore capitulated in 1799; the Company took over the Carnatic in 1801; and the final defeat of the Marathas occurred in 1817–18. By this date, either through conquest or through alliances with the 500-odd princely states (a few, like Hyderabad, almost as large as Ireland, but mostly very small principalities), a large part of the sub-continent had fallen under British control or influence.

The days of the Company as a trading concern were, however, numbered. As the Company gradually took over administration and collection of revenue in the conquered territories, the British government became more interested in Company activities and the fortunes being amassed by private individuals to the detriment of Company trade. General Clive, for example, extorted £234,000 from the Nawab of Bengal. Other traders also made fortunes (Company officials were expected to supplement their meagre stipends by private trade) and rich 'nabobs' (the English version of Nawab) became an increasingly familiar sight in British society and Parliament. Not surprisingly, the British government, with the National Debt at £140 million in 1763, began to demand some return for the military and naval aid given to the Company during the French wars. In 1767 the Company reluctantly agreed to contribute £400,000 a year to the British Exchequer. But even this sum proved too great for the shaky finances of the Company. By 1782 the Company was £1 million in debt and the enquiries of a number of select and secret parliamentary committees led to no fewer than eighteen hostile reports. The result was a series of political enactments which culminated in the assumption of full sovereignty by the Crown in 1858. Each renewal of the Company's charter provided the opportunity for a further liquidation of the Company's powers.

The process began with Lord North's Regulating Act in 1773. In return for the liquidation of the Company's debts, its affairs both in England and India were reorganised. Then, in 1784, by Pitt's India Act, the directors of the Company were divested of their political responsibilities. Political oversight was vested in a Board of Control consisting of six Privy Councillors under a President who later became a member of the Cabinet. The foremost representative of the Company in India, the Governor-General of Fort William in Bengal, became a Crown appointment and three councillors were appointed to assist him. The Governor-General-in-Council was to be the supreme authority in the Company's possessions.

Most subsequent reforms dealt with the commercial business of the Company. The Company lost its monopoly of trade with India in 1813. Twenty years later its monopoly of the China trade went the same way. The Company's trading role was then brought to an end and the Company was left simply as the organ of government in British India. Thus by 1833 the movement of free trade had begun to have an influence on British policy towards India.

The humanitarians and Evangelicals were also influential. In 1833 Thomas Babington Macaulay, the historian, who was then secretary to the Board of Control, enunciated the concept of imperial trusteeship:

> It is difficult to form any conjecture as to the fate reserved for a state which resembles no other in history, and which forms by itself a separate class of political phenomena. The laws which regulate its growth and its decay are still unknown to us. It may be that the public mind in India may expand under our system till it has outgrown that system; that by good government we may educate our subjects into a capacity for better government; that, having become instructed in European knowledge, they may, in some future age, demand European institutions. Whether such a day will ever come I know not. But never will I attempt to avert or to retard it. Whenever it comes, it will be the proudest day in English history.

This new spirit was soon seen to be at work in India.

Lord William Bentinck, an aristocratic Radical and disciple of Bentham, had been appointed governor-general in 1828. He was instructed to carry out several economies but he also succeeded in enacting judicial and revenue reforms as well as encouraging steam transport, tea and coffee cultivation, iron and coal production, the planning of a network of roads, drainage projects and irrigation canals. He is best remembered today, however, for beginning an attack on some of those Indian social and religious customs which were most offensive to Western eyes. His most radical measure was the abolition of *suttee*, the burning of widows on the funeral pyres of their husbands. A campaign was also begun to suppress the bands of *thugs*, groups of robbers and ritual murderers who roamed the countryside waylaying travellers and performing human sacrifices to the goddess, Kali. This campaign was successful in 1836. Bentinck also suppressed ritual child sacrifice and discouraged infanticide.

From the correction of abuses, Bentinck turned to the problem of education. He declared: 'general education is my panacea for the regeneration of India', and he decreed that the content of the learning encouraged should be Western knowledge and that the medium of instruction should be English. English was already the language of government and commerce and had been substituted for Persian in the law courts. Macaulay, who had gone out to India in 1834 as law member on the Governor-General's council, endorsed this innovation in his celebrated Minute on Education in 1835. In language that was scornful of Indian learning and culture Macaulay asserted that Western ideas, taught through the English language, would develop 'a class of persons, Indian in blood and colour, but English in taste, opinion, in morals and intellect'. This policy of 'assimilation', of creating brown Victorians, echoed the sentiments of the Select Committee on Aborigines in 1837 which advocated missionary work and attempts at social and political improvement.

Thus, by the time Queen Victoria ascended the throne, all those influences extant in other parts of the empire — free trade, humanitarianism, evangelicism and utilitarianism — can be seen at work in India. But developments in India in the early Victorian age did not conform to the pattern established elsewhere. There was, for example, no talk by the British of representative institutions and responsible government for this part of the empire. Macaulay, in 1833, had talked of 'an enlightened and paternal despotism' as being the only form of government suitable for India:

> We have to frame a good government for a country into which, by universal acknowledgement, we cannot introduce those institutions which all our habits — which all the reasonings of European philosophers — which all the history of our own part of the world would lead us to consider as the one security for good government.

This was not the only difference. Far from it being an age of laissez-faire in India, the state seemed to interfere more and more; the alleged policy of free trade also seemed to resemble the techniques of mercantilism. And far from witnessing refusals to annex or only limited territorial expansion, the early Victorian age experienced the most rapid extension of British influence and control in India of the whole Victorian period.

Mercantilist techniques

Adam Smith referred to the East India Company as the body 'for the appointment of plunderers of India'. The early profits of trade and the fortunes amassed by individuals supported this contention. One Company ship, the *Berrington*, left England in 1784 with a cargo valued at £27,300 and returned laden with products to the value of £119,304. Thus on one journey alone one ship made a profit of £90,000 — a large enough profit in modern times but an astounding one for the late eighteenth century. Trade with India would have been even larger had the British been able to supply more of the goods in demand in India. Besides small quantities of lead, copper, quicksilver, tin and ivory, British traders could only offer bullion — and the export of precious metals was frowned upon in the age of mercantilism. The object, therefore, was to keep the price of imported goods as low as possible. The Company devised means of its own for doing this: first by extortion and plunder (the very word 'loot' is of Hindustani origin); then, when the Company began to acquire administrative responsibilities, heavy taxes on land were imposed; and, finally, the Company attempted to adjust the economy of India to British requirements. The Victorians benefited from and even continued some of these methods in the so-called age of free trade and laissez-faire.

In 1762 the Nawab of Bengal complained in a memorandum to the English governor about the activities of the East India Company's agents:

> They forcibly take away the goods and commodities of the Ryots [peasants], merchants, etc., for a fourth part of their value; and by ways of violence and oppression they obliged the Ryots, etc., to give five rupees for goods which are worth but one rupee.

This exploitation increased when the Company acquired from the Mughal Emperor, in 1765, the cession of the *diwani* of Bengal — the management and collection of the revenue. This was an equally lucrative business. Although the Company claimed no more revenue than the former rulers, the British were able to enforce its collection. Whereas the last Muslim ruler of Bengal collected a land revenue of £817,553 in 1764, within thirty years the British income had risen to £2,680,000. In Madras the land tax amounted to half the gross product of the land. This income solved the problem of the export of bullion from Great Britain — it paid for the merchandise bought by the East India Company. Company sales abroad, therefore, were sheer profit and, in reality, represented a constant and tremendous drain on the resources of India. This was, in a real sense, legalised exploitation.

Even more harmful was the stranglehold the British obtained on the Indian economy. With the coming of the Industrial Revolution the Company discouraged the manufacturing industries of India and tried to encourage the development of raw materials. This policy affected the basic unit of Indian society — the self-sufficient village. Prohibitive tariffs excluded Indian silk and cotton goods from England. In 1813, for example, a duty of 78 per cent existed on the import of Indian calicoes into Great Britain (otherwise they would have been sold at a price 50–60 per cent lower than that of their English equivalents). British goods, on the other hand, were admitted to India with only a nominal duty. An enquiry in 1840 revealed that British cotton and silk goods imported into India paid a duty of $3\frac{1}{2}$ per cent and woollen goods 2 per cent. Equivalent Indian exports to Great Britain paid an import duty of 10, 20 and 30 per cent respectively. This was one-way free trade: the virtually free entry of British goods into India and heavy tariffs on Indian exports to Great Britain, direct trade with Europe and other foreign countries being prevented by the existence of the Navigation Acts. In this way the Indian textile, shipbuilding, metalwork, glass and paper industries were throttled and the internal vacuum was filled by British goods. Many suffered grievously as India was transformed into a largely agricultural colony exporting raw cotton, wool, jute, oil-seeds, dyes and hides to Great Britain. Only the Indian cotton manu-facturing industry survived.

In India the doctrine of laissez-faire was deliberately ignored. The early Victorians began a whole series of state enterprises — railway and road networks, irrigation schemes, telegraph, postal and banking systems. These developments brought great benefits to India, but it is also noticeable that the commercial and strategic needs of foreign pene-tration were always given priority. And while this new investment involved a major movement of British capital to India, most of the investment, especially that in railways, was at the high and guaranteed rate of 5 per cent interest charged against the revenues of India. In fact, every conceivable expense in governing India was charged against the Indian revenue, from the costs of the army in India to the wages of charladies in the India Office in London. The costs of the mutiny in 1857, the cost of transferring the East India Company's rights to the Crown, gifts to the Zanzibar mission, the expenses of the diplomatic establishments in China and Persia, part of the expenses of the Mediter-

ranean fleet, the cost of the telegraph from England to India and even
the maintenance of a lunatic asylum at Ealing were laid at India's door.
Revenues from India on more than one occasion helped the British
balance of payments.

Thus in spite of Ricardo's doubts about the desirability of British
rule in India and Cobden's condemnations of contemporary imperialism, the Victorians found British rule in India to their liking. Even
John Bright and the majority of the Manchester School supported a
policy of internal development through the promotion of communications and public works. Professor Robin Moore in 'Imperialism and
Free Trade Policy in India, 1853–4' (*Economic History Review*, 1964) has
argued that the desire for Indian cotton involved condoning improvements effected by private capital upon which the returns were secured
against the public revenue of India. That is to say, the Manchester
School exploited India as a source of raw material and as a field for the
guaranteed investment of 'finance capital' and fostered a class of
investors whom J. A. Hobson later described as the 'taproot of
Imperialism'. Manchester manufacturers and Members of Parliament
were certainly in the forefront of the attempts to manipulate the
Indian cotton duties and promote cotton supply, as Professor Peter
Harnetty has demonstrated in his book, *Imperialism and Free Trade:
Lancashire and India in the Mid-Nineteenth Century* (1972). Cobden was in
despair in 1857:

> If you talk to our Lancashire friends they argue that unless we occupied
> India there would be no trade with that country, or that somebody else
> would monopolize it, forgetting that this is the old protectionist theory
> which they used formerly to ridicule. India was a great centre and source
> of commerce for the civilized world before Englishmen took to wearing
> breeches, and it was the renown of its wealth and productiveness which
> first attracted us there. I am by no means as clear as some people that
> we have added greatly to its commerce.

Nevertheless, in contravention of the principles of free trade and
laissez-faire, tariffs were manipulated, products required by British
industry were promoted and the country was opened up for commercial penetration by state enterprise. It was a simple case of commercial imperialism.

The proclamation of British rule

In 1837 Great Britain was indisputably the paramount power in India.
By 1858, the year in which the East India Company was abolished and

British rule was proclaimed, the boundaries of modern India, apart from their north-western and north-eastern extremities, had largely been drawn. Queen Victoria's reign began, however, with a disastrous little war.

The British government was going through one of its Russophobe periods and Palmerston, the Foreign Secretary, saddled the new Governor-General with explicit instructions to watch Russian activities in Afghanistan. The weak Lord Auckland imagined himself to be surrounded by enemies. The result was an invasion of Afghanistan in 1839, ostensibly for the purpose of defeating Russian and Persian ambitions in that country by returning the deposed King Shah Suja to the throne in place of the reigning Amir, Dost Mohammed. Kabul, the Afghan capital, was occupied in August 1839 and Shah Suja was restored to the throne. British garrisons were then entrenched at Karachi, Quetta, Kandahar, and Jalalabad while the new Amir consolidated his position.

In November 1841 the city of Kabul rose in rebellion and the British Resident, Sir Alexander Burns, was murdered. The British were forced to retire. A column of 4,700 British and Indian troops, 12,000 camp followers and a few formidable English ladies, set out for Jalalabad. All the way through the snowy passes the column was harried by tribesmen. A week later a solitary survivor, an army surgeon, reached base. It was a crushing defeat for British policy. British influence in Afghanistan was in ruins, Shah Suja (the original possessor of the fabulous Koh-i-noor diamond) was shortly assassinated, thousands of troops had died and hundreds of thousands of pounds had been wasted. Auckland's successor, Lord Ellenborough, immediately organised an expedition to relieve the besieged garrisons at Kandahar and Jalalabad. The two columns subsequently converged on Kabul and released the remaining British prisoners. The British then hurriedly withdrew, leaving Dost Mohammed in possession of Afghanistan.

The lesson was not lost on the Amirs of Sind who had been forced by Auckland to accept a dictated treaty. The East India Company sent the dictatorial Sir Charles Napier to deal with them. Napier was renowned for his belligerence. In 1829 he had met the objections of the Brahmins of Sind to the abolition of *suttee* in characteristic fashion:

> You say *suttee* is the custom. Well, we too have a custom which is to hang men who burn women alive. You build your funeral pyre and I will build a gallows beside it, and let each of us act according to custom.

He was now of an equally decided opinion:

I do not think the Amirs fools, I think them cunning rascals. They saw
our defeat which encouraged them to break treaties. They hope to have
a second Kabul affair. Now what is to be done? That which is best
for . . . the good government of the population, and we must not
sacrifice it to an endeavour, utterly hopeless I may say, to give to these
tyrannical, drunken, debauched, cheating, intriguing, contemptible
Amirs a due portion of the plunder they have amassed from the ruined
people.

Napier's solution was to provoke a fight. He confided to his diary:

We have no right to seize Sind, yet we shall do so and a very advan-
tageous, useful, humane piece of rascality it will be.

The province of Sind was annexed in 1843. It was such campaigns as
these, together with the occupation of the state of Gwalior in 1843,
that led to the recall of Ellenborough and his replacement by Lord
Hardinge in 1844.

The next troublesome area was the Punjab. After the death of the
Sikh leader, Ranjit Singh, in 1839, the Punjab had begun to fall apart
as civil strife engulfed the state. In December 1845 the Queen Mother,
in an effort to save the boy-King, pushed the army into a war with the
British. The Sikhs were magnificent and well-equipped soldiers with
good artillery. The British Commander-in-Chief, Sir Hugh Gough,
believed in the efficacy of the bayonet. Four costly and bloody battles
ensued which resulted in the Treaty of Lahore in 1846, whereby the
Punjabis paid a war indemnity, admitted a British Resident (Sir Henry
Lawrence) to Lahore and ceded certain lands (including the backward
Muslim state of Kashmir which the British immediately sold to a
Hindu ruler for £1,000,000). It was no more than an armistice. The
second Sikh war flared up in 1848. After further bloody campaigns the
Punjab was annexed by Hardinge's successor, the Marquis of Dalhousie,
and reorganised as a province of British India by the famous brothers,
Henry and John Lawrence.

This was not the end of British expansion. Disputes between British
merchants and the Burmese Governor of Rangoon led to the second
Burmese war in 1852. A small naval force under Admiral Austen
(Jane Austen's brother) was sent to Rangoon and after several skirm-
ishes Lower Burma was also annexed. This was the last of Dalhousie's
conquests but by no means his last annexation. Dalhousie turned next
to the Indian states where misgovernment was rife. First, he took a firm
line with the superannuated King of Delhi who still preserved some of
the trappings of the Great Mughal. He declared that the Mughal

monarchy would end with the life of the present incumbent, Bahadur Shah, who was nearly eighty years old. He then abolished titular sovereignties like Nawab of the Carnatic and the Rajaship of Tanjore. Furthermore, at the death in 1853 of the deposed Chief of the Maratha confederacy, Pershwa Baji Rao, Dalhousie refused to pay a pension to his adopted son, Nana Sahib. Of even greater significance, he refused to recognise the rights of adoption in Hindu states owing allegiance to the British. If a ruler died without natural heirs, the state 'lapsed' to the British government. In this way Satara (1848), Jaipur and Sambalpur (1849), Baghat (1850), Udaipur (1852), Jhansi (1853) and Nagpur, one of the three large surviving Maratha states (1854), came under British control during Dalhousie's period of office. His final act before leaving India was even more provocative: he annexed the rich kingdom of Oudh, one of the last great independent Muslim states in northern India, notorious for its anarchy, misgovernment and corruption. A third of the sepoys in the Bengal army came from Oudh. Significantly enough, the Indian Mutiny in the following year brought to an end one of the most aggressive phases of British expansion in the sub-continent of India.

Dalhousie certainly left his mark on India. He possessed a passion for improvement. He built the first railways in India and two great roads (including the Grand Trunk Road from Calcutta to Peshawar), and established an efficient public telegraph system. He introduced a half-anna letter rate, completed the Ganges Canal, lighted the coasts, improved harbours and reformed everything from forests to jails. He planned a comprehensive scheme of Indian education — primary schools, high schools, colleges and universities — and founded an engineering college at Roorkee as well. The creative and comprehensive nature of his work surpassed that of all other nineteenth-century governor-generals. He was the apostle of a Westernised India. He retired at the age of 44 in 1856 worn out by eight years of service. If he possessed a fault it was that of going too fast. One soldier-administrator, James Outram, believed that 'the Crusading improving spirit of the last twenty-five years would cause a resounding clash'. Among the Indian people all this change and reconstruction gave rise to deep-seated fears and resentments.

To Hindu and Muslim alike, the introduction of English law, language, teaching and religion, in fact any interference with caste and culture, represented an attempt to impose an alien civilisation. If Bentinck had alarmed the orthodox by his reforms concerning *suttee*,

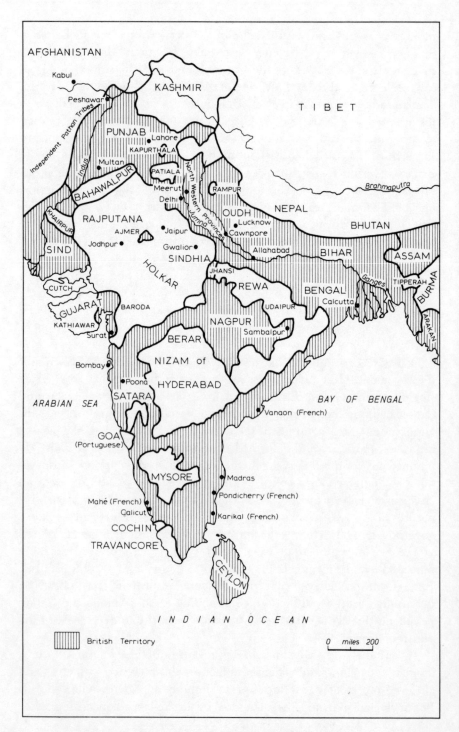

India on the eve of the Indian Mutiny

infanticide and *thuggee*, Dalhousie had threatened vested interests by his doctrine of lapse, his confiscation of estates, the strengthening of the central government and the law of 1850 whereby converts from Hinduism to another religion could inherit ancestral property. The aim was clearly a centrally administered, anglicised India. The attitude of missionaries towards 'unenlightened' and 'ignorant' Indians and the arrogance of educationalists towards Indian abilities and culture were also an affront to national self-esteem. Where would the British stop? Such an atmosphere created the social and political background which allowed a few military grievances to convulse the country.

There had been minor mutinies in 1806 and 1824 and some regiments had refused to serve overseas in 1852. The 1856 General Service Enlistment Act had made such service compulsory when necessary. The atmosphere was suitably charged, therefore, when it was rumoured that cartridges for the new Enfield rifles, which had to be bitten open, were smeared with grease and pig fat. The cow was sacred to the Hindu and the pig was unclean to the Muslim. Despite repeated assurances from British officers, the withdrawal of the order to bite the cartridges open and permission to use their own grease, fears persisted and eighty-five sepoys of the 3rd Light Cavalry Regiment, one of the crack native regiments in India, were arrested at Meerut, the huge Company military station forty miles north-east of Delhi, on 9 May 1857, for refusing to accept the cartridges. The following day their colleagues from three regiments mutinied, massacred their officers, released the prisoners and marched off to Delhi where they proclaimed as Emperor of India the old king, whom they found languishing in his decayed palace. In June the mutiny spread to Cawnpore (North West Provinces), and the British in Lucknow (Oudh) were besieged for eighty-seven days. A semblance of authority was restored in September when Delhi was re-taken. Lucknow was relieved in November. By then the back of the mutiny had been broken but it took eighteen months before stability was finally restored.

It was not a national uprising: two-thirds of the country stayed passive. The Bombay and Madras armies remained loyal, so did most of the Indian princes (except the Rani of Jhansi, one of Dalhousie's dispossessed girl-widows, and Nana Sahib, to whom Dalhousie had refused a pension). The recently conquered Punjab remained quiet. Afghanistan, after the recent assistance from Great Britain when the Persians occupied Herat, provided no help to the mutineers and Nepal sent Gurkhas to aid the British. Resistance occurred mainly in the western half of Bengal. It was largely a soldiers' mutiny; only in Oudh was there the suspicion of a national uprising. It is doubtful whether more than a quarter of the 200,000 sepoys were involved. There was no organised plan of campaign and no recognised leader. The mutiny consisted of a series of local outbreaks and was not a war of independence as some Indian historians have claimed.

Yet it was more than just a mutiny of the Bengal army. The fears and resentments which had built up were widespread and led to several brutal and bloody incidents. The British public was fed on stories of gruesome sepoy atrocities. Several hundred British women and children died, a large number at the instigation of the ferocious Nana Sahib of Cawnpore. Women were also raped. But British vengeance was also terrible. Fates worse than death were devised. Frantic Muslims were sewn into pigskins before execution, Indians were forced to lick up the congealed blood of their victims and were shot from the mouths of cannons. 'Clemency' Canning, Dalhousie's successor, had his work cut out to earn his nickname.

The end result was the abolition of the East India Company. The British were now in India to stay. There was little chance of trusting or handing power to a people who were thought to be something less than human. In November 1858, while war still raged in central India, British rule was proclaimed. The Queen's proclamation announced:

> We desire no extension of our present territorial possessions . . . we shall respect the rights, dignity, and honour of native princes as our own . . . we declare it to be our royal will and pleasure that none be in any wise favoured, none molested or disquieted, by reason of their religious faith or observances, but that all shall alike enjoy the equal and impartial protection of the law. . . . And it is our further will that, so far as may be, our subjects, of whatever race or creed, be freely and impartially admitted to office in our service . . .

It concluded:

> When, by the blessing of Providence, internal tranquillity shall be restored, it is our earnest desire to stimulate the peaceful industry of India, to promote works of public utility and improvement, and to administer the government for the benefit of all our subjects resident therein. In their prosperity will be our strength, in their contentment our security, and in their gratitude our best reward. And may the God of all power grant to us, and to those in authority under us, strength to carry out these our wishes for the good of our people.

Thus the early Victorian age closed with the official declaration of

British rule over the largest area of the British empire. Like most of the developments in early nineteenth-century India, it contradicted the drift of events elsewhere. Yet it is quite clear that no survey of the early Victorian age and no general theory of Victorian imperialism is sufficient which does not take the contradictory elements of Indian history in the first half of the nineteenth century into account. We must now examine some of the more general ideas which have been put forward concerning the framework of Victorian expansion.

PRINCIPAL EVENTS, 1837–58

1835–7	Great Trek in South Africa
1837	Rebellions in Upper Canada and Lower Canada
1838	May–November. Lord Durham's mission to Canada. Apprenticeship system in the West Indies abolished
1839	The Durham Report. Aden annexed. Afghanistan invaded
1840	Treaty of Waitangi with Maori chieftains. New Zealand annexed. Union of the two Canadas
1841	Retreat from Kabul
1842	New South Wales Government Act. Hong Kong annexed
1843	Maori Wars begin (continue until 1847). Natal annexed. Sind conquered
1845	First Sikh war
1846	Earl Grey becomes Colonial Secretary. Lieutenant Governor of Nova Scotia instructed to institute responsible government. British Kaffraria and Labuan annexed
1847	James Stephen replaced by Herman Merivale as Permanent Under-Secretary in the Colonial Office. Elgin becomes Governor-General of united Canada. Governor of Cape Colony becomes High Commissioner for South Africa
1848	January. Nova Scotia first colony with responsible ministry. March. Responsible government implemented in Canada. Second Sikh war. Transvaal and Orange Free State become Crown colonies. Satara, Jaipur and Sambalpur 'lapse' to British Crown
1849	Navigation Acts abolished in Great Britain. Rebellion Losses Bill passed in Canada
1850	Australian Colonies Government Act. Baghat lapses
1851	Australian gold rush. Victoria becomes separate colony
1852	Sand River Convention. New Zealand Constitution Act.

Lower Burma annexed. Udaipur lapses. Representative government in Cape Colony

1853   Jhansi lapses

1854   Bloemfontein Convention. Nagpur lapses. Britain ends sugar protection

1855   British Parliament authorises new constitutions for most of Australian colonies

1856   Responsible government in New South Wales, Victoria and Tasmania. Oudh annexed

1857   May. Indian Mutiny begins at Meerut.
        June. Fall of Cawnpore. Siege of Lucknow and Delhi.
        September. Delhi recaptured by British.
        November. Lucknow finally relieved.
        Responsible government in South Australia

1858   British Columbia established. Gold rush.
        November. Queen's Proclamation of British rule over India.
        Government of India Act

Further Reading

J. H. Rose, A. P. Newton, & E. A. Benians (eds), *Cambridge History of the British Empire*, Vol. II, *The Growth of the New Empire, 1783–1870*. Cambridge University Press (Cambridge, 1940).

D. M. Young, *The Colonial Office in the Early Nineteenth Century*. Longmans (London, 1961).

P. Knaplund, *James Stephen and the British Colonial System, 1813–47*. Wisconsin University Press (Madison, 1953).

G. R. Mellor, *British Imperial Trusteeship, 1783–1850*. Faber (London, 1951).

E. Williams, *Capitalism and Slavery*. University of North Carolina Press (Chapel Hill, 1944).

R. T. Anstey, 'Capitalism and Slavery: A Critique', *Economic History Review*, 2nd Series, Vol. XXI, pp. 307–20, 1968.

E. A. Walker, *The Great Trek*. Black, 4th ed. (London, 1960).

O. Ransford, *The Great Trek*. Murray (London, 1972).

P. Burroughs, *The Canadian Crisis and British Colonial Policy, 1828–41*. Arnold (London, 1972).

C. New, *Lord Durham's Mission to Canada*. Oxford University Press (London, 1929).

G. M. Craig (ed.), *Lord Durham's Report*. McClelland & Stewart (Toronto, 1963).

G. Martin, *The Durham Report and British Policy*. Cambridge University Press (Cambridge, 1973).

R. L. Schuyler, *The Fall of the Old Colonial System: A Study in British Free Trade, 1770–1870*. Oxford University Press (New York, 1945).

B. Semmel, *The Rise of Free Trade Imperialism. Classical Political Economy, the Empire of Free Trade and Imperialism, 1750–1850*. Cambridge University Press (Cambridge, 1970).

W. P. Morrell, *British Colonial Policy in the Age of Peel and Russell*. Oxford University Press (London, 1930).

J. L. Morison, *British Supremacy and Canadian Self-Government, 1839–54*. Maclehose (Glasgow, 1919).

J. M. S. Careless, *The Union of the Canadas: The Growth of Canadian Institutions, 1841–57*. Oxford University Press (London, 1968).

P. Burroughs, *Britain and Australia, 1831–55: A Study of Imperial Relations and Crown Lands Administration*. Oxford University Press (London, 1967).

J. M. Ward, *Earl Grey and the Australian Colonies, 1846–57*. Melbourne University Press (Melbourne, 1958).

J. M. Ward, *Colonial Self-Government*. Macmillan (London, 1976).

J. M. Ward, *Empire in the Antipodes: the British in Australasia, 1840–60*. Arnold (London, 1966).

A. G. L. Shaw, 'British attitudes to the colonies, ca. 1820–50', *Journal of British Studies*, Vol. IX, pp. 71–95 (1969).

P. Bloomfield, *Edward Gibbon Wakefield: Builder of the British Commonwealth*. Longmans (London, 1961).

K. E. Knorr, *British Colonial Theories, 1570–1850*. Toronto University Press (Toronto, 1944).

J. W. Cell, *British Colonial Administration in the Mid-Nineteenth Century: The Policy-making Process*. Yale University Press (New Haven, 1970).

B. A. Knox, 'Reconsidering Mid-Victorian Imperialism', *Journal of Imperial and Commonwealth History*, Vol. I, pp. 155–72 (1973).

J. S. Galbraith, *Reluctant Empire. British Policy on the South African Frontier, 1834–54*. California University Press (Berkeley and Los Angeles, 1963).

C. W. de Kiewiet, *British Colonial Policy and the South African Republics, 1848–72*. Longmans (London, 1929).

G. D. Bearce, *British Attitudes towards India, 1784–1858*. Oxford University Press (London, 1961).

P. Woodruff, *The Men Who Ruled India*, Vol. I, *The Founders*. Cape (London, 1953).

E. Stokes, *The English Utilitarians and India*. Oxford University Press (London, 1959).

R. J. Moore, 'Imperialism and "Free Trade" Policy in India, 1853–4', *Economic History Review*, Vol. XVII, pp. 135–45 (1964).

P. Harnetty, *Imperialism and Free Trade: Lancashire and India in the mid-nineteenth century*. University of British Columbia and Manchester University Press (Manchester, 1972).

A. T. Embree (ed.), *1857 in India: Mutiny or National Uprising?* Heath (Boston, 1963).

S. N. Sen, *Eighteen Fifty Seven*. Ministry of Information (Delhi, 1957).

M. Edwardes, *Red Year: The Indian Rebellion of 1857*, Hamilton (London, 1973).

Part III
Mid-Victorian Imperialism

According to the accepted hypothesis, the middle decades of the nineteenth century were dominated by an aversion or an indifference to empire. These were supposedly the years when most British economists, politicians and writers unquestioningly accepted the separatist ideas of the Manchester School. The mid-Victorians, it was argued, saw no need for maintaining the imperial tie. In short, free trade had finally made the empire obsolescent and the great 'Age of Separatism' had begun.

Clearly this interpretation ignored the existence of those writers who had constructed a set of doctrines which demonstrated the necessity of empire to an industrial England. It also ignored the continuing expansion of the Indian empire and the use of supposedly out-dated mercantilist techniques to promote economic growth. It contained a number of puzzling paradoxes. Since these could not be explained away, two prominent critics were finally led to conclude that the contradictions arose not from historical reality but from the historian's approach to it.

[12] The Gallagher–Robinson Thesis of Continuity

In their famous article, 'The Imperialism of Free Trade', published in the *Economic History Review* for 1953, John Gallagher and Ronald Robinson rejected the existence of an age of anti-imperialism in the mid-Victorian years. They began by drawing up an impressive (if sometimes misleading) list of imperial annexations between 1840 and 1877. They then posed a series of awkward questions. Why were so many new colonies obtained and new spheres of influence established in an alleged age of indifference? How many colonies were abandoned in this 'Age of Separatism'? Why was the Indian economy developed by the state in the era of laissez-faire? These were facts for which the orthodox view could not account. Indeed, Gallagher and Robinson went on to argue that excessive concentration on formal methods of control had missed the continuous grasp on the West African coast and on the South Pacific which British sea power was able to maintain. Furthermore, even though Great Britain abandoned the Orange Free State and the inhabitants of the Transvaal in the 1850s, effective supremacy over the whole region had been retained by informal paramountcy. Clearly, in more ways than one, there was a continuity of policy which the conventional interpretation missed.

These inadequacies in the accepted hypothesis caused Gallagher and Robinson to question the wisdom of treating the British empire as an historically comprehensible unit. After all, the history of Britain in the nineteenth century was the history of an expanding industrial society. Yet no more than 30 per cent of the 20 million British emigrants during the years 1815–1914 settled in the colonies. And in no year did the empire take much more than one-third of British exports. Of the estimated £1,187 million invested overseas between 1815 and 1880, not more than a quarter was placed in the British empire. Even in 1913, less than half of the £3,975 million of foreign investments lay inside the formal empire. Thus only within the total framework of expansion could the nineteenth-century empire be made intelligible.

The two Cambridge historians then proceeded to suggest an entirely new hypothesis. Defining imperialism as the process of integrating new regions into an expanding economy, they argued that the mid-Victorian years were the decisive stage in the history of British expansion overseas. During these years the combination of commercial penetration and political influence allowed the United Kingdom to dominate those economies which could be made to fit best into her own. Once British political and economic expansion into this 'informal' empire was taken into account, the late Victorian age did not seem to introduce any significant novelty into the process of expansion. Indeed, the main work of imperialism in the so-called expansionist era concerned not the annexation of marginal regions in Africa, but the more intensive development of areas already linked with the world economy.

The distinctive feature of the 'imperialism of free trade', stated Gallagher and Robinson, was a willingness to limit the use of paramount power to the establishment of security for trade. The type of political control could vary from outright possession to informal supremacy depending on the amount of intervention necessary to achieve this end. For example, in Latin America, China and the Balkans, once entry had been gained, the object was simply to encourage stable governments as good investment risks. Only in areas which failed to provide satisfactory conditions for commercial or strategic integration was it necessary to use power imperialistically. Consequently, whether imperialist phenomena showed themselves depended not only on the factors of economic expansion, but also on the political and social organisation of the regions concerned and on the world situation in general. This explained why informal techniques of free trade could be used to promote British interests in China and Latin America at exactly the same time as mercantilist techniques of formal empire were being employed to develop India. 'Formal' and 'informal' empire were, in fact, variable political functions of an expanding British industrial society and the difference between them was not one of fundamental nature but of degree — they were to some extent interchangeable. Throughout the nineteenth century British governments worked to establish and maintain British paramountcy by whatever means best suited the circumstances of their diverse regions of interest.

In Gallagher and Robinson's view, the fact that the mid-Victorians, in the circumstances of mid-century, were not driven to annex territory so often as their late Victorian counterparts should not be allowed to obscure the basic continuity of British policy. Mid-Victorian policymakers did not refuse to extend the protection of formal rule over British interests when informal methods had failed to achieve security. Gallagher and Robinson concluded, therefore, that the usual summary of the policy of the free trade era, 'trade not rule', should be amended to read, 'trade with informal control if possible; trade with rule when necessary'.

It was a fascinating hypothesis, and this analysis led to a great deal of rethinking about the nature of the Victorian empire. The whole framework of Victorian imperialism was examined afresh. Some commentators accepted much of the new thesis but thought the analysis insufficient to account for the whole phenomenon of British imperial expansion, especially the occupation of large areas overseas for non-economic reasons. Others attacked its basic assumptions. The debate has led to a clearer understanding of the Victorian empire.

[13] Criticisms of the Thesis

The first serious attempt at rebuttal of Gallagher and Robinson's ideas came from Professor Oliver Macdonagh in an article entitled 'The Anti-Imperialism of Free Trade' (*Economic History Review*, 1961). Macdonagh denied that the exponents of free trade had ever promoted the growth of an 'informal' empire. The forcible 'opening up' of markets contradicted their pacifist ideals and the empire *per se* fostered wars, squandered resources, reduced commerce and reduced the chance of establishing lasting markets. By illustrating his arguments with quotations from the writings and speeches of Richard Cobden, Macdonagh sought to show that Cobden had opposed imperial growth and exercises *because of* his adherence to free trade. The appellation 'imperialism of free trade', therefore, suggested the opposite of the truth.

Macdonagh insisted that the new terminology was unacceptable. For example, the looseness of the term 'informal' empire created difficulties. Gallagher and Robinson had argued that the nineteenth-century empire should be interpreted in terms of overseas trade, investment, migration and culture. Yet one of the major recipients of these was the United States. Should the USA be included as part of the informal empire? And would it not be equally odd to have to drain Canada of colour on the map while painting the Balkans off-red? Clearly, the criteria of informal empire were not applicable to the areas of formal rule. Were, then, the concepts of 'formal' and 'informal' empire so easily interchangeable? Indeed, one country seemed to defy Gallagher and Robinson's categories altogether. Was Ireland imperialising or imperialised? Admittedly, Ireland was the prime exporter of population from the United Kingdom, but she was also the major exporter of French Revolutionary ideology, Roman Catholic religion and anti-British sentiment. To Macdonagh's mind, overseas trade, investment, migration and culture did not march in the same direction.

Macdonagh also criticised the universality of the new thesis. The framework was too simplified and de-personalised. Imperial problems were often inextricably interwoven with domestic issues, and the relationship of the economic and political arms in promoting British expansion was not simply one of master and servant. Victorian attitudes towards empire were compounded of more elements than self-interest. Furthermore, it did matter which party and men were in power: the existence of an implacable opposition to imperialism had been ignored. Macdonagh concluded that Gallagher and Robinson's approach merely replaced old conceptual difficulties with new. Variations in policy had to be admitted, the existence of a vast range of external factors affecting the formulation of imperial policy acknowledged, and the presence of a strong (if largely ineffective) countercurrent of anti-imperialism taken into account. The term 'informal' empire also had to be made more exclusive.

Many of these criticisms have been reinforced by the research of Professor D. C. M. Platt. In an article, 'The Imperialism of Free Trade: Some Reservations' (*Economic History Review*, 1968), Platt agreed that the British government always did its best to open the world to trade, but he denied that British official policy in relation to overseas trade and investment ever amounted to anything like the energetic promotion and intervention described by Gallagher and Robinson. The scope of government in the first half of Victoria's reign and the limits within which in the age of laissez-faire it was possible to work, were extremely narrow. In fact, British paramountcy was the result of an industrial and financial lead created through the agency of British traders and investors *without* government intervention. Occasionally, British action in opening world markets on equal terms to international trade may have ended in violence, but at no time did a British government attempt to obtain indirect political hegemony over a new region in the interests of future British commercial expansion. Their aim was limited to the creation of a 'fair field and no favour' trade policy.

As for the examples of British intervention in Latin America and the Far East cited by Gallagher and Robinson, these were not typical of British policy but the very reverse of what Gallagher and Robinson claimed. The mid-Victorian Foreign Office did not seek to encourage stable governments in Latin America, China and the Balkans as good investment risks, and to suggest that Great Britain had a political hold on China was to exaggerate beyond recognition. The policy of a laissez-faire non-interventionist government could not realistically be described as 'trade with informal control if possible; trade with rule when necessary'.

In two later articles, 'Further Objections to the "Imperialism of Free Trade", 1830–60' (*Economic History Review*, 1973) and 'The National Economy and British Imperial Expansion before 1914' (*Journal of Imperial and Commonwealth History*, 1973), Platt has denied that the term 'informal' empire can be applied to the years before 1860. In the first half of the nineteenth century foreign trade was relatively unimportant, British industrialists and investors concentrated on the home market and, in an age of short booms, recurrent slumps and slow economic growth, British traders were generally indifferent to marginal markets. Sufficient customers and supplies of raw materials were to be found within the existing markets in Europe, the United States, India, Australasia and Canada. Thus the concept of complementary satellite economies in this period — especially in Latin America, the Levant and China where there was little prospect of two-way trade — is misconceived. In fact, Gallagher and Robinson antedated, by several decades, the importance of the 'informal' empire as a destination for British investment and as a supplier of foodstuffs and raw materials.

Platt argues that this sort of relationship did not develop until *after* 1860. By then the expanding population and developing industries of Great Britain had begun to outgrow her traditional markets and sources of supply. In the second half of the century Britain's economy opened wide. Increased investment overseas and fierce economic competition in European markets forced Great Britain to turn her attention to the underdeveloped world. Then British governments did attempt to annex territory and establish spheres of influence in the interests of commerce and finance. Platt concluded that Gallagher and Robinson had mistakenly transposed back in time this newly acquired scope of government activity — to a period when the economic incentive to further imperial expansion was at its lowest ebb!

What, then, is left of the 'imperialism of free trade'? It must be admitted that Gallagher and Robinson's original list of areas annexed in the early and mid-Victorian periods was misleading and that the annexations which did occur frequently had little to do with the needs of free trade. Rarely did the British government intervene on behalf of British economic interests. The concepts of 'formal' and 'informal' empire are not easily interchangeable. Indeed, the term 'informal' empire makes little sense before 1860.

Nevertheless the area painted red on the map continued to expand throughout the nineteenth century. It does seem reasonable to conclude, therefore, that there was a fundamental continuity in British overseas trade and territorial expansion throughout the nineteenth century, provided it is borne in mind that this expansion was one of *direction* rather than *time* — it proceeded by a series of uneven thrusts which began for particular reasons at different times in different places.

That, mainly for economic reasons, an extension of government responsibility was needed in the late Victorian age to achieve the minimum of security for British trade does not necessarily indicate a

breach in the concept of continuity, but rather a change of gear and
direction in government activity. The methods of the late Victorians
may have been different but, in most cases, they had the same ends in
view as their predecessors.

[14] Mid-Victorian Realism

The years 1846–73 witnessed an age of growing prosperity. During this
period restrictions on the use of capital disappeared, the means of
transport multiplied, shipping prospered and exports soared. After the
Crimean War, Great Britain looked forward to a period of peace and
expanding trade. The other trading nations of the world, unable to
rival British power, were eager to share British wealth. The markets of
the United Kingdom and her huge empire now lay open to them. This
stimulated economic activity, reduced tensions and also encouraged
acquiescence in the British hegemony. For Great Britain the age of free
trade saw something approaching the very mercantilist ideal of an
international monopoly.

In this age of peace, prosperity and security, the whole question of
empire was examined afresh. As regards self-government, much had
been conceded yet still more was demanded. Where was it all to end?
According to the conventional view, most contemporaries concluded
it could only lead to separation — a fate beneficial to colonies and
mother country alike. This interpretation of mid-Victorian indifference
to the empire's future was expounded in two scholarly works: *Studies
in Mid-Victorian Imperialism* (1924) by C. A. Bodelsen, and R. L.
Schuyler's *Fall of the Old Colonial System* (1945). The teachings of those
members of the Manchester School who wished to relieve the mother
country of the burdens of imperial government were assumed to have
dominated the age. The writings and speeches of politicians and pub-
licists insisting that the empire was an expensive anachronism were
cited. Disraeli's reference to a 'millstone round our necks' was a
favourite example. The mid-nineteenth century was the 'Age of
Separatism'.

This interpretation has been seriously challenged by recent writers.
It would seem that too much prominence has been given to isolated
comments referring to specific difficulties, to partisan judgements and
irritated outbursts. It is true that most mid-Victorian statesmen viewed

independence as the natural destiny of colonies of British settlement and that nobody wished to retain them within the empire by compulsion. But not everybody agreed that the framework of empire would disintegrate or that the moment of separation was near. While most critics regarded the empire in economic and political terms as a burden, this did not necessarily imply that they were eager to hasten the day of separation.

One of the most constructive criticisms of the orthodox interpretation appeared in the *American Historical Review* for 1961. In an article entitled 'Myths of the Little England Era', John S. Galbraith argued that charges of 'separatism' against mid-Victorian statesmen could usually be traced to references concerning expenditure on unproductive colonial wars or to the impossibility of defending Canada against aggression from the United States. The problems of Canada probably occupied the attention of the British Parliament more than those of any other part of the empire (India excepted) during the years 1830–60, and British agitation was particularly noticeable when Anglo-American relations were strained. But Professor Galbraith maintained that there was no evidence to suggest that doctrinaire 'Little Englandism' was ever influential in Parliament or Cabinet.

In Galbraith's view the myth of the 'Little England' era sprang from preoccupation with empire in a strictly political sense. During the mid-Victorian age, when Great Britain enjoyed an unparalleled freedom of access to world markets, future continental competitors were eager buyers of British consumer goods and capital equipment. In these circumstances there was, in general, no need to assert sovereignty over new dependencies, to fight expensive wars of subjugation or to establish the costly and complicated machinery of administration. Thus the mid-Victorian years were not really an age of indifference, and the label 'Little Englander' is of doubtful value as a description of a significant British attitude at mid-century. Galbraith concluded that since most mid-Victorian thinkers were agreed on the need to end expensive paternalism, the spectrum of opinion on colonial policy was much narrower than the language of partisan politics suggested. The difference between the views of Russell and Earl Grey, Molesworth and Gladstone, was in fact small.

The deeper this analysis is probed the more just Galbraith's conclusion appears. There was indeed much common ground between the Wakefield School of colonial reformers, benign Liberals and aggressive Radicals. All would probably have approved of a British empire without restrictive political ties and tariffs. By no means all the members of the Manchester School agreed with Goldwin Smith on the need to encourage separation on the grounds of economy. In fact, the Manchester School was little more than a disparate group of economists expressing divergent views. They did not expound any general theory of laissez-faire. It was Cobden's pacifist wing that gave the group its alleged anti-colonial bias. This did not prevent other elements of the school backing state intervention in India or petitioning the Foreign Office to take strong action in China. Thus the alleged centre of 'Little Englandism' did not always hold 'Little England' views. And in the election of 1857, at the time of the *Arrow* episode and the Canton bombardment, the Manchester Radicals were driven 'bag and baggage' from the Commons. 'Little England' sentiments were certainly not universally popular in the age of Palmerston.

Too much has been made of mid-Victorian separatism and indifference. Critics of empire always existed, but apart from the few extremists like Goldwin Smith and Cobden, most so-called 'separatists' did not advocate the actual dismemberment of the British empire. That decisive step was to be left to the initiative of the colonial governments. Even the cry of the Radicals for the abolition of tariff preferences, drastic pruning of the defence estimates, and the cutting of administrative costs, only amounted to a demand for separation if the existing system proved unchangeable. The end of the Old Colonial System and the institution of free trade did not necessarily mean abolishing the empire. Such an idea never sank very deeply into the Victorian consciousness.

The mid-Victorians were realists. The question at issue in the middle decades of the nineteenth century was not whether the empire should be preserved but what form a reorganised empire should take in terms of government and defence. Would the existing bonds of empire hold? The survival of a centralised unit seemed a remote possibility when the American War of Independence, the demise of the Old Colonial System and the ever increasing sphere of self-government were borne in mind. Mid-Victorian statesmen had to face the full implications of the new system of colonial government.

By 1855 the British government's scruples about premature concessions of self-government had been swept aside. Among the established settlement colonies only Western Australia and the South African colonies had failed to demand and receive responsible government. It had been a hurried and disorganised act of disengagement. Control over internal policies had been relinquished but Great Britain still found herself responsible for colonial defence. The problem of Great Britain's overseas garrisons — the major financial burden of empire still remaining — had to be tackled separately. Consequently much talk was heard during the 1850s and 60s of the corollaries of self-government: of self-defence, self-reliance and the privileges of freemen. The acceptance of a definite policy of withdrawing the garrisons culminated in the Defence Review of the 1860s.

[15] The Defence Review of the 1860s

The late 1850s witnessed a series of war scares, apprehension and defensive preparations. Fear of France under Napoleon III and the need to rush troops to Canada during the American Civil War and to New Zealand during the Anglo-Maori wars, highlighted the dualism of Great Britain's international role. She was both a European state threatened by the menace of continental politics and an imperial power with distant obligations. In short, British strength was perilously diffused. Strategists were acutely conscious that the existing system of imperial defence was expensive, inadequate and inefficient. Great Britain's army was ludicrously small. Even in peace time it was difficult to secure regular reliefs for regiments stationed in the tropics. In any case, few imperial garrisons would have been strong enough to meet foreign aggression. Military thinkers were generally agreed that the concentration of a large reserve of troops at home capable (in theory) of being despatched anywhere at short notice, was, along with the Royal Navy, the most effective way of defending the empire. Thus the policy of withdrawing the garrisons was never intended to weaken imperial ties or show any diminution of Great Britain's regard for her colonial possessions. Nevertheless to many of the colonists it appeared that in the era of free trade it was no longer essential to British interests to protect the colonies.

Desire for economy as well as efficiency did, indeed, play a large role in reducing imperial garrisons. One of the main concerns of both Gladstone and Disraeli as Chancellors of the Exchequer was to reduce expenditure. Constant demands for fortifications, arms, and iron warships combined with British commitments in Europe, Africa and the Far East to place a heavy strain on the British economy — especially when a commercial depression hit parts of Great Britain in 1861. Economic retrenchment was no mere party line. The military estimates appeared ripe for the axe. After all, the economic growth of many colonies made British taxpayers feel entitled to some relief from colonial military expenditure. But colonies which had recently achieved responsible government, though insistent on their newly gained rights, were less eager to assume all the duties attached to self-government.

The third Earl Grey had made it clear in 1846 that colonies, excluding imperial military bases and naval stations such as Gibraltar or Malta, could only look to the mother country for military support in cases of danger from external attack. The maintenance of internal security was the province of the local government. Each colony received a quota of imperial troops paid for by the British government. Additions to this force made at colonial request were to be paid for by the colonial government. This scheme proved a suitable basis for reducing imperial garrisons in British North America and Australia, but the 'Kaffir Wars' prevented the system being fully applied to South Africa. The Crimean War put an end to any further changes.

A Select Committee on Colonial Military Expenditure was finally appointed in 1861. The general consensus of opinion was in favour of withdrawing the garrisons. Arthur Mills, the Committee's chairman, introduced an important resolution in the Commons on 4 March 1862:

> That this House, while fully recognising the claims of all portions of the British Empire to Imperial aid in their protection against perils arising from the consequences of Imperial policy, is of the opinion that Colonies exercising the right of self government ought to undertake the main responsibility for providing their own internal order and security, and ought to assist in their own external defence.

The House accepted the motion without a division. This provided an authoritative parliamentary endorsement for, and stimulated public approval of, the government's attempt to reduce expenditure and concentrate imperial troops. The policy was never questioned by any subsequent British government.

A policy of peaceful disengagement had been decided upon. But the decision was by no means easy to implement. The Colonial Office faced difficult situations in New Zealand and British North America. In the circumstances, a policy of withdrawal hardly seemed feasible. In New Zealand the Anglo-Maori wars had flared up in 1860. Thus the withdrawal of British troops was not ordered until November 1865. The New Zealanders continually protested against the withdrawal policy and Sir George Grey, the colonial governor, remonstrated with both the Colonial Office and the local British military commander. Such were the circumstances that in July 1867 the Secretary of State, the Duke of Buckingham and Chandos, decided to withdraw the last British regiment. Even the massacre in November 1868 of thirty colonists at Poverty Bay in the North Island did not affect the Colonial Secretary's stand. The last British troops, however, did not leave New Zealand's soil before February 1870. It had taken nearly a decade to implement the Select Committee's recommendation.

A similar difficulty arose in British North America. After the outbreak of the American Civil War, considerable reinforcements were rushed to Canada to strengthen the existing imperial garrison. Strained relations with the northern states during the *Trent* crisis led to further warlike preparations. By the end of 1862, however, Canada's sole contribution was 18,000 volunteers. In fact, persistent Canadian reluctance to assist in her own defence finally caused the British government to begin withdrawing the garrisons and to concentrate the remaining troops in order to spur the Canadians into action. Thus a British presence continued in Canada after Canadian confederation.

One of the most vehement critics of the government's military policy was Goldwin Smith, the Regius Professor of Modern History at Oxford from 1858 to 1866. Smith was incensed by the refusal of the Canadians to assist the mother country in defending their country and in a remarkable series of letters to the *Daily News* in 1862 and 1863, subsequently reprinted under the title of *The Empire*, he declared that the sooner the connection between Great Britain and Canada were severed, the better it would be for both communities. Ostensibly an impartial observer, Smith was in reality a violent partisan who believed the colonial empire offered no rewards whatsoever. In his emphasis on the pecuniary aspect of the connection, his disgust with the protectionist policies of the colonies, his hatred of militarism and utter disregard for all sentimental considerations, he was a typical exponent of all the extreme views of the Manchester School. In his letters to the *Daily News*, he put the case for colonial emancipation with a clarity and forthrightness unsurpassed by earlier critics. The empire had become a source of expense because the mother country usually had to pay for the military operations caused by the rashness of the colonists in dealing with neighbours and natives. It was also a source of weakness and danger because the garrison system prevented military concentration in Europe whilst leaving individual colonies virtually defenceless against a strong local aggressor.

Great Britain was thereby constantly exposed to the risk of entangle-
ments with foreign powers, the United States in particular.

Smith maintained that the only answer to this situation lay in
almost immediate colonial emancipation:

> That connexion with the Colonies which is really part of our greatness,
> the connexion of blood, sympathies and ideas — will not be affected by
> political separation. And when our Colonies are nations, something like
> a great Anglo-Saxon federation may, in substance if not in form,
> spontaneously arise out of affinity and mutual affection.

In keeping the self-governing colonies in a state of dependency the
mother country was preventing the rise of a genuine sentiment of
nationality. While most mid-Victorian statesmen disagreed with
Smith's more extreme views, they realised there was much truth in
the last point. The self-governing colonies must be obliged to under-
take the responsibilities that their new political status involved.

[16] The Implications of Responsible Government Realised

Smith certainly had a point. The political and military aspects of
colonial nation-building were intimately connected. But the realisation
that if the overseas garrisons were to be withdrawn in their entirety,
it would be necessary to look ahead to the formation of cohesive
national units in Canada, Australia and South Africa to make these
colonies truly capable of an independent existence, was slow in dawning.

In 1858, the Colonial Office had before it two proposals for federation. One came from Canada, the other from South Africa. Sir Edmund
Head, Governor of Canada, had suggested (with the concurrence of
his ministers) dividing the United Province into two colonies, forming
a federal union with the Maritime Provinces and acquiring the
Hudson's Bay Company's territories in order to open up and colonise
the Canadian west. Sir George Grey, Governor of the Cape of Good
Hope and British High Commissioner in South Africa, had proposed
a scheme to federate the British colonies of the Cape and Natal with
the two Boer republics, the Orange Free State and the Transvaal.
Neither proposition was received favourably. Both governors narrowly
escaped recall. Sir Edward Bulwer-Lytton, the romantic novelist at

the head of the Colonial Office, effectively quashed the schemes. Two splendid opportunities for encouraging self-reliance were lost.

However, Bulwer-Lytton's successor, the Duke of Newcastle, eventually came to favour the idea of federation in both these regions. In 1860, Newcastle accompanied the Prince of Wales on a visit to Canada and had an opportunity to study the problems of the provinces at first hand. He later informed the North American governors that while it was not for the British government to initiate any movement towards union, they did not want 'to impede any well considered scheme which may have the concurrence of the people of the provinces'. Privately, Newcastle believed that the day was far off when the link between mother country and colonies would be severed. Nevertheless, he was prepared to admit the logical possibility of an early separation and regarded it as Great Britain's duty to create, as soon as possible, a powerful state out of the disjointed British North American provinces. Then Canada 'would become to us a strong and self-reliant Colony so long as her present relationship with the Mother Country continues and when she separates she would be a powerful and independent Ally and a most valuable, and I believe essential, makeweight in the Balance of Power on the American continent'. This was indeed a prophetic assertion for the 1860s.

Resolutions calling for federation were finally forwarded to the Colonial Office on 7 November 1864. The main impetus towards union had sprung from British North American experience during the American Civil War. After hostilities began, neutral British territory became the scene of activity for fifth columnists from the North and Confederate agents from the South. Canada felt doubly vulnerable when the Union government became involved in disputes with Great Britain. Canadian military weakness provided the final justification for union.

This time the project was endorsed in Great Britain. There can be no doubt as to the reasons for this. Gladstone, the Chancellor of the Exchequer, was quite explicit:

> We must not conceal it from ourselves, that if up to this time the sentiment of British North Americans with regard to self-defence has to some extent separated the burdens of freedom from the spirit of freedom the fault has been mainly ours. . . . We have to bring about a different state of things. The best way to do it is to raise their political position to the very highest point we can possibly bring it, in order that with the elevated position their sense of responsibility may likewise

grow. It cannot be too distinctly stated that it is in this light that we look upon the plan for uniting the Provinces of British North America.

Cardwell also affirmed that it was British policy to form 'great and powerful' communities overseas, capable of defending themselves and standing on their own feet. In fact, he was quite prepared to push the Maritime Provinces into joining the confederation when provincial jealousies threatened to torpedo the scheme. Nevertheless when the British North American Act was finally placed on the statute book in 1867, Prince Edward Island and Newfoundland remained outside the boundaries of the new Dominion. Subsequently, however, the territories of the Hudson's Bay Company were handed over to the Canadian government, the province of Manitoba was created in 1870 and British Columbia was incorporated in the Dominion in 1871. Prince Edward Island eventually joined in 1873. The foundations of the first new nation of the Victorian age were then complete.

After confederation, the British government continued its policy of withdrawing the imperial troops. Reinforcements had been rushed to Canada in 1866 because of the Fenian scare. In February 1868, the Duke of Buckingham, in line with his decision concerning New Zealand, announced the intended withdrawal of the bulk of the remaining troops. By 1871 the implications of responsible government had finally been realised. In the following year responsible government was inaugurated in the Cape Colony. It was a conscious and swift attempt to bring to a logical conclusion a process of disengagement that had been implicit in the initial concessions of responsible government in the 1840s and 1850s. In the mid-Victorian age Great Britain gracefully disengaged herself from a substantial part of her empire. The mid-Victorian assessment of the future of the self-governing colonies was realistic. The burdens of empire had been removed and the ties loosened but relations still remained cordial. As Gladstone stated in 1867:

> The connection between this country and her colonies is not a selfish and sordid connection, and ought not to be so on either side. No, it is at once a connection of interest, of honour, feeling and duty.

It was a connection dependent on the good will and interests of the colonists themselves.

[17] The Mid-Victorian Debate

By the 1860s the British government may have accepted a policy of
'separation by consent'. But this policy was radically different from
what the older school of historians dubbed 'separatism'. As a valid
description of British attitudes in the mid-nineteenth century this can
only refer to a permissive attitude towards separation should the
colonies wish for it. Indeed most so-called separatists looked for the
gradual relaxation of ties, usually by mutual consent over an unspecified
period of time. This would be a prelude to the grant of independence
which, although regarded as inevitable, would not preclude some form
of continuing association. Cobden confessed:

> People tell me I want to abandon our colonies; but I say do you intend
> to hold your colonies by the sword, by armies and ships of war? That is
> not a permanent hold upon them. I want to retain them by their
> affections.

And John Bright admitted:

> I have no dread of separation but I would avoid anything likely to
> provoke it.

In fact, although opposed to the extension of imperial commitments
and additional expense, he did not favour the dismemberment of the
empire at all — except by mutual consent:

> Give up all the colonies & dependencies of the Empire? Can any
> Statesman do this, or any country do this? I doubt it.

Moreover, all the leading Manchester Radicals, Goldwin Smith included, accepted the existence of the Indian empire, believing it would
lapse into chaos and anarchy should the British depart. Thus even those
who regarded the colonies as a burden could subscribe to the belief that
the empire was a trust handed down to them, for better for worse, by
their forefathers. The pragmatic acceptance of obligations once they
had been incurred was almost universal.

This is not meant to deny that some aspects of empire were depre-
cated in the 1860s. Nor to suggest that only cranks thought the empire
added nothing to British strength. But, in practical terms, the 'anti-
imperialism' of the alleged 'Little England' era never amounted to
anything more than the negative assumption that if the colonies were
destined for eventual independence, colonial expenditure should be cut
to a minimum and further expansion avoided. Thus even the most

hostile critics of the existing commitments could freely subscribe to a policy of self-government, self-defence and reduced colonial expenditure. Politicians with such diverse views as Cobden, Gladstone, Adderley, Earl Grey and Disraeli, and leading exponents of such different points of view as Goldwin Smith and Wakefield, were united in support of a policy intended, as Arthur Mills wrote in the *Contemporary Review* for 1869, to ripen the settlement colonies 'to the earliest possible maturity — social, political and commercial — to qualify them, by all the appliances within reach of a parent state, for present self government and eventual independence'. For the extreme critics of empire this was the first step towards the empire's dissolution. For the majority, it provided an opportunity for building a new relationship.

Most empire enthusiasts were aware of the fragility of the existing colonial links. Yet they refused to believe that local independence would inevitably lead to the dissolution of the empire. As Herman Merivale, when Professor of Political Economy at Oxford, wrote in his classic *Lectures on Colonization and Colonies* (1841):

> It does not follow as a necessary consequence that the attainment of domestic freedom is inconsistent with continued dependence on the Imperial sovereignty. The epoch of separation is not marked and definite, a necessary point in the cycle of human affairs, as some theorists have regarded it. . . . The mere political link of sovereignty may remain, by amicable consent, long after the colony has acquired sufficient strength to stand alone.

Thus in the 1860s, while the British government continued its existing policy towards the colonies of European settlement and continued to shoulder its obligations towards the Crown colonies, there seemed little need for supporters of empire to enter into a detailed argument in its defence. And in the House of Commons there always existed a sufficient number of back-benchers committed to the cause of empire to check the influence of Cobden and his few associates who favoured the writings of Goldwin Smith. But such were the uncertainties relating to Great Britain's future connection with her colonies that many colonial commentators felt some contingency plans were called for. Henry Thring, Home Office Counsel, in his pamphlet, *Suggestions for Colonial Reform* (1865), suggested a uniform scheme for the constitutional development of colonial government in four stages, whereby a colony might withdraw from the empire whenever it chose. Viscount Bury, in *Exodus of the Western Nations* (1865), proposed a draft treaty, in the form of 'Articles of Separation', to regulate Great Britain's relations with a colony when independence had been recognised. In 1868 Charles Dilke, who was fervently in favour of the retention of the Crown colonies and Indian empire but believed there was no advantage to be gained from the existing link with the self-governing colonies, wrote in *Greater Britain*:

> Recognising the fact that Australia has come of age and calling on her, too, to recognise it, we should say to the Australian colonists: 'Our present system cannot continue; will you amend it, or separate?'. The worst thing that can happen to us is that we should 'drift' blindly into separation. After all, the strongest of the arguments in favour of separation is the somewhat paradoxical one that it would bring us a step nearer to the virtual confederation of the English race.

Dilke, like many others, objected to the retention of colonies of British settlement in a state of dependency after they were capable of standing alone.

The mid-Victorians were well aware that the traditional colonial links were fast being undermined and that new forms of connection were needed. C. B. Adderley suggested: 'between the alternatives of dependence and separation lies the real secret of a lasting connection — that of common partnership'. But most serious writers, accepting the logical development of colonial independence, regarded the alternatives as being between planned separation and a policy of drift. Since the British government's policy made no specific arrangements for separation, it was usually stigmatised as drift. Hence the abundance of so-called 'separatist' literature in the late 1860s suggesting future paths for the government to take.

Throughout the 1860s, the British government continued to follow a policy of 'separation by consent', refusing to make concrete plans for hypothetical developments in the future or to force the pace of colonial independence. However, Gladstone's election victory in 1868 caused a sudden alarm. Many members of his first ministry were suspected of being strongly against the continuance of the colonial connection. Were the more extreme 'separatist' notions now to be applied to colonial policy? Granville's leanings towards the Manchester School and his actions at the Colonial Office led to the cry of 'the empire in danger' being taken up by certain sections of the press. This was the great empire scare of 1869–70 which was once designated the 'climax of anti-imperialism'.

[18] Gladstone's Views on the Empire

Undoubtedly the 1860s witnessed a difficult period in the history of
Great Britain's relations with her colonies. A series of troublesome
events served to emphasise the burdens of empire and to highlight the
rather haphazard nature of the existing imperial relationship. The
American Civil War and the Anglo–Maori wars resulted in an enlarge-
ment of the British defence budget, mainly because Canadians and New
Zealanders expected the British to defend their homes for them.
Friction on the Gold Coast led to an ill-prepared expedition against the
African empire of Ashanti, with results that nearly ended in the downfall
of Palmerston's last administration. A Select Committee on the West
African Settlements carried out a rapid reappraisal of Great Britain's
position in 1865 and eventual withdrawal from the burdens of empire
in all of these troublesome and unprofitable colonies (except perhaps
Sierra Leone) was recommended. Canada had already started to go
her own way before the foundation of the Dominion in 1867 and the
Australian colonists were demanding greater independence as well,
most immediately the right to establish internal reciprocal tariffs. In
these circumstances, increased colonial autonomy and further reduction
of defence expenditure seemed the natural course for Great Britain to
follow. But it was Gladstone's known views on the existing situation and
his much publicised ideas on the future of the imperial relationship (as
well as the way in which his government began to tackle this problem)
that led to the 'Colonial Question' becoming a subject of intense
debate in 1869–70.

Gladstone had always been averse to imperial expansion: 'the lust
and love of territory have been among the greatest curses of mankind'.
He disliked British rule over alien races. Nevertheless he accepted the
principle of moral trusteeship for backward peoples and, in general,
had no quarrel with the existence of colonies — it was the system of
their government that he objected to. Steeped in classical tradition, he
wished to adopt the Greek model: 'perfect freedom and perfect self-
government'. He approved of the introduction of responsible government into the colonies of white settlement and wished to extend it. As
he said in his lecture to the Chester Mechanics' Institute in November
1855:

> Govern them upon the principle of freedom — let them not feel any
> yokes upon their necks — let them understand that the relations
> between you and them are relations of affection; even in the matter of

continuing the connection, let the colonists be the judges, for they are the best judges as to whether they ought to continue to be with you or not, and rely upon it you will reap a rich reward in the possession of that affection unbroken and unbounded in all the influence which the possession of such colonies will give you, and in all the grandeur which it will add to your renown.

In Gladstone's view, the remaining ties should be of honour, interest, kinship and affection. The ultimate destiny of colonies was independence. To this end Great Britain should promote 'more self-reliance and more self-relying habits'.

Gladstone fully supported the Defence Review of the 1860s. In a speech on the Canadian Railway Loan in March 1867, he declared:

The system of vicarious defence — the system of having the burdens of its frontier defence borne by another — enervates and depresses the tone of the country in which it prevails; and its withdrawal is necessary in order to bring the country to the full possession and enjoyment of freedom.

Otherwise colonists would never truly be 'free men'. It was these views on colonial autonomy, the desire for economy (especially in the realm of defence expenditure), and the election pledge for 'peace, retrenchment and reform', that led many contemporaries in 1868 to expect a radical colonial policy from a government which included in its ranks several critics of the existing imperial relationship.

Among the most prominent elements in the new Liberal government's programme were Cardwell's proposed army reforms. A Royal Commission on recruiting in 1867 had concluded that one of the reasons army service was so unpopular was that two-thirds of the service was spent abroad. Cardwell proposed to remedy this situation by reducing imperial troops stationed in the colonies from 50,000 to 26,000 and thus generating, he hoped, a spirit of British energy and self-reliance. Gladstone and his Colonial Secretary, Earl Granville, endorsed this policy. The Defence Review of the 1860s was to be pushed to its logical conclusion.

It was the hurried withdrawal of the remaining regiments from Canada, New Zealand and Australia, and similar plans for South Africa, which created the mistaken impression that the Gladstone ministry was intent on introducing a new colonial policy. During the years 1868–70, the attitude of the British ministers hardened as developments on the continent of Europe made reforms in British defence strategy more urgent. To the continuing friction with the United States and to the old fear of Russian expansion into the Mediterranean and central Asia, was now added the new fear of Bismarck's Germany. After the Franco-Prussian war and Russia's tearing up of the Black Sea clauses in the Treaty of Paris of 1856, reform of the British army (especially with the concept of concentrating British troops for the defence of the British Isles) assumed a new urgency. It was against this backcloth that the Gladstone government attempted to push through the withdrawal of the overseas garrisons.

[19] Granville's Colonial Policy

Granville took the lead. One of his first actions as Colonial Secretary was to endorse the decision to remove the last remaining British regiment from New Zealand. It was an unpopular act. Not only had relations between the Colonial Office and the New Zealand government seriously deteriorated, but it now appeared that open war might break out in the colony with Maori guerrillas. Granville added fuel to the fire in March 1869 by conveying a curt despatch to the colonists refusing to guarantee a loan for the purpose of internal security. This news was received badly in the southern hemisphere. In London, Sir George Grey (the former governor of the colony) and four prominent New Zealanders wrote to *The Times* declaring that such a callous attitude was calculated to drive New Zealand out of the empire. The *Spectator*, 24 July 1869, concluded:

> It is clear that Mr. Goldwin Smith's colonial 'policy', the policy, that is, of shaking off the colonies . . . has not only been accepted by the existing Government, but they are acting on it.

A general attack was begun on Granville's 'heartless' policy.

Granville hardened his heart. Some plain speaking followed. He proceeded to announce in October 1869 that British troops could not be retained under any circumstances. As the New Zealanders had failed to raise their own military force, yet persisted in antagonising the Maoris by confiscating their lands, Great Britain was not acting as a friend to New Zealand in encouraging a policy 'pregnant with danger' by providing a 'delusive shadow of support'. Such a forthright statement was guaranteed to attract the wrath of the New Zealand ministers. Many contemporaries became convinced that it was the Gladstone government's intention to sever the colony's connection with the empire.

In fact, it was not until after the last British regiment had been withdrawn from New Zealand in February 1870, and after Granville's policy had been debated in Parliament and the press, that the Colonial Secretary consented to disavow any wish to abandon New Zealand. In a conciliatory despatch of March 1870, he rather belatedly informed the colonial ministers:

> The refusal to retain troops in N.Z. did not proceed from any indifference to the true welfare of the Colony but from a conviction that . . . the employment of British troops in a Colony possessed of responsible Government was objectionable in principle except in the Case of foreign War and . . . it is not for the interest of the Colony itself that New Zealand should be made an Exception from that rule, which, with due consideration for circumstances is in course of application to other colonies.

Granville, amidst a storm of critical comment, had finally achieved the removal of one of the remaining anomalies of responsible government and forced the New Zealand ministry to face the consequences of its own internal policy. It was the most important aspect of the period which some historians have since dubbed the 'climax of anti-imperialism'.

The Gladstone government's policy towards Canada raised a similar controversy. Once again the government was intent on withdrawing as many British troops as possible — in this case at a time when the United States apparently harboured annexationist ideas and the young Dominion faced raids by the Fenians and risings by its own part-Indian *métis*. The home government seemed determined not only to remove the burden of Canadian defence from the British taxpayer but, as in New Zealand, to sever most of the connections with the colonial military system.

The bulk of the controversy which the government's Canadian policy aroused in 1870, however, was largely the personal responsibility of Granville. On 14 June 1869 he informed the Canadian Governor-General in a confidential despatch that the existing imperial relationship was dependent on the goodwill of the Canadians themselves:

> The greatness of England consists not in the geographical extent of her Empire, but in the spirit which animates those who inhabit it, and the traditional regard of her allies. It will be far more truly consulted by retaining Canada as an ancient, prosperous and cordial friend, than as a

half-hearted Dependency. H.M. Government believe that hereditary cordiality is best secured by not only treating the continuance of the imperial authority as dependent on the interest of Canada, but by holding the statesmen and people of the Dominion to be the proper judges of that interest.

Granville then added in his own handwriting the following often-quoted sentence which has usually been used to demonstrate that he was a separatist:

You will also be good enough to bring to my notice any line of policy, or any measures which without implying on the part of H.M. Government any wish to change abruptly our relations, would gradually prepare both countries for a friendly relaxation of them.

This despatch led Sir John Young, the Canadian Governor-General, to announce in July 1869 that Canada's destiny lay in her own hands. It was for Canadians to decide whether to continue the existing relationship or substitute some other form of alliance. Hostile critics in Great Britain and Canada immediately interpreted this as a reference to union with the United States. Sir John Young had to clarify his position in a later speech. It was clear that the Canadians wished to remain as they were. Granville's approach, whatever had been his intentions, came to nothing.

Granville's dealings with Canada and New Zealand aroused a great deal of suspicion. Was the British government trying to sever the remaining links of empire in the hope that the colonists would then stand on their own feet and in the not too distant future secede from the empire? Those who chose to place this interpretation on the government's actions did not have to look far to find further evidence to support their views. Granville succeeded in stirring up a hornets' nest during his short stay in the Colonial Office.

Granville's offer of the K.C.M.G. to Alexander Tilloch Galt, the Canadian Finance Minister, seemed to confirm the uneasy feelings about the British government's colonial policy. Galt was a prominent Canadian denigrator of the imperial connection who believed that Canadian confederation was but a preliminary step towards an imminent declaration of independence. When he was accused of being disloyal to the Queen in the Canadian Parliament in February 1870, he retorted that a policy of independence had been arrived at by the Imperial government. As Granville refused to publish for the British Parliament all of his correspondence with Galt, another storm of critical comment arose.

Certainly for a man renowned for his charm and tact, Granville upset numerous colonies with his extremely uncharacteristic disregard for the susceptibilities of others. Colonists in British Columbia complained of being pushed into the Canadian confederation and the Cape Colony was equally indignant at being prodded towards the acceptance of responsible government. In the Legislative Assembly of the Cape, Governor Sir Philip Wodehouse voiced a widespread feeling:

> In Northern America we have unmistakable indications of the rapid establishment of a powerful independent State. In Australia it is probable that its several settlements with their great wealth and homogeneous population will see their way to a similar coalition. In New Zealand, the severance is being accomplished under very painful circumstances.

The intentions of the government seemed separatist beyond all shadow of doubt when, in June 1870, Granville announced the proposed abandonment of the colony of the Gambia to France in return for a few gains elsewhere on the West African coast. The government, it was alleged, had shown its true colours at last.

A crisis of opinion

These events led some historians to regard the years 1869–70 as the years when the British government came closest to dismembering the empire. According to this interpretation the year 1870 was the great divide in the history of the nineteenth-century empire. Recent research, however, has emphasised the basic continuity of British imperial history. How, then, does the 'climax of anti-imperialism' fit into the history of Victorian imperialism?

The first Gladstone government was clearly intent on making self-government work and bringing the colonies to accept the burdens attached to responsible government. To this end the imperial military presence was withdrawn as far as was practicable. After all, internal security was a corollary of responsible government and, in Gladstone's eyes, a necessity if 'free' communities were to be established. All this was in perfect conformity with liberal doctrines of responsible government, free trade and self-reliance. But Granville's actions in 1869 must also be viewed against the background of immediate needs: the commitment to economy, Cardwell's proposed army reforms, and the need to foster good relations with the United States and to meet European obligations. These factors caused the British government to force the pace of colonial development. It was Granville's misfortune that the steps taken occurred at difficult moments in New Zealand and Canadian history. Such treatment regardless of all mitigating circumstances, at a time when anti-empire sentiments were receiving widespread publicity, not unnaturally led to controversy. A policy followed throughout the 1860s did indeed reach its climax at the turn of the decade.

But was it a separatist policy? Granville always denied this. In fact, when Lowe, the Chancellor of the Exchequer, objected to the eventual promise of a guarantee for a loan to New Zealand, Granville was quite emphatic on this point: 'I don't wish them to separate, and if they do, it will do us politically a little harm — but they will not separate.' He was convinced that the time for separation was yet to come. In the case of Canada he minuted in the Colonial Office's records that whether the connection continued 'in precisely the same form, or whether at some future time the strong but elastic bond between them should be further relaxed . . . feelings of the strongest affection and mutual respect' would endure. His own views were probably most accurately summed up in another confidential minute:

> The friendly separation of Canada from this country, and a declaration of its independence would relieve Great Britain and the Dominion from some present embarrassment, and from future risks. But I should regret that this country should appear to adopt any abrupt proceeding which may alienate the Canadians.

In the long term, Granville was prepared to conciliate the colonists. In fact, his views coincided with the liberal idea of separation by consent provided the mother country retained the right to initiate a friendly separation. His sounding of the Canadian Governor-General's views in June 1869 was his only attempt to put this philosophy into practice.

Gladstone had foreseen that Granville's colonial policy would be discussed and attacked in Parliament. He wished to show that it was the decided policy of the government. When a Select Committee to examine colonial policy was called for in April 1870, therefore, he seized the opportunity to intervene in the debate in order to remove the existing misconceptions. He denied that the government had attempted to introduce a new colonial policy:

> There is no question of any new policy at all; but there is a question of the successive development and application of admitted principles to one colony after another, according as circumstances allow and invite their application.

Gladstone was intent on ensuring conditions for a peaceful separation in the future. 'Freedom and voluntaryism' was to be the basis of the connection. But no community could be free unless it enjoyed the burdens as well as the privileges of freedom. Colonies must be taught to be self-reliant. This was 'the sense, the principle and the secret of our policy'.

It was hardly an outright disavowal of separatism. In May 1871, however, Knatchbull-Hugessen (the Liberal spokesman for the Colonial Office in the Commons), in sheer exasperation, declared that the government did not wish to dismember the empire. Self-reliance

> did not mean separate existence, for a Colony might be great and self-reliant, and still maintain an intimate connection with the mother country. The government wished to retain the colonies; but they wished to retain them bound to this country by ties of kindred and affection.

After such a forthright statement the 'empire scare' faded.

What, then, are we to make of Granville's colonial secretaryship? Clearly, while Granville remained at the Colonial Office, domestic politics and the needs of British foreign policy dominated colonial policy. The Chancellor of the Exchequer, the Foreign Secretary, the Secretary of State for War and the Prime Minister all intervened in colonial affairs without much resistance from the Colonial Secretary. And in the Cabinet (which contained men with such differing points of view as Gladstone, Bright, Fortescue and Forster) each issue was probably debated on its merits. While most members would probably have agreed with Gladstone's emphasis on the desirability and inevitability of colonial devolution, not all were prepared to accept the outbursts of Bright and Lowe. Kimberley, who succeeded Granville at the Colonial Office, was certainly more sanguine than most. He could see no need for a separation in the foreseeable future. In July 1870, he recorded in his private journal:

> Those who know Canada best are convinced that Canada would fall into the hands of the Americans if she were to cease to be British, unless she had become much stronger & more populous than she can be for some time to come . . . the question of independence ought not to be regarded as a practical one in our time. It is reduced to a mere speculation as to the future.

Even Kimberley agreed with Gladstone, however, that the 'frothy talk' about cementing the bonds of empire was nonsense.

It was precisely this refusal on Gladstone's part to associate himself with the growing agitation for 'consolidation' that allowed rumours concerning the intentions of the government towards the colonists to persist, even within the Liberal party. Yet the policies Granville pursued were by no means original. They had all been inaugurated many years earlier and had been approved at the time by the Conservative party. Even the proposal to exchange the Gambia had been raised and eagerly endorsed by the Conservatives in 1866. Granville was doubly unfortunate that so many issues came to a head when the British government was intent on reducing its overseas commitments.

Granville was, however, in part at least, responsible for the outcry his actions caused. He never gave an adequate explanation of his policy and allowed a ripple of discontent over the treatment of New Zealand, expressed by a few sympathisers in London, to erupt into a full-scale parliamentary and press campaign. On the other hand, his most commendable acts received no publicity. The transfer of the Hudson's Bay Company's territory to the Dominion of Canada, the establishment of the Order of St Michael and St George as a colonial decoration, and the tactful handling of the New Zealand approaches to the United States concerning possible annexation were ignored. Even his concessions to the colonists were misinterpreted. His belated decision to support an imperial guarantee of a loan to New Zealand and the decision to send a British expedition to fight on Canadian soil to quell Riel's rebellion on the Red river, were seen as acts of capitulation. For this bad publicity the government had no one but themselves to blame.

The strength of the opposition and the extended campaign against the alleged policy of Granville seem to have shaken the government. After Disraeli's 'exhausted range of volcanoes' speech at Manchester in April 1872 and his insinuations at the Crystal Palace banquet in June 1872, the Liberals trod warily. Indeed, by 1872 the government had rapidly declined in popularity. Various government measures — Cardwell's army reforms, the Education Act, Ballot Act, University Test Act and Licensing Act — had alienated influential interests. The government's foreign policy had also been rather lacking in successes. The Alabama arbitration, Russia's tearing up of the Black Sea clauses in the Treaty of Paris, the German annexation of Alsace–Lorraine and a rather fanciful German invasion scare made the British electorate feel uncomfortable. The early 1870s had also seen a rise in prices, a series of strikes and a couple of uninspired budgets. In all, the Liberal administration was becoming increasingly unpopular. Further controversial measures were best avoided. As the government tottered on throughout 1873 (Gladstone actually resigned but Disraeli refused to form a

minority government), talk of colonial separation disappeared and even
the Liberal Cabinet was forced to consider the possibility of British
expansion in the tropics. By 1875 W. E. Forster could ask, 'Who talks
now of casting off the colonies?' Federation, not disintegration, became
the subject of discussion. In the mistaken belief that Granville was about
to cut the colonies adrift, certain defenders of the imperial connection
had gathered their forces and attacked an almost universally held
belief. A core of resistance to the ideas of separation by consent and
general public indifference to the empire came into being. Within a few
years separatist ideas became unfashionable.

Consequently in the 1870s there were two easily identifiable schools
of thought as regards the empire. One school followed Gladstone's
concept of voluntary ties, a largely self-governing empire held together
by ties of kinship and affection. The opposing school wished to re-
construct the empire as a centralised unit. This group believed in
imperial federation, an idea hotly debated in the 1870s, leading to the
formation of the Imperial Federation League in 1884. The two great
political parties came to be associated in late Victorian minds with one
of these concepts. Gladstone and most Liberals believed in 'freedom and
voluntaryism'; the exponents of the opposite school of thought called
on Disraeli to take up the cause of empire unity. In 1872, at the Crystal
Palace, Disraeli had belatedly attacked the colonial policy of the
Liberals. Some historians have dated the beginnings of the 'New
Imperialism' from this speech. It is true that a number of assumptions
characteristic of the British imperialism of later decades were added to
the British imperial outlook during Disraeli's second ministry, but in
general Disraeli's attitudes and policy have been much misunderstood.

[20] The Disraeli Legend

Disraeli's views on the British empire have long been a subject of disagreement. In particular, controversy has raged round a speech he
made at the Crystal Palace on 24 June 1872 at a banquet following a
conference of the National Union of Conservative and Constitutional
Associations. In this speech Disraeli outlined the three great objects of
the Conservative party. These were to maintain the ancient institutions
of the land, to uphold the empire of England and to elevate the condition of the people. His comments on the empire were extremely slight

but it was all good party propaganda, making the most of the recent outcry against Granville's conduct of colonial affairs.

Disraeli maintained that the Liberals had spent forty years trying to disband the empire. They had done their best to convince everybody that the empire was a costly burden to be shed as soon as possible. When self-government was introduced, it seemed as if the last imperial ties were about to be cut. Disraeli argued that self-government

> ought to have been conceded as part of a great policy of Imperial consolidation. It ought to have been accompanied by an Imperial tariff, by securities for the people of England for the enjoyment of the unappropriated lands which belonged to the Sovereign as their trustee, and by a military code which should have precisely defined the means and the responsibilities by which the colonies should be defended, and by which, if necessary, this country should call for aid from the Colonies themselves. It ought, further, to have been accompanied by the institution of some representative council in the metropolis, which would have brought the Colonies into constant and continuous relations with the Home Government.

In the future, he concluded,

> no minister in this country will do his duty who neglects any opportunity of reconstructing as much as possible our Colonial Empire, and of responding to these distant sympathies which may become the source of incalculable strength and happiness to this land.

Fortunately, public opinion after thirty years had now veered in favour of the second great object of the Tory party — the maintenance of the empire of England.

It was a typical piece of political propaganda. It contained nothing particularly original. It is Disraeli's motives for making the speech, however, that have attracted attention. Only six years previously he had made his famous reference to 'colonial deadweights'. Why, then, in 1872 did he suddenly wear the empire on his coatsleeve? The suggestion of G. E. Buckle, Disraeli's biographer, that the speech reflected Disraeli's genuine interest in the empire and was an example of his prophetic vision, met with a strongly worded rebuttal in the pages of the *Canadian Historical Review* for 1920. Professor J. L. Morison, in an article entitled 'Disraeli's Imperial Ideas', asserted that Disraeli had no real understanding of the empire and could not even cope with the most ordinary difficulties of colonial administration. He merely used the empire for political advantage and his imperialism was a sham which brought discredit on Great Britain.

This interpretation was warmly endorsed by Professor C. A. Bodelsen in his *Studies in Mid-Victorian Imperialism*. Bodelsen believed that Disraeli's Crystal Palace speech was due less to his own dedication to the cause of imperialism than to the realisation that here was a new chance of 'dishing the Whigs'. He based this belief on two extracts from Disraeli's letters which have since become famous. In 1852, Disraeli had informed the Earl of Malmesbury: 'These wretched colonies will all be independent, too, in a few years, and are a millstone round our necks', and in 1866 he had enquired of Lord Derby:

> What is the use of these Colonial deadweights which *we do not govern?* . . .
> Leave the Canadians to defend themselves; recall the African Squadron;
> give up the Settlements on the west coast of Africa, and we shall make
> a saving which will, at the same time, enable us to build ships and have
> a good budget.

Bodelsen argued that Disraeli had only shown an interest in empire when he saw some advantage for the Conservative party. He did nothing to implement his Crystal Palace ideas after 1874. This, in fact, was a superb example of Disraeli's opportunism. In 1872 he had jumped on to a popular bandwagon and craftily annexed the new empire sentiment to the Conservative party.

This view soon became the orthodox historical interpretation of Disraeli's imperial ideas. Professor Richard Koebner and H. D. Schmidt in their semantic survey, *Imperialism: The Story and Significance of a Political Word, 1840–1960* (1964), repeated many of these ideas. Disraeli's sudden interest in empire in 1872 was totally new and unexpected. He was merely indulging in a piece of demagogic self-advertisement. His speech was not a statement of Conservative policy but a criticism in retrospect of the Liberal party. There was little historical truth in his survey of Liberal actions and the ideas he put forward were completely unoriginal. However, it was quite mistaken to believe that the speech gave the empire a new standing and direction. It did not inaugurate a new Conservative colonial policy. The renown of the Crystal Palace speech was totally unjustified.

Since Koebner wrote, Disraeli's imperial ideas have been examined afresh. His earlier writings, letters and speeches have been studied in detail by S. R. Stembridge and W. D. McIntyre and the ideas he expressed in 1872 have been traced back to the 1830s and 1840s. This has enabled an entirely different interpretation to be placed upon Disraeli's interest in the British empire. It is possible to trace continuity in Disraeli's ideas and to show that much of the criticism levelled at his Crystal Palace speech was misguided. Numerous references to the problem of colonial tariffs and a customs union, the preservation of waste lands, the need for a defined system for imperial defence and the idea of a representative council in the metropolis can be found in the pages of Monypenny and Buckle. Disraeli had even equated the Liberals with the separatists in 1863. In fact, the whole of the Crystal Palace speech was very much in line with Disraeli's earlier expressions on the subject.

It is misleading, therefore, to suggest that the ideas Disraeli put forward in 1872 had been suddenly adopted for political gain. It is equally mistaken to criticise Disraeli's ideas as being impractical in the 1870s. As Professor Koebner stated, the speech was a criticism in retrospect, not a programme or statement of policy. Disraeli had attacked the Liberals for not adopting a policy of 'imperial con-solidation' in the 1850s. There is no evidence to suggest that he in-tended to implement his ideas in the future. Disraeli was simply indulging in a piece of political propaganda. In this sense his words at the Crystal Palace do not merit the significance which has been attached to them by later commentators.

Disraeli's position has been misunderstood. Whereas his lack of interest in colonial affairs after 1872 has been held to demonstrate the Conservative leader's insincerity and opportunism, in reality this criticism springs from a basic misconception of Disraeli's ideas. Disraeli was not interested in the parochial problems of individual colonies. He was more interested in the empire as a source of power and prestige. It was the part the possession of empire could play in assisting Great Britain's role in world affairs that concerned him most. He was deter-mined that this advantage should not be frittered away by misguided Liberals with their 'Little England' tendencies. Disraeli was con-cerned with the maintenance of British power in general. It was quite natural, therefore, that his major concerns as Prime Minister should be the Indian empire and British foreign policy in the east.

Disraeli had always believed that England's greatness was founded on her commerce, navy and empire. Although he later came to accept the 'quiet revolution' in colonial policy (and was instrumental in persuading the Conservatives to abandon their opposition to the policies of free trade and responsible government) at the time he feared such policies would lead to the dissolution of the imperial connection. This led him at the end of the 1840s to look round for alternative means of 'reconstructing' the empire. For two years he toyed with proposals for establishing a colonial *Zollverein* and with making the colonies an integral part of the United Kingdom with full representation in Parliament. However, a Conservative programme for imperial consolidation was of no interest to Lord Stanley, the Conservative leader.

Disraeli was most appalled by the anomalies left by the grant of responsible government. In particular, because of the haste with which internal self-government had been conceded, reasonable measures for self-defence had never been insisted upon. A new military code was desperately needed. Disraeli constantly returned to this theme in Parliament in the late 1850s and early 1860s. He was particularly forthright whenever major military expenditure in the event of a possible Canadian-American war was discussed. But Disraeli never suggested, unlike many other critics of Canada, that the imperial links should be severed. Indeed, in 1863 he attacked the separatists with his famous jibe against 'prigs and pedants'. In a debate on Canada in 1865 he reaffirmed that it was Great Britain's duty to defend the empire: it would be fatal and disastrous to Britain's future greatness, he maintained, to 'shrink from the duty which Providence has assigned us to fulfil'.

Disraeli's much quoted references, therefore, to 'a millstone' and 'colonial deadweights' are by no means representative of his general views. It is noticeable that both outbursts concerned Canadian relations with the United States: the three-mile fishing limit in 1852 and the Fenian attacks in 1866. On both occasions Disraeli as Chancellor of the Exchequer had to deal with politically embarrassing issues which interfered with his budget plans. These were moments of despair for Disraeli. Developments he had long foreseen were about to become costly realities. In this context his irritation is perfectly understandable. It would be wrong, as S. R. Stembridge has argued in his 'Disraeli and the Millstones' (*Journal of British Studies*, 1965), to infer from these statements a general aversion to empire.

Disraeli, then, was not a separatist in the 1860s; nor was he an expansionist in the 1870s. He was not interested in colonies as such or in British expansion in the tropics. On the contrary, he was solely concerned with utilising the British possessions to increase British power and influence. The empire of England was the visible expression of the power of England in the affairs of the world. Consequently, Disraeli's interest in empire did not affect colonial policy: it lay in the realm of foreign affairs. This became only too obvious when Disraeli became Prime Minister once again in 1874.

[21] Disraeli in Power, 1874–80

Disraeli's second administration has always had an important place in the interpretation of Victorian imperial history. Even if the conventional view that an age of anti-imperialism gave way in the 1870s to a 'New Imperialism' advocated by Disraeli is no longer acceptable, there was certainly an increased amount of imperial activity at this time. The list is impressive: modest extensions of British control in West Africa and the Malay States, the annexation of Fiji in 1874, the purchase of the Suez Canal Company shares in 1875, the Queen's new title of Empress of India in 1876, the annexation of the Transvaal and the establishment of the Western Pacific High Commission in 1877, the occupation of Cyprus in 1878, and the attempts at British expansion in Zululand and Afghanistan in 1879. But the idea that Disraeli was responsible for a series of forward movements in the early years of his administration and for an aggressive expansionist policy in the late 1870s has recently been disputed.

Disraeli was an elderly widower of seventy when he formed his second administration. His health was poor: 'Power! it has come to me too late', he complained. Disraeli lacked the robust stamina of Gladstone and was unable (even if he had so wished) to oversee the work of the various government departments. Consequently, Conservative policy was often the result of a series of uncoordinated developments which did not always meet with Disraeli's personal approval. Disraeli was interested in ideas. He could never be bothered with details. But in 1874 even ideas seemed to be in short supply. According to the new Home Secretary, R. A. Cross, the Conservative administration had great difficulty in framing the Queen's Speech. It is not surprising then, as recent research has shown, that most of the achievements of this administration were the result of the individual work of such men as Cross, Sclater Booth and Viscount Sandon.

Foreign affairs apart, Disraeli seems to have expected individual policies from his ministers. He certainly had no wish to dictate colonial policy. This was left in the capable hands of his colonial specialist, the Earl of Carnarvon. Carnarvon was a man greatly concerned with good government in the empire, with economy and with security. He was not the sort of man to introduce an expansionist policy. The Foreign Secretary, the Earl of Derby, was an equally cautious statesman. Indeed, he was one of the most isolationist Foreign Secretaries that Great Britain has ever experienced. These were not the men to indulge in expansionist ventures. Eventually both Derby and Carnarvon resigned from the government because of Disraeli's handling of the Eastern Question. It was not until Lord Salisbury became Foreign Secretary that the government presented a united front to Europe. Before 1878 British foreign policy was tempered by Derby's passivity. Disraeli's inflated view of empire and his wish for a greater display of British power never reached beyond the realms of imperial rhetoric and the Queen-Empress's new crown.

Disraeli and colonial affairs

In these circumstances it comes as no surprise to learn that Disraeli played little part in the various extensions of British territory and influence made in 1874. But Professor W. D. McIntyre, in his analysis of *The Imperial Frontier in the Tropics 1865–75* (1967), has gone further than this. He has shown quite conclusively that the alleged 'forward movements' of 1874 were a myth. They did not result at all from a change of personnel in Whitehall and were not part of any consistent Conservative philosophy.

When the Earl of Carnarvon received the seals of the Colonial Office there were several outstanding problems demanding his immediate attention. These problems concerned West Africa, the Malay States and the South Pacific. The Conservatives had taken office just as the Ashanti War of 1873–4 on the Gold Coast was drawing to its close. The British government found itself without a policy once again. Carnarvon decided to meet British obligations in the most economical way: the Gold Coast forts were added to the island of Lagos further round the coast to form a new Crown colony. A new administrative authority was also assumed in the hinterland of the Gold Coast, known at this time as the 'protectorate'. It was a modest advance of British influence. At the same time a similar advance was made in the western Malay States. The previous Liberal government had requested a new governor of the Straits Settlements to enquire and report on this area. But, as so frequently happened, the governor exceeded his brief and arranged for British residents to act as advisers to two of the Malay rulers. The British government was faced with a virtual *fait accompli*. Carnarvon was left to deal with this insubordination and he ended by endorsing the governor's actions. Once again another modest advance had been made and the beginnings of British political control in Malaya emerged.

It was in the South Pacific, however, that the new Conservative attitude to empire seemed to be most apparent. In October 1874 the

Fiji Islands were annexed to the British Crown. The former Liberal government had been under great pressure to annex these islands but Gladstone had refused to do more than send two commissioners to survey the scene. Once again the commissioners exceeded their instructions. In the end Carnarvon's decision was dictated by the actions of others. He bowed to the pressures for annexation and later established the Western Pacific High Commission in an attempt to solve the remaining problems of the area. It was the government's intervention in these three regions that led some historians to suggest that here was the beginning of a 'New Imperialism' launched by Disraeli.

Nothing could be further from the truth. The Conservative government had been extremely reluctant to make any moves which involved further commitments or extensions of territory. Carnarvon's decisions had sprung from the reappraisal of the British position in these areas carried out by his Liberal predecessor. Kimberley had already decided that it was necessary to take a firmer grip of administration on the Gold Coast and to appoint residents to the Malay States, and he had also urged Gladstone to annex the Fiji Islands. Carnarvon simply went ahead with most of Kimberley's plans. The change of government in 1874 made little effective difference to colonial policy. Each decision was taken on its merits in response to an individual problem. The decisions were not the result of a new Conservative 'imperialism'.

Disraeli's role in all this activity is most revealing. Apart from the occasional letter of encouragement he hardly figured in it at all. Carnarvon was left to his own devices. The Prime Minister showed little interest in events in West Africa and the Malay States and when the problems of the Fiji Islands demanded an answer, Disraeli was more concerned with the fate of the government's Public Worship Regulation Bill which Carnarvon and Salisbury had attacked in the Lords. As the Cabinet was heavily divided on this bill, he positively refused to hold a Cabinet meeting. He wrote to Carnarvon, 'I must leave the matter entirely to your discretion'. Thus in October 1874 the Fiji Islands were added to the British Crown at the discretion of the British Colonial Secretary!

But what of the annexation of the Transvaal in 1877? Surely Disraeli must have played a more positive part in this? In fact, yet another example of Disraeli's 'imperialism' crumbles on examination. Once again Carnarvon was the man behind the policy. The instability of the two Boer republics and the African resistance they provoked compromised the security and prosperity of the British possessions. It seemed to

Carnarvon that there was a growing possibility of a general African uprising in South Africa. In 1875, therefore, he launched an attempt to federate the four British territories — Cape Colony, Natal, Basutoland and Griqualand West — with the Orange Free State and the Transvaal. But conditions for a spontaneous federation did not exist. The Boers were resentful of previous attempts to stifle their economy by preventing them from having independent access to the sea. They had also been alienated by the British annexation of Basutoland in 1868 (as the Orange Free State Boers were about to pick up the spoils of war) and by the British seizure of Griqualand West in 1871, after the diamond rush. For its part, the Cape Colony had no wish to shoulder the finance and defence burdens of less affluent neighbours. Carnarvon's heavy-handed approach to the situation only increased the colonists' deter-mination. His directives seemed to impinge on the Cape's powers under responsible government, and his extremely undiplomatic envoy, the historian J. A. Froude, made matters worse. A conference held in London on this subject in 1876 was an abject failure. Consequently Carnarvon decided to put pressure on the Boer republics. An oppor-tunity soon arose when the Transvaal, on the verge of bankruptcy, suffered a reverse in a war with one of its African peoples, the ba-Pedi. As Zulu power was also being revived and the Swazis were also adopting a threatening stance, Carnarvon prevailed upon the Transvaal Boers to accept annexation. Disraeli showed little concern: 'In all these affairs I must trust to you, and you are a person in whom I have much trust. Do what you think wisest.' Another significant addition to the empire was made without the Prime Minister showing much interest.

The impressive list of Disraeli's 'forward movements' involving a new and dynamic Conservative 'imperialism' is beginning to look very depleted. We are left principally with the aggressive policies of his later years — the Zulu and Afghan wars. But once again the pattern is all too familiar. The last thing Disraeli wanted was a series of imperial wars to drain the British treasury and to complicate his conduct of British foreign policy in the east.

In 1878, Sir Michael Hicks Beach became Colonial Secretary. He had no previous experience of colonial affairs and found it difficult to restrain Sir Bartle Frere, the forceful Governor of the Cape Colony and High Commissioner for South Africa, who had been the chosen instrument for Carnarvon's policies. The new Colonial Secretary had no clear conception of what Frere was doing. In fact, the British High Commissioner was intent on establishing British paramountcy over all

the African states south of the Zambezi so that the internal security of
the South African colonies could be assured. Unfortunately, after the
annexation of the Transvaal, the British had inherited frontier disputes
with the Zulus. As the whole Zulu structure was geared to warfare,
Frere decided that the Zulu power would have to be broken. He
determined on a preventive war.

Hicks Beach seems to have been totally unaware that force would be
the only means of subordinating the Zulus to a British protectorate.
The Cabinet were in equally blissful ignorance. Disraeli was furious
when the course of events finally became clear in the closing months of
1878. The Colonial Secretary immediately warned Frere to abandon
his expansionist plans. But Frere plunged recklessly ahead with an
ultimatum which it was virtually impossible for the Zulu ruler to
accept. The result was a disastrous war which began with the ignomini-
ous British defeat at Isandhlwana and the heroic defence of Rorke's
Drift. Eventually the British forces were victorious, but Gladstone, in
his attack on 'Beaconsfieldism', made great political capital out of
Disraeli's misguided ambition for territorial aggrandisement.

Disraeli, however, had not wanted the Zulu war. But since Hicks
Beach and the Queen strongly supported Frere, he bowed to their
pressure. Despite his condemnation of the proconsul in private, he
supported Frere's actions in public and opposed all demands for
Frere's recall. In reality, the Zulu war was the product of Disraeli's
weakness as Prime Minister, not the product of an aggressive intent.

Exactly the same may be said about the Afghan war. Great Britain
was dragged into yet another unwanted war by a forceful man on the
spot. In 1877, Disraeli and Salisbury decided the time had come to
establish information posts beyond the north-west borders of India to
watch the Russians in central Asia. A new Viceroy, Lord Lytton, was
appointed with the deliberate intention of persuading the Amir of
Afghanistan to accept British resident agents. The Amir, naturally
suspicious of such a proposal, refused to cooperate. But when an un-
heralded Russian mission suddenly arrived in Kabul, Lytton decided
to despatch a British mission as well. The British government urged
caution and sent off a diplomatic protest to Russia. But Lytton,
determined on action, ordered the British mission to enter Afghanistan.
It was turned back at the frontier and war ensued. Disraeli was beside
himself with rage:

> When V-roys and Comms-in-Chief disobey orders, they ought to be
> sure of success in their mutiny. Lytton by disobeying orders, has only

secured insult and failure. . . . To force the Khyber, and take Cabul is a perilous business.

In public, however, the Prime Minister supported the rebellious Viceroy and talked grandly of securing a 'scientific frontier'. At first all went well: the Afghans were defeated and a British mission was installed at Kabul. But a few months later the mission was massacred and a second punitive war had to be fought. Gladstone had a field day attacking the grandiose foreign policy of Disraeli.

Yet, as is by now only too apparent, Disraeli had not made any plans for an Afghan war. Once again, it had been his own weakness as Prime Minister and the blundering of his Secretary of State for India, Lord Cranbrook, that were responsible for the mess. Gladstone's attack in his Midlothian campaign on Disraeli's aggressive imperialism was undeserved. The Zulu and Afghan wars were not part of an imperial vision. Disraeli's contribution to these events was purely negative: a failure to oversee Cabinet ministers and to control the men on the spot. Disraeli was not the expansionist he is commonly alleged to have been. Disraeli was too vain a man, and too conscious of his role as a political leader, however, to admit that any developments in his ministry did not spring from decided policy. Gladstone took him at his word and historians have subsequently done so as well.

Is, then, the fabled connection of Disraeli with the empire undeserved? Did he contribute nothing to the British imperialism of later decades? This conclusion would be misleading. Disraeli's contribution lay in a different sphere, in the realm of foreign policy.

Disraeli, India and the Eastern Question

It was Disraeli's concept of the British empire in world affairs, increasing the power and influence of Great Britain, that caused observers to link Conservatism and empire. During Disraeli's premiership, discussions concerning Indian interests and the threat of Russian expansionism became increasingly more frequent. As time progressed, India came to dominate both Disraeli's foreign policy and his concept of empire.

In the mid-nineteenth century, India was indeed the greatest jewel in the imperial diadem. In 1870 the British had some £270,000,000 invested there — about one-fifth of Great Britain's entire investment overseas. India also took nearly one-fifth of total British exports and was an increasingly vital market for Britain's cotton goods. Equally important, India controlled the trade of the Far East through her export surplus with that area. But the economic sphere was only one aspect of India's strategic importance to Great Britain. India also provided the grand base for British power in the eastern hemisphere. At various times in the nineteenth century, the Indian army was used as the long arm of the British empire in China, Persia, Ethiopia, Egypt, Afghanistan, Burma, the Sudan, Nyasaland, Uganda, Hong Kong and Singapore. Economically, politically and militarily, India was one of the keys to Britain's greatness. Disraeli understood all this. His purchase of the Suez Canal Company's shares, the Royal Titles Act making the Queen Empress of India, the sending of Indian troops to Malta and the occupation of Cyprus were all intended to reaffirm British power in the east. The defence of British naval life-lines and the approaches to India was one of the main focal points of British foreign policy in the nineteenth century.

Disraeli's actions first displayed imagination when he discovered in November 1875 that the bankrupt Egyptian Khedive was negotiating with a French syndicate the sale of his shares in the Suez Canal Company. Disraeli persuaded the Cabinet that control of this important imperial seaway could not be allowed to fall entirely into French hands. In a dramatic personal coup, he raised a loan from Rothschilds and purchased 44 per cent of the Suez Canal Company's shares for £4,000,000. It was a purchase, he informed the House of Commons, made in the interest of imperial greatness.

The following year Disraeli set about making the Queen Empress of India. The Royal Titles Bill was introduced in the Commons in February 1876. But when it became known that the new title was to be 'Empress', with all its alien and continental associations, there was an immediate outcry. In response, Disraeli made a series of impressive rhetorical speeches — which showed he had as little knowledge of Indians as of colonists in general. Eventually the bill was passed out of deference to the known wishes of the Queen. But Disraeli had nearly come unstuck. He was much more circumspect in his use of fine imperial language in the future.

In fact, although Disraeli had entered office in 1874 determined that Great Britain should once again have a voice in European affairs, apart from making the Queen into an Empress (in part a gesture against Russian advances) he seems to have had very few notions about what to do. As Robert Blake found, once Disraeli achieved power he had curiously little idea what to do with it. Disraeli's foreign policy lacked direction. Lord Salisbury concluded in 1877: 'English policy is to float lazily downstream, occasionally putting out a diplomatic boat-hook to avoid collisions'.

While Lord Derby remained at the Foreign Office, Disraeli's desire that Great Britain should have a leading voice in European affairs was countered by the inactivity of his own Foreign Secretary, and it was over British foreign policy in the Eastern Question that the two men clashed most frequently.

In June 1876 the Bulgarian atrocities hit the headlines. Some 12,000 Bulgarian peasants (the contemporary estimate was double this number) had been massacred by Turkish irregular troops. There was a tremendous outcry in Great Britain and Gladstone emerged from retirement with his best-selling pamphlet *Bulgarian Horrors and The Question of the East*. The misgovernment of the Porte was a scandal of long standing. Yet Disraeli persistently refused to endorse the demands of the European powers for immediate Turkish governmental reforms. Indeed, the presence of British warships just outside the Dardanelles seemed to be encouraging the Turks in their obstinacy. Disraeli, who had been loath to admit that any atrocities had occurred (some of his speeches on the subject were regarded as flippant), was accused of supporting the Turkish policy of repression.

Disraeli did not share the Liberal and humanitarian outcry against the Turks. He was not pro-Turk, however. His interests lay elsewhere. He was much more concerned with adopting an independent British line and with striking a blow at the Dreikaiserbund. But when Russia declared war on Turkey in 1877, he immediately decided on the necessity of preserving Turkish territorial integrity. With the Russian advance on Constantinople, Disraeli had visions of the British and Russian empires meeting in the Mediterranean as well as on the frontiers of India. Possessing no ideas other than the traditional Palmerstonian conception of British interests, he reverted to Palmerston's ideas of defence strategy.

Palmerston had always sought to uphold the status quo in the east by preventing the emergence of Russia as a Mediterranean power and the possibility of a Russian advance overland towards the Red Sea or the Persian Gulf. Adopting this line of reasoning, Disraeli seems to have believed in a Russian menace over the whole area of central Asia, Asia Minor and south-eastern Europe. To Disraeli's mind Constantinople was the 'Key to India'.

Most British politicians were agreed on the need to safeguard the routes to India and the status quo in the Dardanelles and the Persian

Gulf. But not all agreed on the wisdom of shoring up Turkey. Salisbury felt quite strongly on this:

> I feel convinced that the old policy — wise enough in its time — of defending English interests by sustaining the Ottoman dynasty has become impracticable, and I think that the time has come for defending English interests in a more direct way by some territorial re-arrangement.

But Disraeli would have none of it — whoever held Constantinople could threaten Egypt and the Red Sea. This was a remote possibility at best, a product of muddled thinking and small-scale maps.

Thus, when hostilities began between the Russians and the Turks, Disraeli was convinced that British interests were at stake. He proceeded to embark on a series of grand military schemes: a £6,000,000 vote of credit was requested from Parliament, a British fleet was sent to Constantinople, and a British expeditionary force under Lord Napier of Magdala was discussed. It was all part of a grand military game aimed at intimidating Russia.

Disraeli's brinkmanship, however, caused most concern in Great Britain. There was an uproar in the country. Carnarvon resigned in the early stages of the crisis, the Cabinet was hopelessly divided and the Opposition was bent on securing the Prime Minister's head. Disraeli remained undeterred. The Peace of San Stefano, signed in March 1878, endorsing Russian gains in the Balkans and Armenia, threatened British interests. Through her influence over Albania and an enlarged Bulgaria, Russia would become a power to be reckoned with in the Mediterranean. According to Disraeli, such a disturbance of the balance of power imperilled the empire. His hare-brained schemes now increased. He talked rather wildly of a British expeditionary force sailing secretly from India to seize Cyprus or Alexandretta. This caused the Foreign Secretary, Lord Derby, to follow Carnarvon and resign. In the end an expedition of 7,000 troops did sail from India: but it went to Malta instead. Disraeli also mobilised the reserves. The excitement in Great Britain was tremendous. Such brinkmanship was a dangerous game. The Opposition was furious. For three nights the despatch of Indian troops was debated in the Commons. Disraeli was accused of violating the Bill of Rights. The government put up a spirited defence and escaped censure.

Disraeli then achieved his long-desired success. The Russians, exhausted after the recent war, agreed to an international conference, to discuss the San Stefano treaty. Salisbury, the new Foreign Secretary, prepared the ground well. Disraeli dominated the summit meeting in Berlin and returned home triumphantly proclaiming 'Peace with Honour'. The 'big Bulgaria' had been broken up and British interests secured in Asia by a new military alliance with Turkey and by the occupation of Cyprus. Once again the Liberal Opposition was aghast. Foreign commitments had been made without the authority of Parliament and a new military concept of empire which had emerged at government level during the crisis had been flaunted before the British public. The British empire, it seemed, was rapidly becoming a centralised military unit to be used by the British Prime Minister for furthering purely British ends. Imperialism and Conservatism became linked in the minds of contemporaries, and it was Disraeli's handling of the Eastern Question that caused the Liberals to censure so severely Disraeli's dreams about empire.

[22] Gladstone and the Debate on the Character of the British Empire

Gladstone had been in the forefront of the attack on Disraeli's foreign and imperial policies, believing that they amounted to nothing less than a calculated policy of imperial aggression. He feared that the empire (which to Gladstone symbolised freedom and voluntaryism) was being turned into a military machine. Indeed, the term was becoming increasingly associated in the late 1870s with military and political power over vast alien populations.

   Gladstone carried his attack from the floor of the House of Commons into the pages of the monthly reviews. In August 1877, he became involved in an acrimonious debate with Edward Dicey, the editor of *The Observer*. In an article entitled 'Aggression on Egypt and Freedom in the East', Gladstone replied to arguments put forward by Dicey in earlier numbers of the *Nineteenth Century*, advocating an occupation of Egypt in the interests of empire security. Dicey had argued that the power and greatness of Great Britain depended on her imperial position. Gladstone asserted that this concept was utterly mistaken:

> The root and pith and substance of the material greatness of our nation lies within the compass of these islands, and is, except in trifling particulars, independent of all and every sort of political Dominion beyond them.

Our only interest in the empire was the well-being of the constituent parts. The empire was a burden of honour.

Dicey rejected outright the Liberal concept of empire. He insisted that although the British empire had given great benefits to mankind, basically the empire was for the sole benefit of Great Britain. It was part of Great Britain's greatness and had a role to play in defending British interests against Russian expansionism. It was this militant (and illiberal) empire spirit which emerged during the crisis in the Near East that Disraeli fostered in 1877–8.

Disraeli defended every move he made in the Eastern Question as being in the interests of peace and of the British empire. The Prime Minister often adopted a grand imperial tone in his statements in Parliament, making numerous references to the 'millions who are bound to us by our military sway'. After his return from the Congress of Berlin he paraded the military might of the empire before the House of Lords:

> England must have seen with pride the Mediterranean covered with her ships; she must have seen with pride the discipline and devotion which have been shown to her and her Government by all her troops drawn from every part of the Empire.

Salisbury adopted a similar tone when he announced, at a banquet in Knightsbridge in July 1878, that the British government was 'striving to pick up the thread — the broken thread — of England's old Imperial traditions'. Great Britain's foreign policy could not but be an imperial one.

The whole character of the empire seemed to be changing. Gladstone returned to the attack in the September 1878 edition of the *Nineteenth Century* with an article entitled, 'England's Mission'. Where was the peace with honour? Where was the honour, he asked, in coming to terms with the Turks, occupying Cyprus, and annexing the Fiji Islands and the Transvaal? The British empire did not need Bosnian submissions in which the British could only remain as masters. There was no high moral purpose in this. It was a case, as he later said, of 'Liberty for ourselves and Empire over the rest of mankind'. In November and December 1879, Gladstone transferred his attack from the printed page and stormed north in a 'pilgrimage of passion' (as Disraeli called it) to engage the support of the Scots.

Gladstone repeatedly referred to foreign affairs in the many speeches he made during his triumphant tour of Midlothian. It was a magnificent *tour de force* as he stood hatless surrounded by huge crowds spellbound by his powerful oratory. Gladstone bitterly attacked the foreign ventures of the Conservative government. What had the British gained from all the annexations and occupations, from interfering in the affairs of the Malay States, the Gold Coast and Egypt which might yet prove to be the embryo of an African empire? Where was the glory to be gained from the Zulu and Afghan wars?

> We have gone up into the mountains; we have broken Afghanistan to pieces; we have driven mothers and children from their homes to perish in the snow; we have spent treasure, of which a real account has never yet been rendered; we have undergone an expenditure of which as yet I believe we are aware but a little.

Disraeli, he said, was no respecter of human life, of individual liberties or of the British purse. He revelled in military dominion over alien peoples. Great Britain had been led to overreach the limits of prudence and had incurred obligations she could not hope to meet. 'Remember [intoned Gladstone] the sanctity of life in the hill villages of Afghanistan is as inviolable in the eye of Almighty God as can be our own.' The empire was a sacred trust, not an object for exploitation. Great Britain had no right to interfere in developments that affected every avenue of approach to her eastern possessions: 'That, Gentlemen, is a monstrous claim'.

Gladstone's performance, repeated in January 1880, was a magnificent propaganda victory. Although Disraeli boasted that he had not read a single line, the absence of any attempt at contradiction from senior Conservative ministers was a damaging blow for the Conservative ministry directly prior to a general election. Gladstone's accusations remained unanswered and his denunciation of imperialist ventures, costly foreign policy and unpopular wars made 'imperialism' a damaging smear-word in the election of March 1880. Disraeli's policies were decisively rejected at the polls. Gladstone's harangues, combined with an agricultural and industrial depression, had sealed the government's fate.

[23] Disraeli's Contribution to British Imperialism

Disraeli's contribution to the character of British imperialism needs to be reassessed. He showed no interest in the details of colonial problems. He ignored Canada, Australia, New Zealand and the Cape and played little part in the formulation of colonial policy towards the dependent empire. With the so-called 'forward movements' of the early years of his administration he had almost nothing to do. With the policies of 'Beaconsfieldism' in India and South Africa he also had little sympathy. In general, his contribution was a purely negative one: a failure to oversee departmental policies, restrain Cabinet ministers and control the man on the spot. But he was highly successful at one thing. He was adept at turning a series of disconnected and unforeseen events into (to use his own words) 'the semblance of deep and organised policy'. His success lay in convincing contemporaries and later generations alike that he possessed a grand imperial vision.

Disraeli's apparent endorsement of expansionist policies belonged solely to the realm of histrionics. In this sense he was no 'imperialist'. But in Disraeli's handling of the Eastern Question his one fundamental belief does emerge — that of a powerful, united, military empire reinforcing the strength of Great Britain in her role as a world power (with India providing resources and armies largely beyond the control of the British Parliament). Gladstone recognised the empire of Disraeli's dreams and fought a running battle with the Prime Minister over the future character of the empire in the mud-slinging campaigns of the years 1877–80.

In fact, Disraeli's imperialism added little tangible to the empire's strength. Cyprus never proved a worthwhile asset and Salisbury's policies in India only succeeded in stretching the strained resources of trained manpower even further. Great Britain's voice had been re-asserted in the affairs of Europe, it is true, but the *Pax Britannica* rested on an even flimsier basis than before. It was only towards the end of the nineteenth century that Disraeli's reputation soared to new heights and a legend of Disraeli's percipience and imperial vision began to grow. Disraeli was then remembered for all his imperial rhetoric and for his ideas of an expanding militant empire linked with an undemocratic and illiberal spirit glorifying British achievements and rule overseas. It was a concept that added a new dimension to the British imperialism of the late Victorian period. It was this contribution which linked Disraeli's name with the empire.

In 1880, however, the British electorate rejected what they conceived to be Disraeli's grandiose and costly schemes. The Conservatives were heavily defeated in the election and a triumphant Gladstone returned to Downing Street comparing the disappearance of Beaconsfieldism with 'the vanishing of some vast magnificent castle in an Italian romance'. The Liberals were restored to power complete with their mid-Victorian philosophy of limited, economical government, informal rule and free trade, and their policies of limited intervention and minimum responsibility. The clock seemed about to be put back ten, even twenty, years. Yet the 1870s had witnessed some significant landmarks in the history of Europe. Great Britain was about to enter a new phase of her history as an imperial nation and as a world power. Things could never be the same again. Very much against their will, the late Victorians found themselves enmeshed in the 'New Imperialism' of the last two decades of the nineteenth century.

PRINCIPAL EVENTS, 1859–80

1859 Queensland becomes separate colony

1860 Cobden Treaty with France. Anglo-Maori wars flare up again in New Zealand (last till 1870). Bay Islands ceded to Republic of Honduras. Prince of Wales visits British North America. Sir Frederic Rogers succeeds Merivale at Colonial Office

1861 Select Committee on Colonial Military Expenditure. Indian Councils Act. Lagos annexed

1863 Ashanti invasion of Gold Coast protectorate

1864 Ionian Islands ceded to Greece

1865 Select Committee on West African Settlements. Governor Eyre suppresses Negro rising in Jamaica. Colonial Laws Validity Act

1867 British North America Act establishes Dominion of Canada. Straits Settlements become a Crown colony. Gold discovered at Tati. Diamonds discovered in Griqualand West

1868 Gladstone becomes Prime Minister and Earl Granville Secretary of State for the Colonies. Basutoland annexed

1869 Suez Canal opened. Hudson's Bay Company cedes its territorial rights to the Dominion of Canada

1870 Cardwell's army reforms. Last British troops leave New Zealand. Riel Rebellion. Manitoba created

1871 British Columbia joins Dominion. Leeward Islands federated. Griqualand West annexed. Sir Robert Herbert succeeds Rogers in the Colonial Office as Permanent Under-Secretary

1872 Responsible government implemented in Cape Colony. Disraeli's Crystal Palace speech

1873 Prince Edward Island joins the Dominion. Ashanti War

1874   Disraeli becomes Prime Minister. Fiji Islands annexed

1875   Suez Canal Company shares purchased. Carnarvon launches plans for South African confederation

1876   Victoria becomes Empress of India. Public Debt Commission established in Egypt. Bulgarian atrocities

1877   Transvaal annexed. Western Pacific High Commission created. Russo-Turkish war

1878   Treaty of San Stefano. Congress of Berlin. Cyprus occupied. Dual Control established in Egypt. Afghan war begins

1879   Zulu war. Gladstone's Midlothian campaigns

1880   March. Gladstone's election victory

Further Reading

J. A. Gallagher & R. E. Robinson, 'The Imperialism of Free Trade', *Economic History Review*, 2nd Series, Vol. VI, pp. 1–15 (1953).

O. Macdonagh, 'The Anti-imperialism of Free Trade', *Economic History Review*, 2nd Series, Vol. XIV, pp. 489–501 (1962).

D. C. M. Platt, 'The Imperialism of Free Trade: Some Reservations', *Economic History Review*, 2nd Series, Vol. XXI, pp. 296–306 (1968).

D. C. M. Platt, 'Further Objections to an "Imperialism of Free Trade", 1830–60', *Economic History Review*, 2nd Series, Vol. XXVI, pp. 77–91 (1973).

D. C. M. Platt, 'The National Economy and British Imperial Expansion before 1914', *Journal of Imperial and Commonwealth History*, Vol. II, pp. 3–14 (1973).

W. R. Louis (ed.), *Imperialism: The Robinson–Gallagher Controversy*. Watts (New York, 1975).

C. A. Bodelsen, *Studies in Mid-Victorian Imperialism*. Fertig (reprinted New York, 1968).

J. S. Galbraith, 'Myths of the Little England Era', *American Historical Review*, Vol. LXVII, pp. 39–42 (1961).

C. C. Eldridge, *England's Mission: the Imperial Idea in the Age of Gladstone and Disraeli, 1868–80*. Macmillan (London, 1973).

J. Morley, *Life of Gladstone*. Macmillan, 3 vols (London, 1903).

P. Magnus, *Gladstone, A Biography*. Murray (London, 1954).

P. Knaplund, *Gladstone and Britain's Imperial Policy*. Allen & Unwin (London, 1927).

C. P. Stacey, *Canada and the British Army: A Study in the Practice of Responsible Government*. Longmans (London, 1936).

W. L. Morton, *The Critical Years: The Union of British North America, 1857–73*. McClelland & Stewart (Toronto, 1964).

A. J. Harrop, *England and the Maori Wars*. New Zealand News (London, 1937).

B. J. Dalton, *War and Politics in New Zealand, 1855–70*. Sydney University Press (Sydney, 1967).

The Boers who trekked northwards from Cape Colony during the years
of the Great Trek endured many physical hardships traversing difficult
mountainous terrain and facing attacks from hostile Africans. The journey
was dangerous and slow.

In 1839 Afghanistan was invaded and a British Resident, Sir Alexander Burns, was murdered when the city rebelled in 1841.

Below: In 1849 an angry mob burned down the Parliament Buildings in Montreal after the Earl of Elgin refused to veto the controversial Rebellion Losses Bill.

Top right: Indian Mutiny. Hanging was a comparatively civilised fate for these mutineers. Muslims were frequently sewn into pig skins first. Others, less fortunate, were obliged to lick up the congealed blood of their victims and were shot from the mouths of cannon.

Bottom right: Bones and skulls litter a courtyard in Lucknow after the relieving army had bayonetted 2,000 sepoys.

When British rule was proclaimed following the Indian Mutiny, the Viceroy, 'Clemency' Canning, decorated the loyal Indian princes on the Queen's behalf.

THE LION'S SHARE.

left: In 1875 Disraeli purchased the Khedive's Suez Canal shares for four
ion pounds.

ve: Disraeli guides the Empress of India through the 'dangerous waters'
nperialism.

w: The 'Fathers of Confederation' met at Charlottetown, Prince Edward
nd, in 1864.

Top right: Bales of wool on the road to the docks in Australia.

Bottom right: Dr Jameson taken prisoner by the Boers in January 1896.

Above: General Gordon, sent out to supervise the evacuation of the Sudan, died when the dervishes captured Khartoum in January 1885, two days befor Sir Garnet Wolseley's relief expedition arrived.

In 1897, Queen Victoria's Diamond Jubilee procession, a great imperial pageant, contained troops of 'every colour, every continent, every race, every speech. . . . A living gazeteer of the British Empire' (Daily Mail).

THE BATTLE OF OMDURMAN
BRITISH TROOPS ENTERING THE CITY   René Bull

MAHDI'S TOMB
SHOWING THE EFFECT
OF THE SHELLS

Top left: Lord Curzon treated the rulers of Indian states as unruly schoolboys. Here, His Highness the Nizam of Hyderabad is seen sitting between Lord and Lady Curzon.

Bottom left: The Mahdi's tomb was desecrated after the battle of Omdurman. Here, British troops pass the shelled remains as they enter the city.

Below: The European Legations in Peking were constantly under siege during the Boxer Rebellion of 1900.

One of the last photographs of Cecil Rhodes seen here, accompanied by Dr Jameson, on his arrival in South Africa in February 1902. The Anglo-Boer war finally ended on 31 May 1902. By that time Rhodes was dead and 'imperialism', with the publication of Hobson's book *Imperialism: A Study,* was firmly installed in the international vocabulary as a term of abuse.

W. P. Morrell, *British Colonial Policy in the Mid-Victorian Age*. Oxford University Press (London, 1969).

W. F. Monypenny & G. E. Buckle, *The Life of Benjamin Disraeli, Earl of Beaconsfield*. Murray, 6 vols (London, 1910–20).

J. L. Morison, 'The Imperial Ideas of Benjamin Disraeli', *Canadian Historical Review*, Vol. I, pp. 267–80 (1920).

S. R. Stembridge, 'Disraeli and the Millstones', *Journal of British Studies*, Vol. V, pp. 122–39 (1965).

R. Blake, *Disraeli*. Eyre & Spottiswoode (London, 1966).

W. D. McIntyre, *The Imperial Frontier in the Tropics, 1865–75*. Macmillan (London, 1967).

C. W. de Kiewiet, *The Imperial Factor in South Africa*. Cass, 2nd ed. (London, 1965).

C. F. Goodfellow, *Great Britain and South African Confederation, 1870–81*. Oxford University Press (Cape Town, 1966).

D. R. Morris, *The Washing of the Spears*. Cape (London, 1966).

G. D. Clayton, *Britain and the Eastern Question*. University of London Press (London, 1971).

W. E. Gladstone, *Midlothian Speeches*. Leicester University Press (Leicester, 1971).

Part IV
The New Imperialism

[24] A Fit of Absence of Mind

The scramble for territory in Africa, Asia and the Pacific in the late nineteenth century took the British by surprise. Gladstone was extremely reluctant to indulge in the new madness but in the end he became caught up in a current of expansion which he did not understand and could not check. Salisbury, who probably put more red paint on the map of the world than anyone else, was equally mystified. He recalled that in 1880 'nobody thought about Africa'. Yet, when he returned to office in 1885, he found the whole of Europe was scrambling for the continent: 'I do not know exactly the cause of this sudden revolution. But there it is.' We may wonder if the noble Marquis initially had much idea of what he was doing as he sat on the lawns of Hatfield House or in his room in the Foreign Office drawing arbitrary lines on the map of Africa.

In the last two decades of the nineteenth century the tempo of European overseas expansion suddenly and rather mysteriously quickened. Whereas previously a few European powers, principally Great Britain and France, had made extremely selective acquisitions of territory, there developed after 1880 a rush of annexations and a headlong partition of large sections of the world. In the last quarter of the nineteenth century more territory fell under foreign rule than had been absorbed into empire in the previous seventy-five years. It has been calculated that in the years 1878–1914, the European colonial powers, the United States and Japan acquired about 17.4 per cent of the world's land surface at an average rate of some 240,000 square miles a year. Thus the amount of territory either annexed or partitioned into spheres of influence and the speed with which it was done; the very unselective nature of the new acquisitions and the new areas of the globe involved; and the participation of new agents — Leopold II, Germany, Italy, the United States and Japan — all with their own motives for participation, suggested that a 'New Imperialism' had appeared on the world scene.

The causes of this phenomenon have exercised historians ever since.

If such important participants in the New Imperialism as Lord Salisbury could speak in such puzzled terms about Great Britain's involvement in the scramble for territory, it is little wonder that the whole process should have been viewed at the time as something of an accident. In his oft-quoted lectures on 'The Expansion of England' in 1881, Sir John Seeley, Regius Professor of Modern History at the University of Cambridge, when referring to British expansion in the eighteenth century, uttered that extraordinary statement: 'We seem, as it were, to have conquered and peopled half the world in a fit of absence of mind.' Whatever delusions Seeley's contemporaries may have been acting under, such an explanation hardly seems a plausible one for the actions of the late Victorians. Outside Seeley's ivory tower the contemporary advocates of expansion had much more practical reasons for their views. Anti-slavers, philanthropists, missionary societies, traders and chambers of commerce had very definite ends in view. Some British politicians, like Lord Carnarvon, talked grandly of 'duties to ·be performed', 'obligations to be redeemed', even of a 'civilising mission'. Joseph Chamberlain frequently observed that in bringing security, peace and comparative prosperity to countries that had never known their blessings before, Great Britain was fulfilling her 'national mission'. In fact, that rather overworked cliché, 'Commerce, Christianity and Civilisation' has been used to sum up the varied motives of the late Victorians. Cecil Rhodes, in a rather more down-to-earth fashion, talked of 'Philanthropy plus five per cent'. But in the case of the British South Africa Company, while the company retained the reins of administration the philanthropy was doubtful and the 5 per cent non-existent.

However, the *potential* economic rewards for opening up a vast and unknown continent such as Africa were certainly one of the principal arguments used at the end of the nineteenth century to justify European actions. Sometimes, admittedly, this was a deliberate cloak to mask political and nationalist aims; at other times it may just have been a subconscious rationalisation; on most occasions it was a sincerely held belief. At any rate, even if profit was not the prime motive, it was certainly the excuse used by such advocates as Joseph Chamberlain, Leopold II, Leroy-Beaulieu and Jules Ferry to popularise among their countrymen participation in the scramble for colonies. Africa, for example, was optimistically regarded as a new El Dorado. Biblical tales of Ophir, of the lands of King Solomon's mines and the fabulous riches of the Queen of Sheba, excited Victorian minds. It is not surprising, then, that the first systematic explanation of the factors behind the New Imperialism was couched in language that the late Victorians would understand: empire was to do with profits.

[25] The Theories of Capitalist Imperialism

In the early 1830s Edward Wakefield had argued that empire-building was essential to Great Britain. Undeveloped lands were needed to absorb her surplus population and to provide markets for her manufactures. Like most nineteenth-century economists he believed that the normal tendency of the rate of profit in industrialised societies was to decline. To maintain the existing rate he urged that surplus capital should also be invested in fertile virgin lands overseas. Thus the theory of the declining tendency of the rate of profit at home came to be used as one of the arguments for colonisation.

Before 1870, such a theory was never put forward as an explanation for the existence of colonies. It was quite apparent that surplus capital was going to independent countries, chiefly the United States. However, once the principle that capitalist societies needed to export surplus capital was used by European politicians to argue in favour of colonies previously annexed or about to be acquired, writers such as Friedrich Engels and Achille Loria began to think in these terms. In 1902, J. A. Hobson, an English journalist and economist, first gave general currency to a theory of Capitalist Imperialism by fusing the principle of 'underconsumption' with a dogmatic interpretation of recent historical events.

The ideas of Hobson
Hobson's experiences in South Africa, where he covered the Boer War for the *Manchester Guardian*, convinced him that imperialism was a direct product of capitalism. In his book, *Imperialism: A Study*, therefore, he denounced imperialism as being promoted by manufacturers of war materials, industrialists who required export markets for their surplus goods and capitalists (mainly Jewish financiers) with idle funds. From the figures for Great Britain's National Income he deduced that only about one-forty-fifth of this income derived from external trade. As only a fraction of this trade was with the newly acquired tropical possessions, profit from foreign trade was small. But profits from colonial and

foreign investment were enormous. The investment of surplus capital in overseas railways, mining, shipping, plantation development, armaments and foreign and colonial public securities clearly benefited certain business interests who alone profited from imperialism.

In Hobson's view surplus capital, and consequently imperialism, was the product of an inequitable distribution of wealth which left too high a proportion of profits in too few hands. As a result, consumer power was not greatly increased and this artificially limited the natural expansion of industry at home. On the other hand, a more just distribution of wealth would remove the surplus income and broaden the home market sufficiently to permit it to absorb the goods and capital which had previously been shipped abroad. Thus to Hobson 'underconsumption' by the wage earner was responsible for the recurrent slumps, low interest rates and continuing unemployment. Accordingly, the answer to Great Britain's economic problems was to give the lower classes a higher share in profits by raising wages and improving their conditions, thus providing an internal stimulus to the expansion of the British economy. By removing the surplus capital imperialism would become redundant.

For Hobson, then, the New Imperialism of the years after 1870 was an external symptom of the malfunctioning of the capitalist system in all the metropolitan countries. Domestic pressure for overseas investment in order to sustain domestic rates of profit had led to the acquisition of colonies:

> Overproduction in the sense of an excessive manufacturing plant, and surplus capital which cannot find sound investments within the country, force Great Britain, Germany, Holland, France to place larger and larger portions of their economic resources outside the area of their present political domain, and then stimulate a policy of political expansion so as to take in new areas.

To demonstrate the connection, Hobson printed a list of territories acquired by Great Britain since 1870 and compared this with a table showing the increase in British overseas investments during the same period. The result is striking. To use his figures, during a period when the British empire expanded by some 4,754,000 square miles and absorbed a population of some 88 million, returns from British overseas investments increased from £144 million in 1862 to £1,698 million in 1893. Hobson concluded:

> It is not too much to say that the modern foreign policy of Great Britain is primarily a struggle for profitable markets of investment.

But was it? The new colonies did not attract, either before or after annexation, a high proportion of the new investment. In fact, Hobson failed to distinguish clearly enough in his tables between investment made in other industrial nations (which Great Britain had no power or wish to annex), investment in the older colonies such as Canada and Australia, and investment in the areas which Great Britain had recently annexed or declared to be protectorates. The connection, therefore, remained unproven. Unperturbed, Hobson completed his denunciation of the investor. However much it might appear that colonial acquisitions came about as the result of the efforts of missionaries, humanitarians, patriotic pressure groups, empire-minded politicians or the men on the spot, and were undertaken in the interests of Christianity, civilisation, great power status or personal ambition, in reality a capitalist conspiracy provided the 'economic taproot' of imperialism:

> Finance manipulates the patriotic forces which politicians, soldiers, philanthropists and traders generate. . . . An ambitious statesman, a frontier soldier, an over-zealous missionary, a pushing trader, may suggest or even initiate a step of imperial expansion, may assist in educating patriotic public opinion to the urgent need of some fresh advance, but the final determination rests with the financial power.

Fundamentally, the flag was planted where it was profitable to plant it. A small rich class was able to divert the policies of the industrial nations to its own profit. Poor wages and under-consumption at home, over-production of manufactures caused by the adoption of new mechanical processes and surplus capital led to a search for new outlets for investment. In essence, the New Imperialism was the result of a breakdown in the capitalist system at the end of the nineteenth century.

Clearly, whatever the weaknesses in the argument, Hobson had arrived at a comprehensive theory for explaining imperialist motives. Superficially it seemed to fit the facts. Since 1870 industrialisation had so increased production that supply outstripped demand in home markets at a time when Germany, the United States and Belgium began to challenge Great Britain's virtual monopoly of world markets for certain classes of manufactured goods. Consequently, new markets had been sought in underdeveloped countries, markets which were frequently closed as continental powers resorted to a policy of protective tariffs. As a result British diplomacy and arms had also resorted to annexation and the forcible opening up of markets. This led to wars which brought little profit to the trader but were a source of incalculable gain to investors in such places as Egypt and the Transvaal. Such an interpretation had wide appeal in 1902. Furthermore, beside his economic analysis Hobson wove into his tapestry a discussion of non-economic motives for expansion and thus arrived at a comprehensive and apparently convincing explanation for the events of the last quarter of the nineteenth century.

It was not Hobson alone, however, who gave general currency to a theory of Capitalist Imperialism. Marxist writers soon used Hobson's ideas for purposes of their own. It was Lenin, in fact, who gave the world the theory of Capitalist Imperialism as it is generally understood today and it is Lenin's interpretation, the best-known Marxist explanation of imperialism, which is accepted by most of the communist world in the 1970s.

The ideas of Lenin

While in Switzerland in 1916, Lenin wrote a polemical pamphlet entitled *Imperialism, The Highest Stage of Capitalism*, designed to show that capitalism inevitably resulted in imperial expansion. This led to world wars which could only end in a revolution by the oppressed workers of the world. Bourgeois capitalism, therefore, was approaching the apocalypse Marx had foretold. Even the workers of a backward capitalist state like Russia could now spark off a series of explosions which would bring down the capitalist system in the West. Where a revolutionary situation existed, it was the duty of a disciplined Communist party to mobilise and lead the proletariat to victory. The pamphlet was clearly a tract for the times which overturned many previous Marxist ideas. But, coming from one of the great revolutionary leaders of the twentieth century, this analysis of the capitalist system and imperialism achieved greater popularity than any academic monograph could hope to match.

Lenin adopted many of Hobson's ideas but stripped them of much of their moderation and qualifications and put them to an entirely different use. He argued that until 1860 capitalism was a system of free competition. By 1900 the system was the opposite of competition — monopoly. Imperialism, in fact, was the 'monopoly stage of capitalism'. Lenin traced the pattern of development in the following manner. Technological advance, new organisational developments and the introduction of modern mechanical processes transformed competitive capitalism into monopoly capitalism with its characteristic agencies, cartels, trusts and tariffs. The banks and trusts gradually formed great financial combines which came to control capital itself and, in turn, dominated governments. These 'finance capitalists', in order to main-

tain their profit margins, invested capital abroad. At home this could
only increase production and lower prices. Under monopoly conditions,
therefore, it became necessary not only to exploit the existing markets
but to invest surplus capital in countries like Africa and Asia or semi-
colonies such as Egypt and the Argentine. But this had an additional
corollary — in order to gain the highest returns from overseas investment it was necessary to regulate the economy of these areas to the
investors' advantage. Only in colonies could such comprehensive
economic and political controls be implemented. Consequently, the
need to exploit capital, to secure more raw materials and larger protected markets, necessarily ended in rivalry for colonies after 1870. And
the New Imperialism would continue until the major capitalist powers
had shared the whole 'uncivilised' world between them. Then there
would be wars (like the First World War) for the redivision of empires.
World wars would lead the oppressed masses to rebel against the system,
capitalism would be overthrown, socialist states would arise and
imperialism would disappear from the face of the earth. This was a bold
analysis indeed. According to Lenin, in 1916 the world was on the brink
of a massive social revolution. There could be no break in the grim
cycle of capitalism: exploitation, empire, war, revolution and then,
finally, the extinction of the capitalist system itself. Thus many of
Hobson's ideas had been used to reinforce the Leninist theory that
capitalism was destined to evolve along predictable lines and be
destroyed. While Hobson had been a doctor prescribing a remedy,
Lenin was a prophet forecasting disaster.

The two conceptions were basically incompatible. To Hobson,
imperialism was the result of a malfunctioning of the capitalist system
which was capable of reform. To Lenin, imperialism was the highest
and final stage of inevitable capitalist development. Hobson regarded
imperialism as the export of capital accompanied by force: Lenin
simply equated imperialism with capital export and the dumping of
surplus produce. Hobson had no illusions as to the lack of rewards
provided by the New Imperialism: his 'imperialists' needed to corrupt
British public opinion through the press. Lenin's 'finance capitalists'
automatically dominated governments. In fact, in Lenin's theory there
was no room for explaining the actions of governments in terms other
than those of economics. Hobson's more complex analysis, allowing for
non-economic drives and a broader basis of 'economic necessity', had
been swept away. Above all, while Hobson was concerned with the
motives of the New Imperialism *prior* to the Boer War, Lenin concen-

trated on the twentieth-century world and the genesis of the war in Europe *after* 1900. It is particularly unfortunate, therefore, that many critics have mistakenly linked the two theses. Both deserve to be examined separately. To rebut one thesis is not necessarily to destroy the other.

Criticisms of the theories

It is not unnatural, perhaps, that this particular economic interpretation of imperialism, which retains an attraction as dogma throughout a large part of the world, should have been subjected to extremely critical scrutiny by non-Marxist writers and by Western scholars in general. Even before the First World War, Sir George Paish in an article entitled, 'Great Britain's Investments in Individual Colonies and Foreign Countries' in the *Journal of the Royal Statistical Society* for 1911, had detected Hobson's sleight of hand in equating British extensions of territory in the last quarter of the nineteenth century with the expansion of her overseas investments. Since the First World War numerous economists have examined the problem in greater detail.

One of the first articles of faith to be challenged concerned Lenin's thesis that the overseas empires were not an option but a necessity — that colonial annexations were the result of metropolitan powers being forced to export their capital because of the lack of profitable outlets at home. One of the most striking facts is that, far from being creditor nations, many of the countries which expanded their territories during this period were heavily in debt and did not have any surplus capital to invest. Russia, Japan and Italy fall into this category; Portugal was virtually bankrupt and Leopold II had no adequate financial backing when he embarked on his venture in the Congo. This is the first feature ignored by Lenin.

Secondly, if Hobson and Lenin's theses were genuine historical explanations, one would expect to find a strong correlation between the desire of European powers to export their capital, the fields in which investments were made and the annexation of territory. It is true that in such places as Tunis, Morocco, Egypt and the Transvaal investments were made and territory acquired. It is also true that before 1914 substantial investments were located in the Gold Coast, Malaya and parts of Indonesia. But it would be misleading to suggest that this colonial investment was the norm. In fact, these regions were by no means typical of the colonies acquired during the New Imperialism. These areas were the plums, it has been suggested, which would have attracted capital even if there had been no possibility of control. The metropolitan powers did not, in general, invest on such a large scale in their newly acquired colonies. France, for example, invested most of her surplus funds in Europe: in Russia, Rumania, Spain, Portugal and the Ottoman empire. Germany was more interested in the United States and her own European neighbours, placing a mere 3 per cent of her overseas credit in Africa and Asia, with only a small fraction of this going to her own colonies. For her part, the United States invested in Latin America, Canada and Europe. American investment in colonies was negligible. And can we believe that Fiji, New Guinea and Upper Burma, countries annexed by Great Britain, were fields of existing investment or were thought of as such for the future?

British capital tended to bypass the primitive tropical economies. By 1913 less than half of Great Britain's £3,975 million of foreign investment lay within the British empire and £999 million (over a quarter of it) was to be found in Latin America. The new colonies seem to have attracted very little capital indeed and to have been of only marginal economic importance. After 1870, British capital tended to flow to the well-established areas within the empire — Canada, Australia, India and New Zealand. And elsewhere Russia, China, the Argentine and the United States continued to attract capital because of the existing favourable economic conditions. There were plenty of desirable places for capitalists to invest. There was certainly no need to create opportunity by annexing economic backwaters.

Some of the most frequently cited cases of capitalistic imperialism — the machinations of the bondholders in Egypt and of the financiers in Rhodesia and the Transvaal — have also been undermined by recent research. Other reasons, as important as the profit motive, if not more important, were involved in the occupation and annexation of these areas. In Egypt, the defence of the Suez Canal and of the routes to India was at stake. Annexation of the Transvaal occurred less to satisfy the wishes of the British investors in the gold mines, who were already amassing very nice fortunes in Kruger's republic, than to prevent Boer domination of the Cape (thus challenging British control of the other important sea route to India, the Far East and the South Pacific). Similarly, when the French annexed Tunisia in 1881, they had in mind, beside their own economic interests, the security of Algeria and the need to forestall a possible Italian take-over. In none of these cases was it simply a financial question. Even that classic example of economic imperialism, the Boer War, which Hobson had to the fore of his mind, has fallen from grace. Certain recent studies of this war by Robinson and Gallagher in *Africa and the Victorians* (1961), J. S. Marais, *The Fall of Kruger's Republic* (1961) and G. H. Le May, *British Supremacy in South Africa 1899–1907* (1965) have challenged this once widely-accepted case. It would appear that the all-embracing nature of the argument concerning the primacy of economics is by no means satisfactory.

Hobson's theory concerning overseas investment in colonies not only fails the simple test of geography, but falls down over chronology. It is not only necessary to establish a correlation between the field of investment and the acquisition of colonies: if Hobson's postulations are correct, the export of European capital should have occurred mainly in the 1880s and 90s or shortly afterwards. Yet during the years 1875–95, European overseas investment actually declined. As Lenin indicated, the great age of monopolistic trusts and cartels did not come until after 1900, *after* the great scramble for territory, even in Germany, the country whose industry was most advanced along these lines. But even Lenin's thesis seems questionable. Trusts and cartels played little part in the British and French economies. True, in Great Britain the Salt Union of 1888 and the United Alkali Company of 1897 (plus other examples in shipping, steel and textiles) could be cited, but these were exceptions, not the rule. According to Lenin's definition, British capital remained competitive. On the other hand, the United States with its vast industrial and financial combinations remained until the 1898 episode largely, and, according to Lenin's argument, unaccountably, anti-imperialist.

Economists have also suggested that overseas investment was of an entirely voluntary nature. Lenin's model was much too simple. For example, Professor A. K. Cairncross in his *Home and Foreign Investment, 1870–1913* (1953), has demonstrated that overseas investment was very much part of Great Britain's trade pattern. The United States, Canada, Australia, South Africa and the Argentine, all places where the British invested most, produced the primary goods the British economy needed or required capital investment to meet this need. Therefore, it was virtually an investment in the primary sectors of the British economy — the return was not in profits but in cheap and plentiful raw materials and food which were essential in maintaining British living standards. Consequently, it also kept up profits *and* employment *and* wage levels. British overseas investment during this period was greatest in the 1880s when the terms of trade were most against Great Britain. The returns in raw materials, foodstuffs, and to a lesser extent in profits,

Cairncross believes, played a vital part in pulling Great Britain through the great depression at the end of the nineteenth century — however much Marxist historians of today (like E. J. Hobsbawm in his *Industry and Empire* (1968)) may argue that there was insufficient investment of capital in the home market.

In fact, in the 1880s overseas investment equalled only 5 per cent of the Gross National Product and this fell to 2 per cent in the 1890s. Yet in 1900 the returns on such investment equalled $6\frac{1}{2}$ per cent of the total National Income. These figures suggest that the accruing profits of mid-Victorian investment paid for the new investment of the 1880s and 90s and also helped to cushion the British economy, since the late Victorians must have taken a slice of overseas profits for home consumption. L. H. Jenks in *The Migration of British Capital to 1875* (1927) has also argued that, in an average year, investment in Indian railways caused a demand for £2 million worth of British iron and shipping services. It was this sort of demand which permitted large-scale economies in the British iron industry, without which the housewife's cooking pot would have been more expensive. Capital export also spread purchasing power and facilitated multilateral payments. Thus it would seem that until the school of 'New' economic history can produce alternative computer-processed statistics, argument concerning the profitability to a national economy of home as compared with foreign investment is likely to continue. But, whatever may have been the case, it is quite possible to argue that British capital was not attracted abroad by the simple expectation of higher rates of profit.

Indeed, both Hobson and Lenin accepted the rather facile assumption that direct political control, and therefore exploitation of labour and resources, enabled capitalists to maximise profits. This does not necessarily seem to have been the case. The Imperial British East Africa Company, for example, never paid out a penny and it was many years before Rhodes's British South Africa Company started paying dividends. The rich South African 'Rand Lord' with his Park Lane mansion may have seemed the prototype of all successful financiers, but not all mines produced large profits. In his *Capital Investment in Africa* (1938), Professor S. H. Frankel calculated that the mean annual yield of capital in the Rand mines during the first forty-five years of their effective exploitation amounted to no more than 4.1 per cent. In 1911, Sir George Paish calculated that over 60 per cent of Great Britain's foreign investment had gone into the construction of railways which yielded even more modest returns. Of course, speculators prepared to risk their capital placed their investments where the opportunity arose, regardless of whether the territory fell within the empire or not. Rash speculators, however, were few compared with the more numerous rentiers who wanted a modest but safe return. Even so, losses must have been tremendous. Punters do not brag about their losses; would-be magnates of the Stock Exchange broadcast their miscalculations even less. In fact Mark Blaug has suggested ('Economic Imperialism Revisited', *Yale Review* (1961)) that the yield of capital is generally higher in a capital-rich economy than in an underdeveloped country because the latter lacks social overhead facilities such as roads, railways, harbours, docks, dams, power plants and schools. Since this infrastructure had usually to be created from scratch, many early investors failed to make money during the scramble. Once again one of the basic assumptions of Hobson's and Lenin's theses remains in doubt.

Clearly, the 'theory of Capitalist Imperialism' has never been really *proved*. Nevertheless, it has remained an accepted approach to imperialism for many commentators and politicians. Kwame Nkrumah, the President of Ghana, extended the thesis to its logical conclusion when he maintained in his *Neo-Colonialism: the Last Stage of Imperialism* (1965) that the metropolitan countries were giving the colonies their political independence but retaining the economic strings in their own hands. Despite all the attacks of economists and historians the theory is still very much alive and still capable of adaptation and extension. The existing mythology is probably immune to demolition by mere facts.

Unfortunately, for many critics, the theories have become so outmoded that the works of Hobson and Lenin are no longer considered to be worth reading. Consequently, their analyses have become united into one thesis and are frequently misunderstood. Even academics are liable to over-react. Two timely articles have served as useful correctives to the rather over-simplified glosses on the works of Hobson and Lenin. Eric Stokes in 'Late Nineteenth-Century Colonial Expansion and the Attack on the Theory of Capitalist Imperialism: A Case of Mistaken Identity?' (*Historical Journal*, 1969) reminds us that Lenin viewed the years 1870–1914 as an age of transition, that his analysis relates to the years *after* 1900 and that he was concerned not with partition but with the *redivision* of the world. And T. O. Lloyd in 'Africa and Hobson's Imperialism' (*Past and Present*, 1972) has pointed to the original complexity of Hobson's arguments; to the increase in overseas investment during the years of the chartered companies, 1883–90; and to the enormous importance even a comparatively small amount of investment

had in Africa. Also, the lack of large-scale profits does not remove the
original (if mistaken) hopes of economic gain.

The economic interpretation (to which it will be necessary to return
later) is not a mere figment of the imagination. But it has been too
tempting for anti-Marxists, concentrating their attack on the narrow
basis of Hobson's and Lenin's ideas, to dismiss completely the economic
factor and consequently to erect in its place a new set of myths for the
causes of the phenomenon they are seeking to describe.

[26] Alternative Interpretations

Political motives

One of the foremost critics of the 'theory of Capitalist Imperialism' in
recent years has been the Oxford historian, D. K. Fieldhouse, who has
marshalled the evidence against the ideas of Hobson and Lenin and
synthesised a fashionable trend away from the economic interpretation
of the scramble for colonies. In an article ' "Imperialism": An Historiographical Revision' (*Economic History Review*, 1961) Fieldhouse reviewed
the writings of the critics of the 'Hobson–Lenin thesis' and concluded
that imperialism could not be explained in simple economic terms.
Instead, he argued that colonisation was more the product of political
ambitions, international rivalries, and complex situations in the non-
European world. In short, he asserted that the New Imperialism was
principally a political phenomenon.

Fieldhouse argued that in previous centuries European motives for
acquiring colonies had been the product of two basic drives: the need
to promote a lucrative trade for the metropolitan country and the clash
of political and military rivalries. National power was often as important
as economic advantage and the wars of the eighteenth century involving
the struggle for territory in America, India and the East had been more
a product of European power politics than of strictly economic competition. However, Hobson had assumed that the coming of free trade
had made the economic and political criteria of earlier times irrelevant.
Both he and Lenin had concluded that the renewal of the desire for
colonies after 1870 was attributable to a new factor — the unprece-
dented need to export surplus capital. Fieldhouse disagreed. In his
opinion the outstanding feature of the new situation was the subordination of economic to political considerations.

Basing his arguments on the political upheavals in Europe after 1870 and the subsequent formation of alliances, Fieldhouse argued that the balance of power became once again the dominating consideration of international relations. This led to a return to neo-mercantilist ideas concentrating on national strength, the power to make war and the achievement of national self-sufficiency through protective tariffs. Colonies became part of the international game once Bismarck made his sudden grab for territory in 1884. After that the process assumed its own momentum. Political tensions and the fear of being left out forced even a reluctant Britain to join in. As an impasse had been reached in Europe, the political struggle was extended to the periphery and new worlds were brought into existence in the vain hope of redressing the balance of the old.

It was a persuasive argument providing an attractive alternative interpretation to the purely economic approach. Far from the traders, investors and speculators dictating the tune, politicians, faced with the embarrassing alternatives of taking action or allowing a rival to step in, used the claims of such pressure groups to provide valid grounds for intervention. Their role was thus the reverse of that assigned to them by Hobson. But there were also other impulses which pushed frequently reluctant politicians forward. By the end of the century, when it was being realised that the new colonies were white elephants, colonies had become a psychological necessity and imperialism the property of the almost hysterical masses: politicians, under pressure from a public demand which they could not control, continued, with increasing bellicosity, to scrape the bottom of the barrel for yet more colonial burdens for the white man to carry. With these facts in mind, Field-house concluded that imperialism was a sociological phenomenon with roots in political facts and could properly be understood only in terms of the same social hysteria that had since given birth to other and more disastrous forms of aggressive nationalism. This reassessment at least provided a commendable counterbalance to Lenin's narrow economic arguments and, even with its weaknesses, presented an analysis as sophisticated as Hobson's.

Emotional factors
While economic and political interpretations must remain central to the argument, 'emotional' factors must also be taken into account: ranging from humanitarianism, missionary zeal, nationalism and chauvinism to militarism, international rivalry and plain greed. Hobson, of course, had always maintained that finance was only the

'engine' of imperialism, and did not provide the fuel. This was supplied by the 'enthusiasm' of patriots, militarists, philanthropists and the like. Beside the selfish minority of capitalists and the sectional interests (arms manufacturers, shipbuilders, etc.) Hobson had also included members of the armed services, the colonial and Indian services, and the aristocratic and wealthy classes — all groups with a professional interest in empire — in his 'expansive' forces.

In similar vein, in 1919 Joseph Schumpeter, a distinguished Austrian economist, published a brilliant essay, *Imperialism and Social Classes*, in which he suggested that imperialism was the product of certain war-oriented forces, principally of a ruling class which was becoming an anachronism. Schumpeter regarded imperialism as social 'atavism', an irrational phenomenon in a capitalist society. In his view capitalism was a force for peace and opposed to empire, but pre-capitalist traditions had survived among the aristocracy fostering war-like instincts. This survival of the attitudes of a past age resulted in the 'objectless' disposition on the part of a state in the late nineteenth century to unlimited forcible expansion. Consequently he saw 'expansion for the sake of expanding, war for the sake of fighting, victory for the sake of winning, dominion for the sake of ruling'. Thus Schumpeter found strong social and psychological reasons for imperialism.

However, his analysis was not entirely satisfactory. The attitudes of the governing classes were not simply outdated throwbacks. Nor were the detailed calculations made by such great statesmen as Salisbury and Bismarck concerning the advisability of annexing certain regions entirely irrational. They may have been mistaken, their hopes of economic gain remaining unfulfilled, but they were not therefore necessarily irrational. Schumpeter also ignored genuine humanitarian pressures: idealism, philanthropy and missionary zeal. These have been considered more fully by subsequent writers.

In 1941, Carlton Hayes, writing in his still-popular text-book *A Generation of Materialism, 1871–1900*, described the New Imperialism as a nationalist urge, a psychological reaction springing from an ardent desire to maintain or recover prestige. This thesis has received important confirmation in Henri Brunschwig's *Myths and Realities of French Colonialism* (1960). Brunschwig concludes that the rising colonial movement in France found its principal supporters among journalists, bureaucrats, geographers, and other academics who preached imperialism as a means of restoring national greatness and winning back the glory lost in the Franco-Prussian war. Similarly, in Germany, recent research suggests that colonialism, like Pan-Germanism, obtained most of its support from nationalist professors, teachers, civil servants and soldiers. It would seem that nationalism was an important factor in the New Imperialism. Yet it is a phenomenon as yet little understood. European racism has also received insufficient attention. On the other hand, the importance of the missionary and humanitarian factor has recently been recognised. European administrators frequently followed in the footsteps of pioneer missionaries and humanitarians.

Strategic motives

But Schumpeterian sociology, psychological reactions, social hysteria, prestige seeking, missionary zeal and humanitarian idealism are all difficult to measure. Not until the diplomatic documents of the European powers for the period 1870–1914 were published after the First World War could historians examine the facts more closely. The expansion of the nationalist states was then documented in some detail, incidents of imperialism were reconstructed, and the very first acquisition of colonies by some European countries was investigated. And so diplomatic historians working on diplomatic documents produced a diplomatic solution to the New Imperialism: a chess game focused on the balance of power in Europe, played out on comparatively safe tournament grounds in Africa and the Pacific.

A later generation, however, nourished in an age of 'global nuclear strategy', was not content with such a limited perspective. Believing that the aged Lord Salisbury and others in Whitehall accepted that statesmanship was concerned with the preservation of national security and power, Robinson and Gallagher suggested that the British role in the New Imperialism was dictated by strategical motivations. In their important book *Africa and the Victorians* (1961) these two Cambridge historians argued persuasively that the late Victorians were led to intervene in Africa because the collapse of the Khedive's regime in Egypt and the growth of Boer power in the Transvaal threatened the security of the Suez Canal and Cape routes to India, the Pacific and South-East Asia. The British needed to control the Nile and to encircle the Transvaal in order to maintain British supremacy over the life-lines of empire. These actions led an embittered France to retaliate by annexations in West Africa and a jealous Germany to act aggressively in both East and West Africa primarily for diplomatic ends. Thus, it was argued, Great Britain's strategic motives determined the timing and the manner of the scramble for Africa.

It is an attractively simple explanation (to be discussed more fully in Section 30) and brings to the fore another element in the New Imperialism. But if Robinson and Gallagher were right in believing that military strategy dominated Salisbury's ideas, as has since been shown in an impressive book by J. A. S. Grenville, *Lord Salisbury and Foreign Policy* (1964), such a consideration (which seems to apply to Great Britain alone) cannot be regarded as the key to our understanding of the beginnings of the scramble for territory. It raises immediate problems. Why, for example, did Disraeli commit Great Britain to endorsing the possible annexation of Tunisia by France in return for French acceptance of the British occupation of Cyprus in 1878? Would not the French with naval bases at Toulon and Bizerta then be able to threaten the strategic British naval route through the Mediterranean — in fact the very life-line of her empire? And if strategy alone dominated the thinking of statesmen, why did Salisbury temporarily agree in 1886 to German establishments in East Africa which could threaten Uganda, the Sudan and consequently the headwaters of the Nile? Unfortunately, this explanation is as open to argument as Hobson's capitalist conspiracy.

The emphasis on events in Africa is, however, a corrective one. But in their chapter, 'The Partition of Africa' in volume XI of the *New Cambridge Modern History* (1962), Robinson and Gallagher push their argument much further. They assert that the theorists of imperialism, in scanning Europe for causes, have been looking for the answer in the wrong place. The crucial changes were taking place in Africa. They link the partition to imbroglios with Egyptian revolutionaries, Mahdists, Muslims of the Western Sudan and Christian nationalists in Ethiopia. In short, to what they term 'proto-nationalist' awakenings. It is this concentration on the problems of the local situation that leads us to our final set of motives. All previous discussion has revolved round the Eurocentric factor: it is now time to extend the discussion to the periphery of empire.

The local factor
Since the Second World War, there has been an increasing study made of the regional histories of Asia, Africa and the Pacific. This has frequently been done by national historians specialising in their own cultures, who were thus best able to interpret the complex and often puzzling history of their homelands and to exploit to the full the information to be obtained from oral traditions. Such an accumulation

of new material has added a further dimension to our understanding of the New Imperialism.

Of course, the innate capacity of an empire to extend its frontiers has long been understood. The history of the East India Company in the eighteenth century and of Russia in central Asia in the nineteenth century are obvious examples of the 'turbulent frontier' thesis. D. K. Fieldhouse has dubbed this the 'contiguous area' theory. He suggested that colonies in a power vacuum would inevitably tend to expand until they reached some immovable political or geographical obstacle. There were many reasons for this: the European search for land or cheap non-white labour; the need for military security or administrative efficiency, or for the protection of native peoples on the existing frontiers of empire. All these factors could lead a European state, for humanitarian, strategic or economic reasons, to step in and establish a framework of stability and organised government.

This was well understood by one mid-nineteenth-century Colonial Secretary who minuted in the Colonial Office files:

> looking as I do upon all further extension of dominion in these countries with jealousy and apprehension, I look with most consolation to the map where I think I see some certain boundaries (however wide) placed by Nature to the progress of that process of absorption which seems to accompany our rule wherever we come into contact with tribes of savages or peoples of heathen and barbarous origin.

Indeed, in pointing to the clash of cultures, the Duke of Newcastle had put his finger on one fundamental reason for European expansion. Explorers, labour recruiters, missionaries and traders frequently undermined the fabric of indigenous societies without realising it, as H. C. Cairns has shown in his *Prelude to Imperialism: British Reactions to Central African Society 1840–90* (1965). In general, most indigenous political systems were unable to cope with the economic, military and political problems arising from direct contact with the Western world. 'Imperialism' could, therefore, be the completely unexpected and undesired product of this clash of cultures. It created a number of different frontiers. Indeed, the obvious dynamic of expansion as a reaction to local factors has led recent historians to write in terms of the traders' frontier, missionary frontier, military frontier, various agricultural frontiers, even the frontiers of the hunter, the miner and the civil service and (perhaps most important of all) the gunpowder frontier, since the new firearms fundamentally affected the balance of power between black and white and between black and black. Thus continuing over-

seas expansion can, at least in part, be explained quite satisfactorily
without assuming any new expansive movement in Europe, and a study
of peripheral situations can lead to a very different interpretation of the
New Imperialism than that which begins in Europe itself.

Indeed, European overseas expansion was, in many cases, connected
as much with European activities on the circumference of empire as
with expansionist forces in Europe. European agents rarely found virgin
lands in which to operate. Consequently in Africa, Asia and the Pacific,
they frequently clashed with indigenous societies, which were sometimes
as ancient as their own, and, not understanding the power struggles that
went on around them, tended to take sides in local disputes which had
affected the commercial or political status quo. The natural result of
such intervention was deeper commitment from which the metropolitan
country experienced difficulty in extricating itself. Colonial governors
and men on the spot often presented the home government with a *fait
accompli* when, for a variety of motives — personal ambition, ignorance,
local stability and economic viability among them — they exceeded
their instructions and meddled in unsettled regions. They were often
encouraged in such actions by local opinion. Existing colonies sometimes
became more imperialistically-minded than the mother country; witness, for example, the ambitious ideas of the Australian colonists and
the New Zealanders in the South Pacific in the late nineteenth century.
We must not leave what has been called 'sub-imperialism' out of
account.

The role of local personalities, European and indigenous, is now
recognised as having been an important factor in imperial expansion.
Once historians began to see African states, not as curious museum-
pieces whose affairs were only intelligible to anthropologists, but as
polities sharing many basic aims with governments everywhere, their
whole perspective began to change. The trail was blazed by Professor
K. O. Diké's pioneering study, *Trade and Politics in the Niger Delta,
1830–85* (1956). In his analysis of European–African relations during
the earlier nineteenth century, Diké had demonstrated that the scramble
which began in West Africa in the early 1880s was but the climax of an
extended period of Anglo-African relations. Such events needed to be
viewed in long-term perspective. After all, the 'Scramble for Africa' was
but a short episode in African history. And as our understanding of
Islamic revolutions in the Sudan, Bantu migrations in southern Africa
and the various wars and power struggles of West Africa has increased,
it has become possible to write of the establishment of European rule in

Africa in terms of the interaction of two sets of human beings and two societies, rather than in terms of 'advanced' or 'civilised' West Europeans dealing with 'backward', 'child-like', almost sub-human 'natives'. African nationalism was not always simply a product of imperialism; sometimes it was local nationalism that called imperialism into being.

Thus indigenous rulers rarely played a passive role. Absorbed in their own power struggles and rivalries they often tried to use the power of the foreigners to further their own ends. Professor J. D. Hargreaves in his *Prelude to the Partition of West Africa* (1963), has suggested that some African chiefs had clear aims in view. Although African rulers were often the tools of Europeans, they were sometimes successful in using Europeans for the advancement of their own objectives — elimination of commercial rivals, enhancement of personal power, or safeguarding the independence of their own kingdoms. The men on the spot could, on occasion, therefore, become their dupes. Sometimes European intruders were played off one against the other. Abyssinia, for example, was the one African state to ward off foreign domination at this time and also the one black state to increase its territory. Similarly, because of the skill of Chinese diplomatists during the scramble for 'spheres of influence' and leases at the end of the century, China remained territorially intact. The kings of Siam also managed to maintain their country's independence by playing off the foreigners. Thus the possibility exists that the New Imperialism could also have been influenced by the activities of a number of minor, and hitherto little known, African, Asian and Pacific Island rulers who used the rivalries and emotions of the Great Powers for their own ends.

However, these new dimensions to the older, purely Eurocentric approach to the New Imperialism should not be over-emphasised. Recent historiography has laid much stress on these local developments. But it must be remembered that while the local factor can help to explain some cases of colonial acquisition, it would be an exaggeration to suggest that Europeans were not generally masters of the colonial situation. The superiority of Western technology, economic and organisational resources and the superiority of European arms and military potential saw to that. The disparity in material power was too great. The scope for African initiative was, therefore, limited.

[27] Economics Once More

In attempting to dissect the anatomy of the New Imperialism, historians
have clearly progressed a long way from the rather crude explanation of
Lenin and the rather more sophisticated reasoning of Hobson. Political,
emotional and strategical factors have been taken into consideration
and, during the last decade or so, there has been a marked trend away
from a purely Eurocentric approach to the problem. To some extent,
this latter development has been overdone. In the same way, as a result
of the attacks on Hobson's and Lenin's theses which were marshalled
on a very narrow front, historians have over-compensated by playing
down the economic motive and regarding the New Imperialism as a
purely political phenomenon. Fieldhouse's article 'Imperialism: A
Historiographical Revision' (1961) suffered in this respect. And even
though the 'Gallagher–Robinson thesis' in 1953 began by defining
imperialism as the process of integrating new regions into the expanding
economy of Great Britain, the Atlantic, and then the whole world, the
'Robinson–Gallagher thesis' as defined in *Africa and the Victorians*
ended by arguing that the partition of Africa preceded the penetration
of British trade and capital and that it was the extension of territorial
claims which in time required commercial expansion.

But does this remove the economic motive entirely? Surely Fieldhouse's division between political and economic motives is a little
unreal, and even Robinson and Gallagher's arguments concerning
strategy only place the economic motive back one stage — the defence
of imperial communications with India, which in herself was economically important to Great Britain and militarily important in
defending British (commercial) interests in the eastern hemisphere. In
effect, the economic motive seems to have been placed in the centre of
the stage once again.

However, the new protagonist in the field who has recently done
most to reinstate the economic motive is D. C. M. Platt, the critic of the
Gallagher–Robinson thesis of continuity. In his book, *Finance, Trade and
Politics, British Foreign Policy 1815–1914* (1968), and in an article
entitled 'Economic Factors in British Policy during the "New Imperialism" ' in *Past and Present* for the same year, Platt returned to a semi-
Hobsonian analysis of the British economy of the late nineteenth
century. Admitting that it is difficult to support the view that faceless
financiers manipulated government policy in order to secure profitable
outlets for their surplus capital overseas, Platt argued that Hobson's

basic 'economic necessity' resulting from increased foreign competition, revived protectionism and the closure of overseas markets was real enough. Whereas government intervention had been virtually non-existent in the earlier Victorian years when Great Britain possessed a virtual monopoly of much of the world's trade, the situation changed when Germany, the United States and France became more industrialised, began to rival British production, increased the volume of their exports at a faster rate and reverted in the late 1870s to protective tariffs. After 1880 British traders began to fear discrimination as a result of pressure by foreign diplomatists on behalf of their nationals in Oriental courts and because of the closure of European, and possibly colonial, markets by revived protectionism. At a time of European depression the prospects for British overseas trade looked bleak. Consequently, since Great Britain was not prepared to manipulate tariffs as a bargaining counter, pressure for imperial expansion was increased. This was the 'economic necessity' behind the New Imperialism.

Inevitably, it is the limited commercial and financial return of the colonies subsequently acquired that has called the economic argument into question. At the time the precise value of the new markets was unknown; but the potential seemed tremendous, provided tariff barriers did not soon close them to international trade. The late Victorians were mistaken in their assessment, but the economic drive nevertheless remains as one of the basic factors in their (misguided) calculations. Such a reluctant empire-builder as Lord Salisbury, and such a positive champion of empire as Joseph Chamberlain, as well as empire-builders in the field such as Sir Harry Johnston, all justified colonial annexations on the basis of preventing other powers who practised a discriminatory tariff policy from monopolising new markets in the underdeveloped areas. This was one of the basic reasons for Great Britain's participation in the scramble for Africa and is even more demonstrably true of Britain's participation in the dangerous policy of defining spheres of influence in China at the end of the century. Platt concludes that although there is much in late Victorian imperial expansion which cannot be explained by economic factors, there is much that can be, especially in West Africa, China, the Levant and the South Pacific. No British government could stand aside while the whole future of British trade and investment overseas was placed in jeopardy. Dr Fieldhouse has acknowledged the strength of this argument and in an important book, *Economics and Empire, 1830–1914* (1973), has modified the stance he adopted in his earlier writings. He still maintains, however, that the British government intervened only when economic problems had, to some extent, become 'politicised'. Economic solutions were normally found to economic problems, it was only when other factors complicated these problems that the political solution of annexation was resorted to. Even so, it remains abundantly clear that to attempt an analysis of the causes of the New Imperialism without giving an important place to the economic motive makes no sense at all.

[28] An Assessment

The reasons put forward to account for the sudden flood of European overseas expansion in the last two decades of the nineteenth century, when nearly a quarter of the land surface of the earth and about one-tenth of its inhabitants fell under European, American and Japanese rule, have been many and varied. The New Imperialism was clearly a complex affair, probably incapable of easy and simple explanation. In fact, 'imperialism' is a word which covers many different and un-related developments which have only one thing in common – the final exertion of some form of political control in the non-European world. It would seem, therefore, that no one theory could be sufficiently comprehensive to provide a satisfactory explanation for the actions of various countries in many different regions of the globe, during a quarter of a century of the world's history.

The explanations put forward vary from a simple fit of absence of mind, promoting 'Commerce, Christianity and civilisation', 'philan-thropy plus five per cent' or the 'white man's burden', to the most sophisti-cated (and controversial) theories. These include imperialism as the final stage of capitalism, the search for raw materials and markets, outlets for surplus capital, over-production, under-consumption, trade rivalries, tariff warfare, humanitarianism, missionary zeal, militarism, national-ism, chauvinism, racism, social darwinism, new ruling elites, the yellow press, fear, hysteria, social atavism, power politics, strategy, national prestige, emigration, individual glory, contiguous development, in-subordinate and ambitious men on the spot, scheming local potentates, black nationalism, local power vacuums, the collapse of indigenous societies and collaborating cliques, and the clash of cultures. The list is overpowering, to say the least, and seems to touch upon all of man's activities. *All* of these things, naturally, contributed to the history of the period 1870–1914. It would seem that each of the various, and apparently unconnected, chains of events which constitute the New Imperialism had multiple causes which must be given their due weight in any general historical explanation. The New Imperialism, in other words, was a multifarious response to a fundamental and continuing shift in the balance of power both within Europe and between Europe and the rest of the world.

Indeed, at the end of the nineteenth century the disparity in power between the developed and the undeveloped parts of the world was greater than ever before. It is impossible to separate the events of the period from the conditions of the period: the changes in the European balance of power after 1870; the revolutions in technology, communications, marine science, business organisation and armaments; the new race theories and a cheap national press which provided part of the momentum of the movement at a time of increasing depression and fierce trade competition which eventually led to the adoption of neo-mercantilist doctrines. In all these events, developments in the metropolitan, international and local spheres must be taken into account. Individual cases of annexation must be examined in all three contexts, and the reasons for the need to annex must be ascertained at the local, as well as the governmental, level (they may well have been different). Commercial rivalry, internal crises and power vacuums in existing colonies and spheres of influence, and local friction between individual powers on the periphery of empire explain much, especially when seen as the culmination of relations over a longer period. Nevertheless it is in Europe that the impulses for expansion must primarily be sought: European political and commercial rivalry electrified the atmosphere and led to large-scale partition. And in Europe, political and economic motives, in varying degree, dominated the policies of most European powers. Only towards the end of the century did 'emotional' factors become important when imperialism became (or was made) a popular creed with the masses. In general, the economic motive entered everybody's calculations but it was frequently subordinated to considerations of power politics, prestige, strategy or even the overwhelming demands for intervention from the periphery.

In his survey of *The Theory of Capitalist Imperialism* (1967), Fieldhouse concludes that the historian should begin by studying as fully as possible the general forces operating within Europe and in other parts of the world, then study each particular case of annexation as a special problem and, finally, come to some conclusion about why colonisation occurred in each case. The result will almost certainly be untidy and often highly contradictory, different motives predominating at different times. Fieldhouse believes that the sum of these multiple investigations is the nearest the historian can come to achieving a general explanation of the tendency of Europe to expand after 1870. Anything more comprehensive, he asserts, would almost certainly be misleading.

In a sense the verdict is fair. But it is also most unsatisfactory and inconclusive. For the conclusion that the New Imperialism was the product of a convergence of several chains of events and independent initiatives, each with multiple causes requiring a pluralistic explanation, in reality amounts to a non-explanation. It hardly seems adequate to explain the sudden carving up of the African continent among six European powers, and their attempt within the same three decades to partition other sectors of the world, as simply a series of coincidences. It is the timing of this process which, above all, needs explanation and it is this which pluralistic explanations most noticeably fail to solve.

In order to shed new light on the subject a new approach must be tried. Perhaps historians have concentrated too much on looking for new factors leading to the New Imperialism. Perhaps it would be more rewarding to explain why the previously stable situation was disrupted and why the older stabilising factors disappeared. Professor G. N. Sanderson has recently suggested, in his stimulating article, 'The European Partition of Africa: Coincidence or Conjuncture' (*Journal of Imperial and Commonwealth History*, October 1974), that if such a model could be made to work, the attempts to partition the world would no longer be a simple collection of coincidences — no matter how disconnected the individual initiatives may have been and no matter how many and varied the converging 'forces' were. Clearly, the key questions are: 'Why did the partition of Africa begin when it did?' and 'Why did it develop into almost a world-wide scramble?' We need detailed and empirically verifiable answers to these questions.

Further Reading

M. E. Chamberlain, *The New Imperialism*. Historical Association (London, 1970).

H. M. Wright, *The "New Imperialism": Analysis of Late Nineteenth-Century Expansion*. D. C. Heath, 2nd rev. ed. (Lexington, 1976).

D. K. Fieldhouse, *The Theory of Capitalist Imperialism*. Longmans (London, 1967).

R. Owen & R. Sutcliffe, *Studies in the Theory of Imperialism*. Longmans (London, 1972).

J. R. Seeley, *The Expansion of England: Two Courses of Lectures*. Macmillan (London, 1885).

J. A. Hobson, *Imperialism: a study*. Allen & Unwin, 3rd rev. ed. (London, 1938).

V. I. Lenin, *Imperialism, the Highest Stage of Capitalism. A Popular Outline*. Progress Publishers, 13th ed. (Moscow, 1966).

G. Paish, 'Great Britain's Investment in Individual Colonies and Foreign Countries', *Journal of the Royal Statistical Society*, Vol. LXXIV, pp. 167–87 (1911).

A. K. Cairncross, *Home and Foreign Investment, 1870–1913*. Cambridge University Press (Cambridge, 1953).

L. H. Jenks, *The Migration of British Capital to 1857*. Knopf (New York, 1927).

S. H. Frankel, *Capital Investment in Africa*. Oxford University Press (London, 1938).

M. Blaug, 'Economic Imperialism Revisited', *Yale Review*, Vol. L, pp. 335–49 (1961).

L. C. Robbins, *The Economic Causes of War*. Cape (London, 1939).

K. Nkrumah, *Neo-Colonialism: the Last Stage of Imperialism*. Nelson (London, 1965).

E. Stokes, 'Late nineteenth-century colonial expansion and the attack on the theory of economic imperialism: a case of mistaken identity?', *Historical Journal*, Vol. 12, pp. 285–301 (1969).

T. O. Lloyd, 'Africa and Hobson's Imperialism', *Past and Present*, No. 55, pp. 130–53 (1972).

D. K. Fieldhouse, 'Imperialism: An Historiographical Revision', *Economic History Review*, 2nd Series, Vol. XIV, pp. 187–209 (1961).

J. A. Schumpeter, *Imperialism and Social Classes*. Blackwell, trans. by H. Norden & ed. by P. M. Sweezy (Oxford, 1951).

C. J. H. Hayes, *A Generation of Materialism, 1871–1900*. Harper (New York, 1941).

R. E. Robinson & J. A. Gallagher (with Alice Denny), *Africa and the Victorians: the official mind of imperialism*. Macmillan (London, 1961).

R. E. Robinson & J. A. Gallagher, 'The Partition of Africa', in *New Cambridge Modern History*, Vol. XI. Cambridge University Press (Cambridge, 1962).

H. A. C. Cairns, *Prelude to Imperialism: British Reactions to Central African Society, 1840–1890*. Routledge & Kegan Paul (London, 1965).

K. O. Diké, *Trade and Politics in the Niger Delta, 1830–1885*. Clarendon Press (Oxford, 1956).

J. D. Hargreaves, *Prelude to the Partition of West Africa*. Macmillan (London, 1963).

D. C. M. Platt, *Finance, Trade and Politics in British Foreign Policy, 1815–1914*. Oxford University Press (London, 1968).

D. C. M. Platt, 'Economic Factors in British Policy during the "New Imperialism"', *Past and Present*, No. XXXIX, pp. 120–38 (1968).

D. K. Fieldhouse, *Economics and Empire, 1830–1914.* Weidenfeld and Nicolson (London, 1973).

G. N. Sanderson, 'The European Partition of Africa: Coincidence or Conjuncture?', *The Journal of Imperial and Commonwealth History*, Vol. III, pp. 1–54 (1974).

Part V

Late-Victorian Imperialism

[29] A Revolution in Policy?

Gladstone's election victory in 1880 was intended to herald a return to the economical approach to government at home and to the traditions of non-intervention and minimum responsibility abroad. As the new Prime Minister remarked,

> We believe that the responsibilities of this great empire . . . are sufficient to exhaust the ambition or strength of any minister or any parliament, and we do not wish to overload them or break them down.

In 1880 there were no British plans for an expansionist colonial policy.

Nevertheless, no matter what the attitudes and intentions of the British government, a change had come over the world. Since the Franco-Prussian war and the unification of Germany and Italy the balance of power in Europe had shifted. Germany was a new power in the ascendant; France was nursing her humiliation. Russia was also continuing to expand her frontiers towards south-eastern Europe, the Mediterranean and Asia Minor as well as in central Asia and the Far East. Further afield, the United States had emerged from the throes of her civil war to take her place on the world's stage. With the advancing industrialisation of so many countries, with the innovations in technology, refrigeration, marine science and communications, and with the beginnings of a genuine world economy, the world seemed to have become a smaller place.

Nothing, probably, had done more to alter the geography of the world than the completion of that waterway through the ninety miles of sand which separated East from West. The Suez Canal provided Great Britain with a new and fast route to India, south-east Asia and the Pacific and gave her an increased strategic interest in the eastern Mediterranean and the Middle East. In the same year, the finances of the bankrupt Bey of Tunis, a quasi-independent Muslim ruler under Turkish suzerainty, were brought under a tripartite commission of

British, French and Italian representatives. Unknown to the European powers, this was the beginning of the end for the policy of shoring up existing Muslim states, such as Turkey, Zanzibar and Morocco, in order to maintain law and order inland. And, also in 1869, a huge diamond, the Star of South Africa, was found near the Orange river. Gold had already been discovered at Tati, north of the Vaal, in 1867. Thus in the 1870s Africa began to grip the imagination of European adventurers. The tales of endurance, courage and enterprise of such explorers as Livingstone, Burton, Speke, Grant, Baker and Stanley added an aura of romance to the legendary lands of King Solomon's mines. By the end of the decade, much of the blank map of Africa had been charted and Africa lay open to European penetration. Finally, in the early 1880s, the European powers took the plunge: France occupied Tunis, Britain occupied Egypt, Leopold II of the Belgians established himself in the Congo and Bismarck made his sudden bid for colonies in South-West and West Africa. By 1884–5 the 'Scramble for Africa', as *The Times* called it, had begun, and, with the calling of an international conference in Berlin, black Africa entered the realm of international affairs.

The scramble for Africa was but the most striking example of the New Imperialism in action. In Great Britain Gladstone and Granville were at a loss how to deal with the new phenomenon as events took them by storm. When Salisbury returned to office in 1885, he too was taken aback by the upheaval that European relations had undergone. For the rest of the century the late Victorians strove to retain their position in the world and to keep their markets, sources of raw material and lines of communication open. Late Victorian imperialism, in general, was a defensive reaction to the New Imperialism of others. Far from being the pacemakers the British, although they may have ended with the lion's share, for most of the time struggled to retain parity with the expansionist Schmitts, Ferrys, Crispis and Leopolds of the late nineteenth-century world.

Was there, then, for the British, a 'New' Imperialism? Was there a revolution in policy after 1880? Truly, there was a spectacular change from informal to formal methods of control. The need to maintain a 'fair field and no favour' trade policy certainly required greater government intervention after 1880. Previously, through the superiority of British naval power, industry, commerce and credit, Great Britain did not need to own or govern colonies or to monopolise trade. Provided equality of opportunity existed and free trade prevailed, the British always had a head start. But once this superiority was challenged, greater government pressure was required and annexation became a more frequent result.

But this apparent change of gear in government activity and switch to formal methods of control need not necessarily imply a break in the Gallagher–Robinson theory of continuity in British policy if we remember that laissez-faire alone had never been the sole philosophy of Victorian politicians and that annexation, as always, remained a last resort. It is still possible to fit the late Victorian period into the qualified thesis of continuity suggested earlier. But one further modification must be made. The imperialism of economic penetration and the imperialism of annexation were not simply automatic responses to different conditions, the one in general being more suited to the period of British hegemony, the other to a period of greater international competition. They were not necessarily different methods of achieving one single objective. In the late-Victorian period the imperialism of protection and the imperialism of free trade served different ideologies. Whereas those parts of British industry which were feeling the pinch of foreign competition cried out for protection of British markets and trade and generally looked forward to the creation of a completely self-sustaining empire, those sectors of the economy which had continued to prosper regarded the existing system as essential to their successful operation and wished to retain the whole wide world as their stage.

In 1880 the imperialism of economic penetration was still the basic philosophy of British politicians. While a penny off the income tax remained the symbol of sound financial policy, extensions of British rule were avoided whenever possible. In fact, most 'imperialists' in the early 1880s were federalists (the Imperial Federation League was founded in 1884) intent on strengthening the unity and security of the British parts of the empire. In the early 1880s the principle of expansion was not at issue. The real controversy concerned the means of protecting existing imperial interests. Most liberal-minded politicians wished to counteract anarchy and threats of foreign expansion beyond the existing imperial frontiers by continuing the typically mid-Victorian solutions of informal influence and international agreement. Their opponents argued that in the changed conditions of the time, existing imperial interests could only be safeguarded by formal extension of imperial rule. This division of opinion cut across party lines. While some Liberals such as Lord Rosebery, the Marquis of Hartington, W. E. Forster and G. J. Goschen agreed with the latter argument, most members of the party inclined towards a policy of consolidation. The majority of Conserva-

tives, however, were to be found in the camp of the forward school of
opinion.

At the end of the decade these arguments finally broadened into a
struggle between expansionists and anti-expansionists. The legacy from
the comfortable mid-Victorian era had not lasted long. It had been
dependent on three basic factors: first, British naval superiority; second,
the existence of stable regimes in the area of economic penetration
capable of withstanding the impact of Western ideas, economy and
culture; and third, the absence of, or cooperation with, foreign competitors. These three conditions gradually disappeared. By the early
1880s British naval supremacy had gone. In 1884 France, after an
intensive naval building programme, had as many first-class ships afloat
as Great Britain. Indeed, from 1879 Great Britain's position as the
leading imperial power was thought to be particularly vulnerable after
the experience of the Zulu, Afghan and first Boer wars. Traditional
policies of informal supremacy, moral suasion and confederation had
also begun to break down in the 1870s and Great Britain found it
increasingly necessary to make limited territorial annexations and
extensions of administration and to establish new spheres of paramountcy. Sir Percy Anderson, the head of the Foreign Office's African
Department, commented on West African developments in June 1883:

> Action seems to be forced on us . . . Protectorates are unwelcome
> burdens, but in this case it is . . . a question between British protectorates,
> which would be unwelcome, and French protectorates, which would
> be fatal.

As a consequence Great Britain became more involved in regional
problems. This frequently resulted in a collapse of tribal societies. In
the Gold Coast, for example, by abolishing domestic slavery, the British
destroyed an institution vital to the local economy. In East Africa, by
turning the Sultanate of Zanzibar into an instrument for suppressing the
slave trade, the British provoked a revolt of the slavers. In Ashanti,
Sir Garnet Wolseley's Palmerstonian blow in 1874 succeeded only too
well, destroying the cohesion of the country. In each of these cases the
British were eventually sucked into the power vacuum as mid-Victorian
panaceas of informal influence and of small punitive expeditions to keep
recalcitrant rulers in order ceased to work.

Such moves alarmed Great Britain's rivals. France became increasingly worried that the British doctrine of 'paramountcy', establishing an
exclusive claim to certain areas in West, East and South Africa, the

Malay States and the Pacific, was a deliberate attempt to limit France to her existing possessions. Thus the *modus vivendi* which had existed between the two powers in Africa since 1845 broke down in the late 1870s. In a sense French suspicions were not unwarranted. Sir Robert Herbert, a Permanent Under-Secretary in the Colonial Office, when dealing with British problems in the South Pacific noted in May 1875:

> Further annexation will come at the proper time, but to tell the world (Germany, the United States, France etc.) that we *now* contemplate it would be to defeat the object and prevent us from quietly acquiring paramount influence among the islands.

A year later the Colonial Secretary, Lord Carnarvon, expressed his ideas on Africa in even more forceful terms:

> I should not like anyone to come too near us either on the South towards the Transvaal, which *must* be ours; or on the north too near to Egypt and the country which belongs to Egypt.
>
> In fact when I speak of geographical limits I am not expressing my real opinion. We cannot admit rivals in the East or even the central parts of Africa; and I do not see why, looking to the experience that we have now of English life within the tropics — the Zambesi should be considered to be without the range of our colonisation. To a considerable extent, if not entirely, we must be prepared to apply a sort of Munro [*sic*] doctrine to much of Africa.

It was, however, the apparently aggressive intentions of the Governors of Sierra Leone and the Gold Coast, combined with French dreams of finding a 'second India' in the Senegal hinterland, which caused the French to embark on an expansionist policy of their own during the years 1879–83. This forced the British to retaliate. And once gentlemanly agreements between Britain and France to avoid elbowing each other on the periphery of empire had been replaced by international rivalry, with the arrival of Bismarck, Leopold II and the Italians on the scene, the last assumptions on which the canons of mid-Victorian conduct had been based were gone for ever. Even Gladstone was to find himself painting much of the map red, for it was during his second administration that the scramble for colonies really began. Indeed, one school of thought, far from regarding the late Victorians as laggards in the race for territory, believes that the British dictated the timing and course of the scramble for Africa and asserts that Gladstone was the man who began it. Gladstone's actions and motives, therefore, are worthy of detailed consideration.

[30] The Gladstone Ministry, 1880–5

Gladstone's second ministry was bedevilled by the Irish question. He was never fully in control of affairs from the start. The Cabinet was hopelessly divided and the party schism which occurred at the end of the administration was foreshadowed from its beginning. Imperial questions tended to become secondary aspects of this great domestic struggle.

Broadly speaking, the moderate Liberals stood for consolidation of the empire, while the Radicals and Irish Nationalists tended to be its critics. The Whigs, on the other hand, generally belonged to the forward school of opinion. Thus questions such as the Transvaal and Egyptian issues could be used by Parnellites and Radicals to 'dish the Whigs' and extract concessions on Irish policy. The factions in the Cabinet became even more diverse after 1882 when the international rivalry for colonies gradually became apparent. The Whigs then received unexpected support for their forward policy in Africa and the South Pacific from Joseph Chamberlain and Charles Dilke, two of their bitterest opponents on domestic and Irish issues. So great were the dissensions within the government and so interwoven were the various disputes that it became virtually impossible to follow any consistent Irish, foreign or colonial policy without offending some faction with which it was necessary to work in other matters. Only Gladstone's powerful personality, his popularity in the country and his adroitness at balancing the opposed factions kept the ministry together. Issues were evaded rather than solved. Consequently, government decisions tended to be uneasy compromises which emerged from the confusion of conflicts. As a result the Gladstone government drifted into situations it could not control.

In opposition, Gladstone had denounced Disraeli's 'forward' policies: the annexations of Fiji and the Transvaal, the extensions of administration in the Gold Coast and the Malay States, the occupation of Cyprus, the establishment of British military agents in Asia Minor, the Zulu and Afghan wars and the additions to British territory along the north-west frontier of India. He had virtually committed himself in his Midlothian campaigns to restoring independence to the Boers and withdrawing from Cyprus, Asia Minor and Afghanistan. He was appalled by the thought of a 'system of annexations designed . . . to forestall other countries'. The burdens and realities of office, however, led to a modification of projected policy. The task was made infinitely more difficult by the need to balance the moderate Liberal–Radical wing of the party, who abhorred belligerence and the amoral pursuit of national interests (basing their outlook on moral principle, international arbitration and equal rights for all) against the pragmatic, almost Palmerstonian, Whig members who not only wished to protect national interests at all costs but possessed no sympathy for nationalist movements in the Orient, Ireland or the Transvaal. The basis for a united approach to empire did not exist. Gladstone's crusade for the oppressed peoples of Afghanistan, the Transvaal and Ireland was not to reach fulfilment in office.

Imperial affairs

One of the first problems to confront the new ministry was that of the Transvaal. On achieving office the Gladstone government decided to retain temporarily the services of Sir Bartle Frere and to continue ruling the Boer state. Gladstone insisted: 'Confederation is so important . . . it eclipses and absorbs every other consideration.' Economy, apparently, was now more important than the rights of the Transvaalers to independence. The result was predictable: in December 1880 the Transvaalers rose in armed revolt and a general Boer rebellion throughout the whole of South Africa seemed possible.

This crisis deepened the divisions in Gladstone's Cabinet. Forster and the humanitarian imperialists argued in favour of continued British rule in the interests of native trusteeship. The Whigs, Hartington and Kimberley, argued for continued rule in the interests of prestige and supremacy. Gladstone and the Radicals sympathised with the Boer struggle for independence. Thus the Cabinet division between coercion and conciliation reflected the divisions on the Irish question. Consequently, the Transvaal became caught up in domestic politics and, despite the humiliating British defeat and the death of the Governor of Natal at Majuba Hill in February 1881, the Radicals had their way. In August 1881 the Convention. of Pretoria was signed. Boer self-government was restored while the British government retained nominal control of the Transvaal's relations with Africans and neighbouring territories under a vague imperial suzerainty. It appeared to be a neat compromise to mollify the Whig wing. In effect it was disastrous. The Gladstone government retained responsibilities but not the power of effective control. The situation was made even worse when the convention was re-negotiated in 1884 omitting the reference to imperial suzerainty. The makeshift policy of the Gladstone administration, dictated by internal party bickering, had laid some of the seeds for a future war.

Equally unhappy results sprang from the government's attempts at compromise over the Afghan question. To begin with, the Cabinet was intent on withdrawing from Afghanistan and returning the areas occupied by the Conservative administration to the control of the new Amir, Abdur Rahman. But Lytton's replacement as Viceroy, Lord Ripon, soon came to realise that the withdrawal of British troops from an Afghan kingdom undermined by invasion and torn between British and Russian factions could lead only to anarchy and the possibility of further Russian penetration. As a result another compromise was reached. Great Britain accepted responsibility for the defence of Afghanistan but, in order to pacify the Radicals, the strategically important province of Kandahar was returned to the Amir for reasons (as the Queen wrote) of 'political and Party expediency'.

This was another bad bargain. Responsibilities had once again been incurred, this time without any means of controlling the Amir's activities. When the Russians annexed Merv in 1884 and their frontiers advanced inexorably towards Persia and the undefined Persian–Afghan border, the Amir took events into his own hands. Afghan and Russian troops clashed at Penjdeh in March 1885 and the Gladstone government was called upon to meet its guarantee. Even Gladstone found it necessary to threaten Russia with war. This explosive situation was finally defused when the Russians accepted Afghan control of the all-important Zulficar pass. From 1885 onwards both Conservatives *and* Liberals acknowledged that India would have to be defended beyond the Indus. The North-West frontier ceased to be a party issue. By the end of his second administration Gladstone had thrown over the policy of 'masterly inactivity' and even the traditionally Russophile Liberals had for several weeks been on the brink of war with Russia. It was a significant reversal of policy in which internal dissensions and the realities of central Asian politics had played their part.

If the Liberal confrontation with Russia was unexpected, the deterioration in British relations with 'the unspeakable Turk' was not. In the Eastern Question, Gladstone had been a violent critic of Disraeli's apparently pro-Turkish policy. He had objected to the British occupation of Cyprus in particular. But after Majuba Hill, abandonment was thought to be unwise. Gladstone did, however, succeed in dropping Salisbury's scheme for defending the Turkish empire in Asia. The military 'consuls' were withdrawn from Armenia. At the same time Gladstone organised a naval demonstration which persuaded the Sultan to carry out his promise at Berlin to cede a small strip of territory to

Montenegro and a large undefined area of Thessaly to Greece. The result was the collapse of British influence in Constantinople.

It was part of a deliberate policy of the new British government to dispense with the Turks as allies. Gladstone chose to rely for the defence of British routes to India and her position in the Mediterranean on British naval power, the Anglo-French *entente* and, above all, the Concert of Europe. But he reckoned without Bismarck. Bismarck's secret treaties with Austria–Hungary, Russia and Italy soon removed the Concert from practical politics. Now that British influence at Constantinople was gone, Gladstone had to depend more heavily on the Anglo-French *entente*. It was Gladstone's misfortune that events in 1882 in North Africa caused him to lose the goodwill of the French and a controversy over Angra Pequena in south-west Africa in 1884 led to the alienation of Bismarck. By the time Gladstone's administration collapsed, Great Britain's foreign and imperial policies were in shreds, Egypt had been occupied and the scramble for colonies was on.

The occupation of Egypt

The occupation of Egypt was the last thing Gladstone wanted. It contravened all the high moral principles which he had declared would form the basis of future Liberal foreign policy. Yet despite a belief in the supremacy of moral influence, the Gladstone government entered on an ever-lengthening territorial occupation of Egypt with ever-increasing financial, governmental and defence responsibilities. The result was disliked by Gladstone, the Radicals, the moderate Liberals and the Whigs. Above all it became unpopular with the British people. The stones through the windows of 10 Downing Street testified to that.

Great Britain's vital interests in Egypt had been recognised by Disraeli in 1875 when he purchased the Khedive's Suez Canal Company shares in an attempt to retain parity with French political and commercial influence inside the country. The Khedive's costly reformist schemes for irrigation, agriculture and improved communications had resulted in reckless borrowing at exorbitant rates of interest. In 1876 he was in debt to the tune of £93,000,000. As a result an international Caisse de la Dette Publique (Public Debt Commission) was established to watch over the interests of foreign investors and to handle repayments to foreign bankers. When these arrangements failed, Khedive Ismail was required by the French in 1878 to surrender his autocratic powers, personal revenues and estates to a responsible ministry. This was to include one French and one British minister.

The era of the Dual Control had begun. But the attempts to promote fiscal reform and solvency led to an attack on entrenched privileges, thus uniting the landlords, the army and the depressed peasantry in opposition to the government. When Ismail astutely placed himself at the head of this opposition and in April 1879 dismissed his European ministers, the French and British governments (and Bismarck) persuaded the Turkish Sultan to depose the Khedive and appoint his son, Tewfik, in his place. The new Khedive was given two permanent advisers, a French and a British Controller-General, who, although they no longer held administrative positions, were virtually dictators of Egyptian finance behind the scenes. Furthermore, when the six powers of Europe signed the Law of Liquidation in July 1880 (whereby 66 per cent of the Egyptian revenue was allocated to repayment of the debt) Egypt's financial independence completely disappeared.

To date the British and the French had acted in concert, but the French had always dictated the pace of this exercise in informal supremacy. The British had followed rather reluctantly behind. In fact, the French, in stripping the Khedive of his wealth and turning him into a constitutional monarch, had made him into little more than a Christian puppet and debt-collector for the *effendi*, thus damaging the instrument they wished to rule through. The reaction which occurred against Turkish oppression and Western control, embracing liberal reformers, Muslim conservatives, the landowners, the peasants and a mutinous army under Arabi Pasha, was almost worthy of the name of a nationalist revolt. By the end of 1881 European intervention had brought the country to the verge of anarchy. Affairs finally came to a head when Arabi and his officers surrounded the Khedive's palace and forced him to dismiss his ministers.

Gladstone's reaction was extremely cautious. Joint Anglo-French diplomatic activity would, he believed, be sufficient to restore the Khedive's fortunes and maintain the status quo. If a military expedition had to be sent, both he and Granville, the Foreign Secretary, wished it to be mounted by the Turks. The French, however, did not wish the Turks to intervene. They feared that Arabi's revolt was part of a Pan-Islamic movement which would stir Muslim discontent in Tunisia and Algeria. Gambetta, the French Foreign Minister, preferred a joint Anglo-French military or naval demonstration.

Gladstone wished to stop short of intervention. His Whig colleagues did not agree with him. But the whole Cabinet was agreed on keeping in step with France. It was, therefore, without full consideration of the implications that the British associated themselves with a French declaration assuring the Khedive of their support and announcing their intention to uphold the Financial Control. While the British Cabinet accepted the Gambetta Note of 7 January 1882 as a bluff, hoping it would restore respect for the Khedive's authority and Europe's financial rights, the French were hoping to bind Great Britain to some agreed course of action. Unfortunately, the Note had the reverse of the desired effect: Egyptian opinion rallied behind Arabi and the colonels. In February 1882, Arabi became Minister of War and one of his supporters, Prime Minister. The new government demanded a voice in the formation of the Egyptian budget. The British bluff had been called.

Gambetta insisted that the terms of the Note should now be enforced. The British Cabinet, rent asunder by the Irish crisis, could not agree on any set course. That Britain and France continued to act together at this stage was largely due to the fall of Gambetta on 27 January 1882 and his replacement by the more temporising Freycinet. In May agreement on joint action was finally reached. A joint naval demonstration was to be assembled, and if a landing became necessary, Turkish troops under Anglo-French control should pacify Egypt. The British and French fleets sailed for Alexandria. But at the last moment the French refused to call in the Turk. By itself the naval demonstration was useless. Riots ensued in Alexandria on 11–12 June in which some fifty Europeans died. The crisis had been turned into an emergency.

The British were now on their own. The French government, under attack in the Chamber of Deputies, had withdrawn their fleet to Port Said when the British admiral requested permission to demand the dismantlement of Arabi's new shore batteries which were threatening his ships. Gladstone, deep in a crisis over the Irish Arrears Bill, agreed to the ultimatum being sent in the hope that this action would avert further intervention. But Admiral Seymour misinterpreted his instructions and demanded the *surrender* of the shore forts. When the ultimatum expired on 11 July the bombardment was carried out.

Old-fashioned gunboat diplomacy merely aggravated the situation. The riots spread inland, Arabi proclaimed a *jihad* (holy war) against the British, and the Suez Canal seemed in danger. British intervention was now inevitable. On 20 July 1882 an expedition to Cairo under Sir Garnet Wolseley was decided upon. To please both wings of the Liberal party a short 'Rescue and Retire' operation was planned. That it was to be a solely British venture became apparent on 29 July when the

Freycinet government fell from office and the Italians refused to join the expedition. British operations began on 18 August. The final blow was struck at Tel-el-Kebir on 13 September. The British defeated the Egyptian army, Arabi was imprisoned and the Khedive was restored to power. A surprisingly jubilant Gladstone announced that the country would be evacuated as soon as the Canal was safe and the Egyptians were able to manage their own affairs.

In this muddled way, the Gladstone government, first reluctantly following the French lead then submitting to the pressure of events, ended by occupying Egypt. Their next objective was early evacuation once British supremacy had been established in Cairo. But a speedy 'Rescue and Retire' operation was not possible. The Khedive was no longer capable of standing alone. Indeed, there was no stable authority in the country. The British were trapped. The Radicals wished to hand over power to the Egyptian Chamber of Notables; the Whigs wanted a strong Khedive under British control. Gladstone and Granville decided to appoint a single European Financial Adviser. Thus ended the Dual Control and with it Anglo-French friendship for twenty years.

What was to be done with Egypt? The Earl of Dufferin, sent out to report on the situation, balanced neatly between the two Liberal wings. His prescription was for a dose of financial assistance which would soon put the country back on its feet. The British could then retire. Sir Evelyn Baring (who was in charge at Cairo as Consul-General) was more realistic: speedy retirement and constructive reform were incompatible. It was impossible to restore the status quo. The British would have to stay in Egypt for a good number of years.

Baring's warnings were underlined by events in the Sudan where the Khedive's authority was rapidly collapsing. In 1881 a zealous religious reformer, Mohammed Ahmad, who called himself the Mahdi, rallied round him the pious tribesmen of the Sudan and preached a holy war which would place him at the head of a purified Islam. His immediate military successes turned the movement into a nationalist struggle. The British government ignored the implications of the Mahdist rising until the Khedive's army of 10,000 men under a retired Indian army officer, Hicks Pasha, was cut to pieces by the dervishes in November 1883. It then became apparent that the British could not restore financial order while the Khedive squandered his resources in the Sudan. Moreover, if the Khedive could not hold Khartoum, Egypt itself was in danger.

For once, the British government took a firm stand: the frontiers of Egypt and the Red Sea Ports would be defended but Egypt must

evacuate the Sudan. It was an unpopular decision. It further undermined the authority of the Khedive, killed all hope of Egyptian cooperation and forced Baring to take a firmer grip on the administration
of the country. Gladstone gloomily concluded in April 1884: 'We have
done our Egyptian business, and we are an Egyptian government.'

Worse was to come. The government was under severe attack in the
Commons. The Radicals advocated early withdrawal: the Whigs prolonged occupation. To mollify the critics the Cabinet decided to send
out Major-General Charles Gordon to supervise the evacuation of the
Sudan, with orders to do whatever was possible through personal
influence to secure the Egyptian frontiers.

The government appeared to have taken leave of its senses in its
desire to restore its popularity. Gordon was a man who had enjoyed an
extraordinary military career in China, Africa, India and the Crimea.
He was a popular hero, known to be brave, brilliant and totally undisciplined. On top of this he had been Governor-General of the Sudan
for two years. This made him a most unlikely instrument for Gladstone's
policy of withdrawal. A bible-thumping Christian militant, he could
rival the Mahdi in religious fanaticism. Once in the Sudan he refused
to evacuate Khartoum and waited for reinforcements — troops or
martyrdom.

The relief of Gordon in Khartoum became mixed up in the ministry's
disputes over policy. On 23 April 1884, Northbrook recorded in his
diary:

> Cabinet 3 till 7. Great difference of opinion. Question of immediate
> steps for consideration of expenditure to support Gordon deferred. . . .
> I think Government will probably break up.

Gordon's fate was passed over for the time being while policy in Egypt
was hammered out.

The British position had become acute: heavy budgetary deficits
existed in Egypt and the hostility of Europe was reflected in the Franco-
German *entente* and Russian pressure on the north-west frontier of India.
Throughout May 1884 Gladstone tried desperately to negotiate an
international agreement whereby the Khedive would receive a loan and
Egypt would be neutralised if the British withdrew within the next few
years. But no agreement was forthcoming. France and Germany were
beginning to cooperate elsewhere in Africa. Britain was so tied up in
Egypt that she was highly vulnerable to pressure from the continental
powers. Several spheres of British paramountcy in Africa and Asia were

being invaded and the British found it virtually impossible to retaliate.

Finally, Gordon's danger became so pressing that a relief expedition was agreed upon. The ministers were utterly demoralised, their policy in shreds. By November 1884 the majority of the Cabinet were prepared to throw in the towel. But they could not even agree on how best to quit their responsibilities. They were, however, prepared to barter British supremacy in Cairo. By December 1884 new negotiations were under way with the European powers and, at French insistence, an inter-national loan guaranteed by all six major European powers was accepted. This meant complete European control of Egyptian finances and that all British attempts at reform would be dependent on European consent. So eager were the government to quit that this stipulation was embodied in the London Convention of March 1885, and the Egyptian bâton, which was to bedevil British foreign relations in the next few years, was handed to Bismarck on a plate.

By this time the final Sudanese bombshell had exploded. On 5 February 1885, the British public learned that Wolseley's relief expedi-tion had arrived two days too late. Khartoum had fallen and Gordon was dead. The country was shocked and public reaction was at times almost hysterical. The Queen was beside herself with anger. The British government had abandoned a national hero. Gladstone suffered venom-ous abuse. In the heat of the moment, the Cabinet felt obliged to authorise an advance on Khartoum to break the Mahdi before the British army retired.

This last change of position was too much for the ministry's supporters in the Commons. On 23 February the Conservatives put down a motion of censure calling upon the government to restore order in the Sudan. Northbrook in the Lords and Forster and Goschen in the Commons agreed: it was pointless to smash the Mahdi and then retire without setting up a stable administration. John Morley, the Radical leader, joined in the criticism of the government. As usual the Cabinet had decided 'to go to Khartoum to please the Whigs' and 'to retire to please the Radicals'.

This revolt of the two Liberal wings and the defection of the Parnell-ites reduced the Liberal majority in the Commons to fourteen. But it is clear that most MPs were fed up with the costly and dangerous occupa-tion of Egypt. Even the Tories talked more about Gordon than future policy. After the furore over Gordon's death had died down the Cabinet reverted to their former policy. The Russian war scare following the Penjdeh clash led to the Khartoum expedition being diverted to India.

The Sudan was definitely abandoned. And when the Conservatives achieved office in June 1885 they did nothing to reconquer it. Salisbury even attempted to continue Granville's efforts at securing a neutralisation of Egypt provided the British could return in the event of anarchy or danger to the Canal. The European powers quashed these plans in 1887. One thing is clear, however: British politicians still lacked large-scale territorial ambitions and by 1887 the late Victorians had not donned their imperialist clothes. Indeed, in February of that year, A. B. Winterbotham, a Liberal Unionist MP, observed:

> The jingo fever appeared to be at the very lowest ebb; and the principle of non-intervention had received general support from both sides of the House.

Despite (or perhaps because of) the British experiences in Egypt, mid-Victorian ideas of economy, non-intervention and moral influence still seemed to hold good. The growing school of expansionists were still unable to sway opinions in the Commons. By 1887 expansion was still an unpopular cry.

The Egyptocentric thesis
The Gladstone government had got itself into a mess. British policy had been one of constant compromise. The end product was disaster. The Convention of 1885 was the last of the government's great blunders. Means of withdrawal still could not be found and international fetters now limited Great Britain's freedom of action so that the government of Egypt became even more difficult. France and Russia consistently opposed British plans for Egypt on the Debt Commission; Great Britain had to depend on the cooperation of Bismarck. Bismarck and his successors used this lever to good effect. It caused one of the greatest dilemmas of British foreign policy in the last two decades of the nineteenth century: in Europe Britain found it increasingly in her interests to work with France, the power who opposed her in Egypt and Africa; in Africa it was necessary to work with Germany, the power she found an increasingly difficult and dangerous companion in Europe. Until the Entente Cordiale was re-established in 1904, Great Britain remained in 'isolation'. For this Gladstone's alienation of Turkey, France, Italy, Russia and Germany, but principally his bondage in Egypt, was largely to blame.

The legacy of the Gladstone government was an appalling one. Yet, at first sight, it is difficult to see — apart from the repercussions on international relations — what significance the occupation of Egypt has for Victorian imperialism. It had been carried out only after all alternatives and attempts at European cooperation had been exhausted and was intended to be purely temporary in character. Nevertheless Robinson and Gallagher, who have done so much to increase our understanding of the motives and events of 1882–5, have constructed in their book *Africa and the Victorians*, and in later writings, an elaborate theory whereby the timing and course of the scramble for Africa was dictated by the British occupation of Egypt. In their view, Gladstone and his successors were responsible for the partition of Africa.

Robinson and Gallagher argue that the French were so humiliated after 1882 that they sought 'pin-pricks' in the British side, principally in West Africa. For decades previously there had been a mutually agreed 'hands off' policy in this region. Before the dastardly British invasion of Egypt the activities of the French explorer, De Brazza, were only of passing interest to his government and the schemes of a newcomer, like Leopold II in the Congo, had little chance of realisation. The occupation of Egypt altered all this. The French government immediately endorsed the De Brazza–Makoko treaty and objected when the British tried to protect their interests in the area by concluding an agreement with Portugal. The claims of Leopold II were put forward and the French demanded an international conference to discuss the position in the Congo *and* on the Niger. Bismarck was prepared to sell his services to the highest bidder. In May 1884 he pressed his claims in South-West Africa and a month later joined in the clamour for an international conference.

The results were significant. The British could not afford to antagonise Bismarck, so in the interests of Egypt they accepted his claims for territory in South-West Africa, Togoland and the Cameroons and in New Guinea in the South Pacific. They also decided to do no more than attempt to achieve freedom of trade in West Africa. Thus when the Berlin West Africa Conference met, Leopold's Congo Free State was recognised and a few vague generalisations were made as to the occupation and administration of the West African coast. Britain, France, Germany and the King of the Belgians had now all made advances in Africa. Great Britain also felt compelled to extend her obligations in Bechuanaland, Pondoland and Zululand. The need to provide evidence of occupation and administration on the cheap led to the chartering of commercial companies such as Sir George Goldie's Royal Niger Company and Cecil Rhodes's British South Africa Company. These only increased the momentum for expansion.

Robinson and Gallagher also maintain that Salisbury's decision in 1888–9 — that Great Britain was in Egypt to stay for the foreseeable future — sparked off the second stage in the scramble. Cairo, not Constantinople, soon became the lynch-pin of British strategy and the security of Egypt depended on keeping Uganda and the Nile Valley under British control. The Nile was the life-blood of Egypt. It was feared that a foreign power at the headwaters would be in a position to dam or divert the river and reduce the country to ruin. Salisbury's decision and strategy, therefore, began a more positive phase in Victorian imperialism, and the partition of East Africa was set in motion. First the Germans were persuaded to quit East Africa north of the 1886 partition line and protectorates were later extended over Uganda and Kenya. Then the reconquest of the Sudan was undertaken in 1896 and, in an attempt to uphold British supremacy in the Upper Nile, open war was risked with France at Fashoda in 1898. According to Robinson and Gallagher, the occupation of Egypt was the key to the timing, course and end of the scramble for Africa. Even the final confrontation of the century, the Boer War, was the product of a clash between Boer nationalism and British concern for protecting the Cape route to India. In fact, the partition of Africa was little more than a gigantic footnote to the Indian Empire. As in 1882, so in 1902, strategy dominated the thoughts of the late Victorians.

Robinson's and Gallagher's interpretation is once again persuasively argued. But the academic world has not been entirely convinced. There were so many points of Afro-European contact capable of generating expansive policies of their own, that it is difficult to accept that the partition of Africa was dominated by one motive, was determined from one or two geographical centres, or arose from one single set of causes. In fact, in giving primacy to African crises and regarding rivalries in Europe as only of secondary importance, Robinson and Gallagher are to some extent guilty of putting the cart before the horse. Why were events capable of sparking off the partition? This can only be explained by referring back to relations between the foreign powers and existing vested interests in Africa.

Specialists in West African history were the first to challenge the theory that the partition came about as an accidental chain reaction to the British occupation of Egypt. That this event so angered the French government that they broke their 'gentleman's agreement' not to encroach on the spheres of their rival, has proved the weakest link in the new interpretation. In an article, 'Victorians, Republicans and the

Partition of West Africa' in the *Journal of African History* for 1962, C. W. Newbury, an authority well versed in the records of the French government, argued that there was not a shred of evidence to connect West Africa with Egypt. Similarly Henri Brunschwig, in his *Myths and Realities of French Imperialism 1871–1914*, and the Belgian historian, Jean Stengers, in a review article in the *Journal of African History* for 1962 entitled, 'L'Impérialisme coloniale de la fin du XIXe siècle: Mythe ou Réalité', see the French attempts at aggrandisement as arising out of rivalry not with Great Britain but with Leopold's venture in the Congo. The ratification of De Brazza's treaty with a Congo chief, the Makoko, (which admittedly owed a great deal to French irritation at their exclusion from Egypt) provided the French with a harmless diplomatic success. This unexpected ratification, however, so took everyone by surprise that the King of the Belgians, and the British and Portuguese governments, immediately reacted by staking out their own claims. According to Stengers and Brunschwig, this makes both De Brazza and Leopold II better candidates for setting in motion the scramble for West Africa than Gladstone, Bismarck or anyone else.

However, French interest in Africa did not suddenly spring to life in 1882. It has certainly been convincingly argued (by Newbury and A. S. Kanya-Forstner in 'French Policy and the Origins of the Scramble for West Africa' in the *Journal of African History* for 1969) that the French adopted their more aggressive attitude towards Senegal, the coastal region of West Africa and the Congo in 1879–80. The occupation of Egypt clearly played little part in French calculations. Indeed, the occupation remained a disagreement among friends throughout 1883, and even as late as January 1884 the French consul in Egypt was instructed to cooperate actively with his British counterpart. Not until Anglo-French discussions broke down in June 1884 did the French begin to respond to Bismarck's proposals for 'common action' against Britain in Africa. But even then, French ambitions were concentrated elsewhere. Before 1894 the French focused on the creation of a new continental empire centred on Lake Chad. Thus, the persistent crisis in Egypt can hardly be said to have provided the motive power in the partition of Africa.

In East Africa, however, Robinson and Gallagher's interpretation appears to fit the facts much more closely. The British did play a positive role in the partition of East Africa whereas in the west their motives were entirely defensive, designed simply to retain the existing areas of British commercial predominance. But even in the east the defence of Egypt and the headwaters of the Nile was not the sole factor to be taken into account. The east coast had a strategic significance all of its own because of the Cape route to India. And once the telegraph reached Zanzibar and was intended as Britain's first line of communication with India and the fleet in the eastern waters, it became essential to protect Zanzibar and the port of Mombasa. Uganda and Nyasaland also had a special significance to the British — as Christian barriers to the spread of militant Islam. Perhaps most important of all were the exaggerated hopes of economic gain in this region and the upheavals in Uganda itself.

All in all, while the egyptocentric argument explains much that went on in Africa it does not explain everything. It is of doubtful relevance to the partition of West Africa and it certainly does not explain the propensity to partition large areas of the world. Similarly, Leopold's Congo venture did not really upset the existing situation. More decisive were the French declaration of protectorates in areas directly threatening existing British spheres of informal influence and Bismarck's sudden bid for colonies. Does this remove the argument that the British were responsible for the scramble for colonies? Unfortunately, if Robinson and Gallagher's theory concerning Gladstone and the occupation of Egypt is by no means watertight, Gladstone's role in provoking Bismarck to bid for colonies is equally controversial.

[31] Gladstone, Bismarck and the Berlin West Africa Conference

The reasons for Bismarck's sudden conversion to an expansionist colonial policy have been the subject of endless controversy. Most historians have argued that the Chancellor's actions were the product of motives concerning either domestic politics or foreign policy. But some historians, most notably Miss Sybil Crowe, have suggested that Bismarck did not intend to embark on a colonial policy at all: it was merely an accidental by-product of Bismarck's pique over the procrastination of the Liberal government concerning Angra Pequena. If the latter view is correct, Granville and the Cabinet have much to answer for and the British cannot escape some of the responsibility for all that followed.

In November 1882 the trading company of F. A. E. Lüderitz, a Bremen tobacco merchant, requested consular protection for a trading post they intended to establish at Angra Pequena on the south-west coast of Africa and also the occasional visit of a German warship. Bismarck does not appear to have relished the responsibility of looking after German subjects in such a remote region, and in February 1883 he instructed his embassy in London to ascertain whether the British would be prepared to protect the German merchants. The following September he asked specifically whether Great Britain laid any claim to Angra Pequena. This time, however, no wish to see Great Britain extend 'its efficacious protection' was included. Granville treated the matter casually. One of Bismarck's most important communications (December 1883) was actually left unanswered for six months.

The British government's response proved totally unsatisfactory. The British laid no claim to territory other than Walvis Bay and the Angra Pequena islands, but any foreign claims to sovereignty between the northern boundary of the Cape Colony and the southern boundary of Portuguese Angola would infringe Great Britain's 'legitimate rights'. This assertion of a kind of Monroe Doctrine for Africa annoyed Bismarck intensely. He had by now become more interested in Angra Pequena. But the change in the tone of the notes from Berlin was not perceived by the British government nor, apparently, by the British and German ambassadors. Thus when Bismarck failed to receive a straight answer as to the protection Great Britain could extend to the German nationals, on 24 April 1884 he declared Angra Pequena to be under the 'protection' of the German Empire. The meaning of this statement was deliberately left vague to ensure that the British would have no time to forestall German claims elsewhere in Africa — in Togoland and the Cameroons. Bismarck's new policy in Africa did not become evident until July 1884.

Once Granville had been disabused about the German Chancellor's wishes, the British Cabinet immediately acknowledged the new German protectorates. But it was only the beginning of a new set of problems for the Gladstone administration. Bismarck, alarmed by the Cape ministry's talk of annexing south-west Africa, cooperated with France and sabotaged the London Conference on Egyptian finances in July-August 1884. Furthermore, when the British government annexed Bechuanaland, preventing a link-up between Germans and Boers, Bismarck launched an offensive on another front. He took the initiative in calling together the Berlin West Africa Conference which lasted from November 1884 to February 1885. Gladstone and Granville were to be beaten to their knees. The object was, as Herbert von Bismarck delicately put it, 'to squash Gladstone against the wall, so that he can yap no more'.

As the Reichstag elections approached, Bismarck drummed up another colonial issue and declared a protectorate over the northern coast of New Guinea in December 1884. At the end of the Berlin Conference in February 1885, he announced the chartering of Carl Peters's Colonization Society, thereby imposing German protection on part of the East African coast opposite Zanzibar. Clearly, within two years of German intervention in the African continent the map of Africa had been substantially altered. With the Berlin Conference, black Africa entered the realm of international politics.

Bismarck's motives for intervention have been much debated. Few historians would dispute that they represented a remarkable change of attitude towards colonies. The reasons for this change, which probably occurred in September 1883, have normally been accounted for by reference to his foreign policy or domestic political position. Bismarck always remained a European. One school of thought argues, therefore, that colonies were no more than expendable pawns in Bismarck's game of European diplomacy. Indeed, A. J. P. Taylor in *Germany's First Bid for Colonies, 1884–85* (1938) has suggested that colonies were the accidental by-product of an abortive Franco-German *entente*. So intent was Bismarck (contrary to all the text-books) on obtaining a *rapprochement* with France, that he was prepared to create a grievance against England. Thus the taking of overseas possessions was only a means to an end. This interpretation has been heavily criticised. Bismarck may have been prepared to use colonies as diplomatic counters in his European diplomacy, but this does not prove it was the *reason* for embarking on a colonial policy. In fact, it seems highly dubious that the master diplomat would have saddled his new German Reich with such uncertain and expensive obligations for the purpose of obtaining a possibly unachievable goal when a much less risky alternative lay at hand: cooperation with France against Great Britain in the dispute over Egypt. Taylor's case is clearly unproven.

A much more convincing argument concerns the requirements of Bismarck's domestic policy. Erich Eyck, W. O. Aydelotte, Norman Rich and many other historians have assembled a whole cluster of arguments to support this point of view. After 1879 Bismarck no longer co-operated with the National Liberals. The colonial issue seemed a heaven-sent opportunity to create new political groupings. It would split the National Liberals, appeal to the Bremen and Hamburg merchants, and attract the Conservative party (towards whom Bismarck looked for support for his new protectionist policy), and might even be received favourably by the Catholic Centre Party. Now that colonies were becoming a popular issue with certain sections of the electorate, his new policy would secure him support at the forthcoming autumn elections. In the future, with the health of the aged Emperor William I generally declining, a limited quarrel with Great Britain might prove a useful counterbalance to the Anglophile and Liberal tendencies of the Crown Prince Frederick and his English wife. In general, Bismarck seems to have hoped that his bid for colonies would produce greater national harmony in the Reich, in turn furthering his national policies.

Most recent research (notably by Hartmut Pogge von Strandmann) has supported this interpretation of Bismarck's policy. It is noteworthy, however, that both lines of argument attach ulterior motives to Bismarck's change of mind. Colonies were only a means to an end. That Bismarck become a genuine, if reluctant, convert to the colonial cause has also been suggested, however, by two historians: H. A. Turner, 'Bismarck's Imperialist Venture Anti-British in Origin?' in *Britain and Germany in Africa* (Yale, 1967), and Professor Hans-Ulrich Wehler, 'Bismarck's Imperialism, 1862–90' in *Past and Present* (1970).

Turner argues that Bismarck was worried by the uneven economic development of the Reich. Industrial and agricultural depressions had led him to adopt a protectionist policy in 1879. He then became apprehensive lest the failure to stake out a German claim in the colonial world should have grave economic consequences. If Germany did not have overseas possessions of her own, she would not be able to obtain economic privileges for her subjects through reciprocity agreements. With the well-publicised De Brazza–Stanley race to claim territory along the Congo, Bismarck seems to have been affected by '*Torschlusspanik*', the fear that if Germany did not then participate in dividing up the world she would be left out. These factors, along with domestic political reasons, at a time when Bismarck had committed his government to the task of restoring and furthering the material welfare of Germany and when continued abstention from the colonial arena might have an undesirable effect on the business community, caused the Chancellor to have second thoughts. Professor Wehler shares this view and argues that continuing economic growth and social stability were needed to preserve the social hierarchy and political power structure and also to obtain the support of the conservative elite against the twin challenges of the bourgeoisie and the proletariat. Bismarck needed to convince the Germans that the Reich served their interests. These, it is suggested, were the basic reasons for Bismarck's reluctant change of mind in the late summer of 1883.

Clearly, whatever the reasons, Bismarck's policy was of a deliberate and calculated nature. The incompetence of Granville and the procrastination of the Gladstone government over Angra Pequena, although irritating to Bismarck, were of little real significance. Too much importance should not be attached to the Berlin West Africa conference. The conference was not called to partition Africa. It only incidentally disposed of territory in recognising Leopold's Congo Free State and in acknowledging British claims to the Lower Niger. The vague rules concerning occupation and administration were limited to the coastal regions. At the conference Germany found, much to her surprise, that she had much in common with Great Britain and little in common with France. The new Franco-German understanding quickly evaporated.

Nevertheless fifteen countries had assembled in 1884–5 to discuss black Africa. By this date mere Anglo-French rivalry had been replaced by multi-polar rivalry and the 'scramble', as it was popularly called, had begun. Obsolete British notions of 'informal empire' and 'paramountcy' had been replaced by the new criterion of 'effective occupation'. As time went by this was also applied to protectorate and hinterland areas. Bismarck had succeeded overnight in destroying by international agreement Britain's unofficial empire in Africa. With new rules in operation, the game had to be played afresh. Thus, at the conference, the European theatre finally merged with the minor African stage to form one gigantic international arena. The international cast then performed a play in three acts: the easy, cheap, fairly amicable exercise in cartography of the years 1885–91 (including a few quite severe contests between Britain and France and Britain and Portugal); the more difficult and increasingly expensive exercise during 1891–5 when these claims were taken up; and the climax of the years 1895–1901 when so many conflicts finally came to a head. The years 1901–14 form an uneasy epilogue when most of the remaining disagreements were eventually ironed out. In the whole play, Victorian politicians were, in the main, unwilling actors. The props were to hand but the Victorians had not yet donned their expansionist costumes.

[32] The British Role in the Partition of Africa to 1895

The events of 1882–5 witnessed a remarkable departure from previous policy on the part of a number of European powers and brought about a significant change in the atmosphere concerning colonies in Africa. The change was also becoming evident in the Pacific and south-east Asia. In February 1885, the Radical MP for Newcastle, Joseph Cowen, observed:

> It looks as if an epidemic of mingled acquisitiveness and adventure has set in which will soon leave no eligible slice of the globe's surface without the sovereignty of a civilising power . . . Englishmen may not have mastered the philosophy of Imperial expansion, but their instincts and impulses will prompt them to oppose a spiritless surrender of lands that have been watered by the blood of their best and bravest.

By the mid-1880s the British government had been reluctantly drawn into the tangle. They were indeed intent on maintaining their existing trading facilities and safeguarding the approaches to India. Yet they still betrayed a marked distaste for the responsibility and cost of direct annexations or aggressive territorial policies.

But after 1886 the British government was, at least, able to adopt a more united approach to these tantalising questions. Gladstone's conversion to Home Rule had brought about the long-foreshadowed schism in the Liberal party. In June 1886, ninety-three Liberal Unionists led by Lord Hartington and Joseph Chamberlain voted against the first Irish Home Rule Bill. By 1887 most of these dissidents had formed a Unionist alliance with the Conservatives. The defection of Chamberlain, the Whigs, Forster and Goschen to the Conservatives certainly brought together within one party most supporters of a forward policy. The simultaneous defection of many leading industrialists and financiers endorsed this trend, and as the Liberals gradually became the party of the Celtic fringe, the Unionists became more representative of British commercial, investment and empire interests. The succession of Lord Rosebery (a Liberal Imperialist) to the Liberal leadership in 1894 gave yet another blow to the consolidationist policy of Gladstone, Morley and Harcourt.

At the very end of the 1880s an expansionist policy was gradually becoming more popular. Depression and unemployment were key factors. These were associated with foreign competition and tariff discrimination in overseas markets. As in Germany, the staking out of claims for future prosperity became the popular cry of chambers of commerce and an influential section of the press. With the rapid development of the Witwatersrand gold mines, Africa became more of a commercial proposition and, combined with the cries of philanthropists, anti-slavers and missionaries for civilising the interior, imperial expansion assumed a new appeal. A neat combination of national self-interest, economic, religious and humanitarian motives gave the ideal a high moral tone which had previously been lacking. Salisbury, Rosebery and Chamberlain were gradually converted to the new tropical imperialism. During the depression of the early nineties, overseas expansion was openly advocated as an answer to the economic problem. Economic necessity and humanitarianism were the twin justifications used to convert a doubtful public and a watchful Parliament. The movement did not become generally popular until the late 1890s, and this popularity soon declined. The mid-Victorian ideal of economy was never absent in the late Victorian age and Salisbury and his colleagues only extended the area of formal control when all other diplomatic expedients had failed. Out-dated diplomatic guarantees for free trade, protectorates and spheres of influence remained the stock-in-trade of British politicians. Annexation, as ever, remained a final resort.

In West Africa the British concentrated on the Niger. After the French advance into the hinterlands of the British coastal dependencies and the German erection of protectorates over Togoland and the Cameroons, Great Britain retaliated by declaring a protectorate over the intervening coast from the Cameroons to Lagos. But the Niger Act of Navigation (which accompanied international recognition at the Berlin Conference of a British sphere of influence on the Lower Niger) imposed administrative responsibilities. These were met in 'the cheapest and most effective way' by Granville when a Royal Charter was granted to Sir George Goldie's National Africa Company in July 1886. The new Royal Niger Company, in return for a virtual monopoly of British trade, was to govern in the name of the Crown and to meet the costs of administration out of its own profits. Henceforth British expansion in the area depended upon the ability of the company to make treaties and establish some form of government as proof of British occupation. The rest of West Africa was virtually left to the French. By the conventions of 1889 and 1890, the coastal boundaries of the British possessions and part of the inland borders of the Gambia and Sierra Leone were demarcated. In 1891, only the hinterlands of the Gold Coast and the future Nigeria remained to be decided.

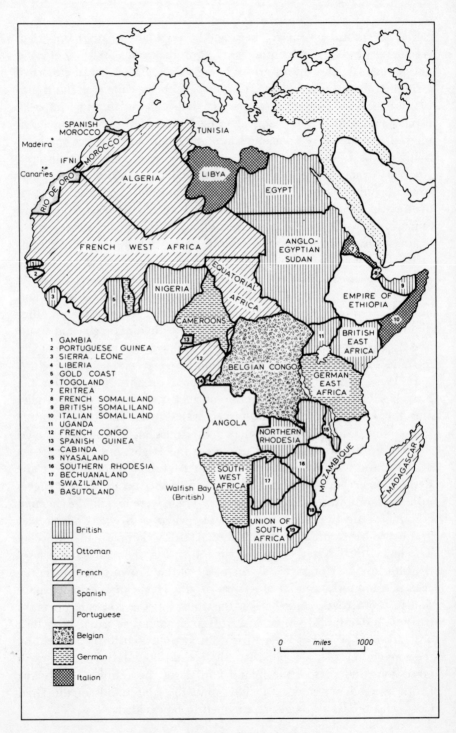

SPANISH
MOROCCO   TUNISIA
Madeira
IFNI   MOROCCO
Canaries   ALGERIA   LIBYA   EGYPT

RIO DE ORO

FRENCH   WEST   AFRICA   ANGLO-
                                                        EGYPTIAN
                                                        SUDAN

2   EQUATORIAL
                         NIGERIA   AFRICA   EMPIRE OF
3   ETHIOPIA
5   6
4   CAMEROONS   BRITISH
                         13   EAST
                                                                       AFRICA
                         12   11
                                    BELGIAN CONGO   GERMAN
                         14   EAST
                                                       AFRICA
                    ANGOLA
                                    NORTHERN
                                    RHODESIA   15
                                                18
                    SOUTH
                    WEST   17
Walfish Bay   AFRICA
(British)
                                                             18
                              UNION OF
                              SOUTH   19
                              AFRICA

1   GAMBIA
2   PORTUGUESE GUINEA
3   SIERRA LEONE
4   LIBERIA
5   GOLD COAST
6   TOGOLAND
7   ERITREA
8   FRENCH SOMALILAND
9   BRITISH SOMALILAND
10 ITALIAN SOMALILAND
11 UGANDA
12 FRENCH CONGO
13 SPANISH GUINEA
14 CABINDA
15 NYASALAND
16 SOUTHERN RHODESIA
17 BECHUANALAND
18 SWAZILAND
19 BASUTOLAND

MOZAMBIQUE

MADAGASCAR

||| British

Ottoman

/// French

Spanish

Portuguese

Belgian

German

Italian

0   miles   1000

The scramble for Africa by 1914

By the same date the partition of central Africa was also complete, at least on paper. Great Britain had few direct interests in this region — apart from the Scottish missions on Lake Nyasa and the Lakes Company which supported them. But the Germans, Portuguese, Transvaalers and Cape colonists all had their eyes on the area. For the Cape colonists this was the road to the north where they hoped to find goldfields in the highlands north of the Limpopo river to match those of the Rand, thus counterbalancing the new wealth of the Transvaal. Unfortunately, the British possessed no claim to this region of Zambezia. So the British government decided to manufacture one. In 1889, they accepted Cecil Rhodes's request for a charter for his British South Africa Company. Thus, in return for extending the Cape railways through Bechuanaland and for relieving the British exchequer of the financial burden of the protectorate, the company was empowered to occupy and govern any areas north of Bechuanaland and the Transvaal which lay outside German and Portuguese occupation. Consequently, Rhodes's agents began by extracting concessions from Lobengula, the paramount chief of the Ndebele, on the strength of which a 'pioneer column' of farming and mining settlers was sent into Mashonaland in 1890 where they established the Southern Rhodesian capital of Fort Salisbury. In 1891 the company was allowed to extend into lands north of the Zambezi which subsequently became Northern Rhodesia (Zambia). Salisbury distrusted Rhodes and disliked his methods but he was prepared to use his great wealth and energy to carve out a series of British territories in the power vacuum of south-central Africa and thus hem in the Boers and Germans from the north.

The only area excluded from the British South Africa Company's sphere was the land south and west of Lake Nyasa where the Scottish missions were hostile to company control. A British protectorate was declared over Nyasaland in 1891. But even here the Chancellor of the Exchequer, G. J. Goschen, refused to sanction grants-in-aid to support a white elephant gained solely for philanthropic purposes. Rhodes came to the rescue by promising to subsidise the protectorate for four years. Thus by 1891 the main lines of the partition of central Africa had also been drawn.

The other area of intense British activity in the initial partition of Africa lay in East Africa. Once again German activities sparked off the rivalry. In February 1885 Bismarck recognised the treaties made by the German explorer, Carl Peters, and arranged a paper protectorate for his East Africa Company on the coast opposite Zanzibar. Salisbury, in need of German support in Egypt, recognised the new protectorate and came to an understanding with Germany. The area was formally divided into two spheres of influence in October 1886 along the line of the present boundary of Tanzania and Kenya from Vanga to Lake Victoria. To act as guardian of the British claims, William Mackinnon, the Scottish shipowner, was given a charter for his Imperial British East Africa Company in April 1888. By this time British policy was becoming more decided.

The major problem confronting Salisbury was Egypt. In May 1887 Salisbury had made his last attempt at evacuation. An agreement with Turkey, whereby the British would leave Egypt within three years provided the European powers guaranteed the inviolability of Egyptian territory and would permit the British to return if the government of the country broke down or a threat developed to the Suez Canal, was wrecked by the French and Russians. Salisbury had to rethink his policy. He was well aware that Great Britain had little influence in Constantinople and that France and Russia were coming closer together, each feverishly building fast cruisers and torpedo boats which would soon challenge British naval superiority in the Mediterranean. These two factors made Egypt a key position in British defensive strategy. With the comforting news that the Egyptian budget was at last showing a surplus, Salisbury announced in a speech at the Guildhall in November 1889 that Great Britain intended to stay in Egypt for the foreseeable future.

This was a momentous decision. Once Great Britain had decided on a prolonged occupation, the defences of Egypt became an important British concern, especially the upper reaches of the Nile where it was believed that sophisticated European technology could dam the river and reduce the country to ruin. Threats to the upper Nile seemed to come from various directions. The Italians were busy establishing themselves in Ethiopia; King Leopold of the Belgians had dreams of extending his Congo empire eastwards; and Carl Peters was intent on organising a German expedition from Witu (an enclave in the British sphere) inland to the Nile. The immediate object of concern was Emin Pasha, Governor of Equatoria, who had survived the Mahdist risings to the north and remained cut off from Europe. In November 1886, William Mackinnon had organised the 'Emin Pasha Relief Committee' and H. M. Stanley had been engaged to lead an expedition. Mackinnon's motives were not entirely humanitarian as he too dreamed of establishing British influence and commerce in East Africa. He was

rudely awakened by Leopold II, however, who refused to release
Stanley from his contract unless the expedition approached the Nile
from the Congo. Mackinnon agreed to the western route and dreamed
instead of a British chartered company in East Africa with Leopold's
Congo schemes providing an outlet to the west coast.

These plans were upset by Peters's hastily organised expedition from
Witu. This aimed at acquiring Equatoria and the lands stretching
southward to Lake Victoria. The British government could no longer
remain aloof. Mackinnon received his charter in 1888 on condition
that he pushed on to Uganda to block Peters's imperialist designs.
However, after Stanley succeeded in 'rescuing' a very reluctant Emin
Pasha a vacuum remained which Peters looked most likely to fill.
Salisbury, therefore, tried on several occasions in 1889 to put the various
British and German claims in East Africa to arbitration. After the fall of
Bismarck in 1890 the situation took a turn for the worse. William II
looked with favour on Peters's activities and allowed a new German
expedition under Emin Pasha to enter the interior. Salisbury decided
that a more comprehensive settlement was now necessary.

The Germans were prepared to negotiate. In March 1890, William II
and Caprivi had decided to abandon the 1887 Reinsurance Treaty
with Russia. Now that France seemed to be gravitating towards
Russia, they were quite willing to establish a *rapprochement* with Great
Britain provided they were not seen to be sacrificing German interests.
Salisbury gauged the situation exactly and had the right plum to offer
— the strategically important North Sea Island of Heligoland. Most
Germans regarded this as a better acquisition than Uganda.

By the so-called Heligoland–Zanzibar treaty of 1890, Germany
gained Heligoland, an extension of the German sphere from Dar-es-
Salaam inland to Lake Tanganyika, and the famous Caprivi Strip
(a corridor of land connecting German South West Africa with the
Zambesi). In return, the Germans recognised a formal British protectorate over Zanzibar, gave up their claims to Witu and conceded
Uganda to the British. Both sides were well satisfied. Salisbury used
the opportunity to secure German recognition of British claims in
Northern Rhodesia, Bechuanaland and eastern Nigeria. At the same
time he concluded a treaty with France agreeing the western boundary
of Nigeria in return for British recognition of a French protectorate over
Madagascar. In the following year, after virtual threat of war, agreement with Portugal was reached in respect of the two Rhodesias and
Nyasaland. The Italians, after their thrust on Kassala, also agreed to

keep away from the affluents of the Nile — in return for recognition of Italian preponderance over much of the Horn of Africa. By signing away huge unoccupied tracts of 'light soil', Salisbury appeared to have bought security in Africa.

By 1891 the paper partition of Africa was virtually complete. But there was still little effective occupation. Most European claims were based on scraps of paper obtained by consuls and concession hunters and signed by African chiefs who had no idea of the significance of their acts and rarely possessed authority over all the areas they allegedly ruled. Consequently when the interior frontiers came to be claimed in the 1890s friction occurred. The European powers now had more men in the field, and occupying forces clashed more frequently both with each other and with the larger, more organised, African states. As the scramble in Africa drew to its close it was inevitably accompanied by greater bloodshed.

The first of Salisbury's schemes to run into trouble concerned Uganda. No British subsidy was forthcoming for the Mombasa–Nyanza railway which was intended to help the I.B.E.A. Company hold Uganda and the Nile headwaters. Without the railway the position of the company was not viable. Mackinnon's finances were failing and the company was obliged to withdraw from Uganda. Would the British government be prepared to pay the costs of administration and occupation? If not, it was feared France would step in and establish a base for expansion into Equatoria and possibly the Egyptian Sudan. It was not Salisbury who had to deal with this problem, however, but Gladstone.

In July 1892 the Queen had to resign herself to having 'that dangerous old fanatic thrust down her throat' once again. She was adamant, however, that the Prince Charming of the Liberals, the Earl of Rosebery, should be appointed Foreign Secretary. She even canvassed in his favour: his appointment was 'necessary to quiet the alarm of the F. Powers'. Gladstone, with a fairly small majority, bent on Irish legislation, could not afford to leave Rosebery out. Rosebery was thus able to dictate his own terms for joining the ministry and virtually became a law unto himself at the Foreign Office. The continuity of Salisbury's policy was assured.

But Harcourt at the Treasury was as successful as Goschen in blocking plans to subsidise the Uganda railway and in freezing funds for a protectorate. Initially the Cabinet decided to evacuate Uganda. But such was the outcry from humanitarian and missionary societies and by chambers of commerce that Rosebery secured the appointment of Sir Gerald Portal to report on the situation. Rosebery secretly gave him a confidential letter recommending retention. The outcome was exactly as he desired: a protectorate was proclaimed over Uganda in June 1894 and was extended exactly one year later to include the land between it and the coast, known as the British East Africa Protectorate (Kenya). In the best Salisbury tradition the British position in East Africa had been upheld.

But the western route to the Nile still lay open. Here Rosebery had to deal with a challenge from Leopold II and from the French. Leopold, to make his Congo venture self-supporting, had tried to take the export trade in ivory and ebony out of the hands of the Arabs. The resulting war drove the Congo deep into the Arab states which lay to the west of the Nile. By 1893 posts were being set up in the Bahr al-Ghazal and Belgian forces had reached Lado on the Upper Nile. To counteract this threat Rosebery agreed in May 1894 to Leopold taking Equatoria and much of the Bahr al-Ghazal. Better the Belgians than the French. But such an obvious attempt to steal a march on his rival only stimulated French desires further. In August 1894 France and Germany insisted on the cancellation of the treaty. Thus, Leopold's expansionist activities, which had done so much to fuel the partition of Africa, were finally brought to a halt. Rosebery had to negotiate direct with France. The French had transferred their ambitions from Lake Chad to the Upper Nile. Argument over the Nile and the Niger now became so heated that in March 1895 Sir Edward Grey, the Parliamentary Under-Secretary at the Foreign Office, announced that any French advance into the Nile Valley would be interpreted as an 'unfriendly act'. Developments were becoming serious by the time Rosebery resigned in June 1895.

The Italian defeat at Adowa in 1896 transformed the politics of the Nile basin and inaugurated the final stage of the partition of Africa. By 1898 the climax had been reached at Fashoda and the scramble was over. The last remaining lines on the map were drawn in 1899 and only minor adjustments, Morocco and Tripoli apart, were made before the First World War. The great age of late Victorian expansion in Africa had ended. It had occupied less than two decades, but a portion of a man's career. The speed, acquisitiveness and aggressiveness of the white man was truly amazing. And the period had also witnessed an astonishing change in public attitudes towards imperial expansion. By 1895 the new tropical imperialism had become accepted. It had assumed a new glamour. In the election campaign of July 1895 Rosebery declared himself to be a 'Liberal Imperialist' which he defined as meaning:

> first, the maintenance of the Empire; secondly, the opening of new areas for our surplus population; thirdly, the suppression of the slave trade; fourthly, the development of missionary enterprise; and fifthly, the development of our commerce, which so often needs it.

Nothing embodied the outlook of the late 1890s better than the expansionist development policies of Salisbury's new Colonial Secretary, Joseph Chamberlain. Chamberlain's period of office, 1895–1903, saw the climax of late Victorian imperialism and also the revulsion against the Boer War. So far as the British empire was concerned, the death of Queen Victoria marked the passing of an age.

[33] The Pacific and South-East Asia

The scramble for Africa was but one aspect of European attempts to partition large parts of the world. Events in Africa were paralleled by events in the Pacific and in south-east Asia: Germany's entry into the Pacific in 1884 sparked off yet another partition. The attempted annexation of eastern New Guinea by the Colony of Queensland in April 1883 had been disavowed by the British government. As always, the mother country did not want the expense or responsibility of governing further acquisitions. To guard their interests the Australians, like the South Africans, were told to confederate. But when Bismarck helped to sabotage the London conference on Egypt in July 1884, even after Granville had backed down in south-west Africa, Hartington, Kimberley, Chamberlain and Dilke had a small victory in the Cabinet. A British protectorate was proclaimed over the south-eastern shores of New Guinea in October 1884. A German protectorate of the northern shores and over the island of New Britain soon followed.

The interested powers then attempted to cordon off their various claims. Great Britain made good her position first by an agreement with Germany in 1886 which recognised her rights in the Gilbert and Ellice Islands and the islands to the south and east; the Northern Solomon Islands and the Carolines and Marshalls to the north were to be in the German sphere. In 1888 she came to a similar understanding with France. A British protectorate was arranged for the Cook Islands (on

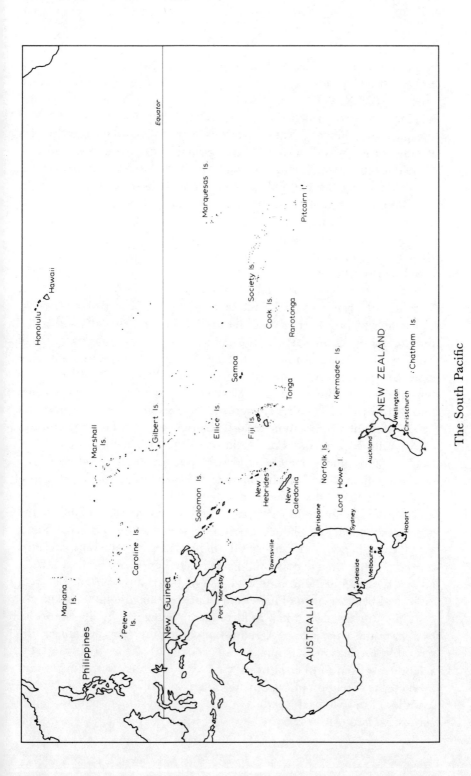

The South Pacific

condition that New Zealand paid for the resident) and a joint Anglo-
French Naval Commission was created to investigate disputes which
arose in the New Hebrides, where strong Australasian Presbyterian
missions had established themselves. This completed the first stage of
the partition. Further rearrangements were made when the Spanish
Pacific empire was dissolved following Spain's disastrous war with the
United States over Cuba. In 1898 America became an imperialist
power annexing the Philippines, Guam and Hawaii. Germany bought
the Caroline, Mariana and Pelew islands and partitioned the Samoan
group with the United States. In return, Great Britain occupied Tonga
and several German islands in the Solomons. It was an amicable
settlement in which the white Europeans decided the future of the brown
peoples of the Pacific.

A similar exercise was undertaken in south-east Asia. Here Great
Britain and France were the major protagonists. The British interest,
as usual, was the defence of India which the French appeared to be
threatening from the east. In 1884 the French began their conquest of
Tonkin and made contact with the Burmese who were behaving
extremely provocatively towards British firms. As a result a British force
occupied Upper Burma in late 1885 and the country was incorporated
into British India. The French were also successful in their conquest and
in 1887 founded the 'Union Indo-Chinoise' in which the protectorates
of Annam, Tonkin and Cambodia were grouped with the colony of
Cochin-China under one Governor-General. Laos and Siam remained
independent and the British concentrated on making the latter into a
buffer state. But the French coveted Laos, which was under the
suzerainty of Siam, and in 1893 invaded both countries demanding the
cession of virtually all Siamese territory east of the Mekong river. Since
Egypt came higher on Rosebery's list of priorities, he reluctantly refused
support for the King of Siam and France kept her prizes. Both countries,
however, recognised the independence of the rump of Siam in 1896.
Siam had been stripped of her empire but she alone remained independent in south-east Asia. She was fortunate in being cast by the European
powers in the same role as Afghanistan, China and Persia. Indeed, the
scramble for leases in China at the very end of the 1890s and the
attempts to partition Persia in the first decade of the twentieth century
marked the extension of the partition mania to the Far East and to the
Middle East. No part of the world appeared to be safe from the
acquisitiveness of Europe.

[34] The Motives of Expansion

Why did it all occur? Even now it is difficult to give a clear and concise answer. Some historians emphasise the political and diplomatic side of the phenomenon, others the economic aspect, and still others the local situations which so often resulted in external intervention. Desire for territory for territory's sake was never an important factor in British policy. 'Our own hands are only too full. We wish for more markets, not for more dominions', declared *The Times* in September 1884. The late Victorians were too economy-minded (almost too Gladstonian in outlook) to welcome the additional expense involved in governing colonies without there being an obvious need or a strong possibility of reward.

Even Salisbury frequently talked in economic terms. In 1884, he criticised Gladstone's anti-expansionist attitude on the grounds that it permitted powers who practised a discriminatory tariff policy to monopolise the new markets in the under-developed areas. As the markets of the industrial world were closed by tariffs, those of the non-industrial world alone remained open and a refusal to annex frequently resulted in their loss. In 1893 he remarked:

> We feel that we cannot suffer, more than we can help, that the unoccupied parts of the world, where we must look for new markets for our goods, shall be shut from us by foreign legislation.

And when speaking in support of a forward policy in Uganda in February 1895, he insisted that dominion overseas was becoming essential to British prosperity and employment as well as world power: in the United States, France and Germany, 'the doctrines of Protection are stronger and stronger, and operate to the exclusion of British commerce wherever their power extends'. On these occasions Salisbury spoke like Sir George Goldie, Sir Harry Johnston, or Captain Frederick Lugard. It could well be that economic considerations loomed larger in British policy than would appear from the Foreign Office files or Salisbury's political correspondence. Maybe Joseph Chamberlain, with his largely economically based arguments and outlook, was not so exceptional a character after all. Disraeli, with his noticeable lack of concern for British trade and concentration on strategy and prestige, was certainly less representative of Victorian politicians than Chamberlain.

And when we concentrate on the partition 'on the ground' it is the rivalry between the localised European economic interests which is immediately most noticeable. It was fear of a French monopoly of the Congolese market that led the British to conclude an Anglo-Portuguese treaty in February 1884. The desire to preserve the 'open door' in the Congo region was the basis of British policy at the subsequent Berlin Conference. Indeed, the delegates at that conference acknowledged the interests 'of the commercial and industrial nations which a common necessity compels to the research of new outlets'. Trade, and the hope of future profit, were important elements in the whole scramble for Africa. Economics usually provided the rationale for the partition if not the motive.

In the Far East, the position was much less complex. The defence of existing trading interests in one of Great Britain's more important overseas markets was clearly the British motive for participating in what looked like a 'partition' of China. The Russians, French and Germans seemed intent on carving out areas of exclusive interest. In 1884 it was noted that Germans and Americans were using diplomatic pressure to promote individual financial enterprises. In June 1885 France made the Treaty of Tientsin with China whereby differential duties and national railway concessions were agreed. This ended international equality and began the policy of concessions which closed with the scramble for leases in 1898. Commercial and financial competition engendered dangerous political rivalries for which the only satisfactory solutions seemed to be mutual agreements defining spheres of interest. In this way commercial rivalry once again ended in imperialist activities.

This underlying theme lends great support to the view that British imperialism was largely a defensive reaction to protect the existing outlets and volume of British trade and investment against assault by foreign competitors. Both the British politicians and Bismarck seem to have been worried by the fear that if they remained passive they would be excluded from the markets of the future. Lord Curzon wrote in his book on Persia in 1892:

> In the furious commercial competition that now rages like a hurricane throughout the world the loss of a market is a retrograde step that cannot be recovered; the gain of a market is a positive addition to the national strength. Indifference to Persia might mean the sacrifice of a trade that already feeds hundreds of thousands of our citizens in this country and in India. A friendly attention to Persia will mean so much more employment for British ships, for British labour, and for British spindles.

Clearly, while the political interpretation of imperialism explains much, it also leaves much unexplained. The economic element remains an important factor and, in certain areas, *the* most important factor in British overseas expansion. Political and economic motives were usually interwoven but they were also capable of operating independently at different levels. Nevertheless, by the mid-1890s the economic motive had become the major *justification* for imperial expansion. In September 1895 the *Spectator* recorded:

> in respect of the opening-up of new sources of demand for British manufacturers. Mr. Chamberlain's large schemes for the development on business lines of the Crown Colonies in the tropics are full of promise of employment, not only for the present industrial population of Great Britain, but for much of that great increase which in any case we must anticipate.

By that date colonial expansion had become a popular panacea for declining trade, over-population and growing unemployment.

[35] The Processes of Expansion

The late Victorians, however, were still dominated by a spirit of financial parsimony, and Conservative politicians in particular remembered the lessons of Midlothian. The British were believed to be notoriously fickle where the empire was concerned and Parliament was against squandering money on 'little wars' and troublesome dependencies. The Earl of Derby expressed a widely-held belief when the questions of New Guinea and Zululand were discussed in the Cabinet in 1883–4: 'the Empire already has black savages enough'. The Earl of Kimberley minuted in March 1884 that the Cabinet 'did not want more niggers' and this point of view was reiterated in 1892 by Sir William Harcourt when he stated:

> We have already as much Empire as the nation can carry. If you give the heart too much work to do by extending the limbs and the frame beyond measure you enfeeble its action, and it succumbs.

Although the anti-expansionist school of Gladstone, Harcourt and Morley declined in influence in the 1890s, many of their basic suppositions remained intact. Even Salisbury aimed at avoiding further direct territorial responsibility by following a policy of expansion by proxy on the principle of 'colonial expansion through Imperial aid'. The burdens of occupation, pacification and administration were normally passed on to British private enterprise or existing colonial governments. In this way Salisbury avoided demands on the British Exchequer and approaches to the House of Commons for legislative authorisation. Throughout the late Victorian period expansion was carried out on the cheap and formal annexations and protectorates were avoided wherever possible. British rule was always extended in the most economical and tentative form. In fact, many extensions of authority took place under the curious fiction that no additions were being made to the empire at all.

In the mid-Victorian period there had been two well-tried means of extending British authority into foreign lands. The first consisted of exercising 'extra-territorial jurisdiction' through the normal consular channels. In countries which did not recognise the concepts of European international law, like the Ottoman Empire, Siam and China, treaties were frequently arranged whereby Europeans were exempted from the processes of local law provided all offences were dealt with in consular courts. By this means some protection (and certain privileges) were extended to the citizens of Europe. Consuls were also of great importance when their influence extended over large adjacent areas which were regarded as 'spheres of influence' in which the British claimed 'paramountcy'. Extra-territorial jurisdiction had been tried (and found wanting) in Fiji before the islands were annexed in 1874; and 'paramountcy' had been increasingly asserted in the Malay States, southern Africa and the South Pacific in the 1870s.

These means were extended in the 1880s. For example, Great Britain effectively ruled Egypt (which remained part of the Ottoman Empire and retained a separate Egyptian government) through Sir Evelyn Baring, the Consul-General in Cairo, after 1882. This position was not altered until 1914. The British Consul-General at Zanzibar from 1864, Sir John Kirk, also built up a remarkable degree of influence in the island and its hinterland. Similarly, the young Harry Johnston, Consul at Mozambique in 1889, signed treaties with the chiefs north of the Zambesi and between Lakes Nyasa and Tanganyika and within a year laid the foundations of British control in Nyasaland and Northern Rhodesia. Consuls were clearly important instruments in late Victorian expansion.

The concept of spheres of influence was also extended in the 1880s. With so many powers seeking to expand their claims, greater efforts had to be made to defend existing areas of paramountcy and to assert British authority. The 'protectorate' or 'protected state' was a suitably vague device. When the Oil Rivers Protectorate in the Niger Delta was declared in 1885, the fiction was maintained that only certain aspects of local sovereignty had been ceded to Great Britain. In effect, the kings and chiefs retained sovereignty over their own people but gave up control of their foreign relations. After a clash with King Ja Ja of Opobo in 1886, however, the nature of the protectorate was redefined. Full sovereignty was claimed. It was then maintained that 'the welfare of the natives . . . taken as a whole' implied a power to veto the activities of individual city-states and put into abeyance individual stipulations of treaties which conflicted with the greater good. Once the Berlin West African Conference had changed the rules of the game the transition from a protectorate to the appearance of a Crown colony was usually an easy one.

Similarly, in the Malay States the Residents gradually came to control the government in the name of the rulers. In this case, to all external observers the difference between a series of protected states and a formal colony must have seemed very small. The same thing occurred in Zanzibar when it became a protectorate in 1890. Although the government continued in the name of the Sultan, its officials were all British and the British Resident became first minister as well. On the other hand, in the Uganda protectorate there were no British officials in the local governments, and even though the protectorate was extended in 1896 over kingdoms to the west and south-west, some of these areas remained outside British control for fifteen years. Thus 'protectorate' was a term which covered many different systems of government and meant different things in different situations to different people.

The conditions stipulated at the Berlin West Africa conference to be observed in the declaration of protectorates included the provision of protection for traders, travellers and the indigenous inhabitants and the establishment of some sort of administration as the symbol of occupation. The late Victorians met these obligations by employing the device of chartered companies. In return for official recognition of land, mineral and trade concessions which gave them legal ownership of these assets, the companies undertook to pacify and administer the territories, to suppress the slave trade and respect native rights. This was a revival of the seventeenth-century practice of empire-building. The East India Company and Hudson's Bay Company had given up their territorial rights as recently as 1858 and 1869 respectively. In 1881, however, the Gladstone government chartered the British North Borneo Company to forestall Spanish claims to the Sulu and Brunei sultanates. Gladstone defended the charter as the cheapest means of shouldering the burden thrust on the government by the 'irrepressible tendency of British enterprise to carry our commerce and the range and area of our settlements beyond the limits of our Sovereignty'. He also chartered Sir George Goldie's company in 1886.

Salisbury was equally astute. He secured the best bargains he could when chartering the companies of William Mackinnon (1888) and Cecil Rhodes (1889). Rhodes agreed to extend the Cape railways into Bechuanaland and to relieve the British treasury of the expense of that protectorate. He later promised to subsidise the Nyasaland protectorate for four years. Mackinnon's Imperial British East Africa Company was to stand sentinel over the British sphere established in East Africa by the Anglo-German understanding in 1886 and also to block Carl Peters's imperialist designs on Uganda. Unfortunately the I.B.E.A. Company, never able to call upon much more than fifty pence worth of capital for every square mile of territory it was supposed to administer and develop, collapsed in 1893. The British government had to establish the Uganda Protectorate in 1894 and the British East Africa Protectorate in 1895. Similarly, northern Nigeria was made a protectorate in 1900. Only the British South Africa Company, with Rhodes's private fortune and the expanding economy of South Africa behind it, remained a viable concern. The 700 police, miners and farmers who entered Mashonaland in 1890 represented an unusually large number. But even this rich company found the administration of Southern Rhodesia expensive and was never able to establish a strong administration in Northern Rhodesia.

Occupation on the cheap was not always effective. All too often the British government found it impossible to control the policies of the newly chartered companies. Only too frequently they were called upon to help the companies out of the scrapes into which those policies had led. In the end the British came to rule large areas of Africa which they originally had little intention of administering. The history of Rhodes's British South Africa Company is an obvious case in point, even if company rule did continue (for once) into the third decade of the twentieth century.

Cecil John Rhodes was indeed one of the greatest imperialists of the Victorian age. His story is an impressive one. The fifth of nine sons of an English parson, he landed in South Africa in 1870 at the age of seventeen hoping to restore his much-impaired health. He soon migrated to the newly discovered diamond fields of Griqualand West where he proceeded to make his fortune with great speed. In 1873 he returned to England to study at Oxford University. As a student, Rhodes's dreams turned to empire-building and the Anglo-Saxon's destiny. According to one biographer, he was much affected by reading the words spoken by John Ruskin during his inaugural lecture as Professor of Fine Art in January 1870:

> Will you, youths of England, make your country again a royal throne of kings; a sceptred isle, for all the world a source of light, a centre of peace; mistress of Learning and of the Arts? . . . this is what [England] must either do, or perish: she must found colonies as fast and as far as she is able, formed of her most energetic and worthiest men; — seizing every piece of fruitful waste ground she can set her foot on, and there teaching these her colonists that their chief virtue is to be fidelity to their country, and that their first aim is to be to advance the power of England by land and sea . . .

So strongly had Rhodes become imbued with this idea that when he made his first will in 1873 he provided for the creation of a secret society to help extend British rule throughout the world and to encourage British occupation of

> the entire continent of Africa, the Holy Land, the Valley of the Euphrates, the islands of Cyprus and Candia, the whole of South America, the islands of the Pacific not heretofore possessed by Great Britain, the whole of the Malay Archipelago, the sea-board of China and Japan, the ultimate recovery of the United States of America as an integral part of the British Empire. . . .

Romantic dreams indeed!

Rhodes entered South African politics in order to further these dreams in 1881. He continued to amass great wealth and after being instrumental in procuring the advance of the British flag into Bechuanaland, he secured through his partner, C. D. Rudd, in October 1888, exclusive mining rights to all the metals and minerals within the kingdom of Lobengula, chief of the Ndebele, in return for 1,000 rifles, 10,000 rounds of ammunition, an armed steamer and £100 a month. Armed with this concession, the charter for his British South Africa Company was granted and a year later — the year Rhodes became Prime Minister of the Cape — the column of pioneers headed for Mashonaland, equipped at company expense, paid 7s 6d a day and promised fifteen gold claims and a 3,000-acre farm each on arrival. Much to Lobengula's dismay, the British flag was raised and Mashonaland was declared to be under British protection in May 1891.

But Rhodes's restless ambition did not rest there. In 1891 the company advanced north of the Zambesi and acquired mineral rights in Nyasaland. The settlers also looked longingly at the fertile highlands to the west where the resentful Ndebele pastured their great herds. How long friction could be avoided was anyone's guess. In the meantime it was arranged with the company that all combatants in any future war would receive 6,000 acres (to be bought back by the company at £1.50 an acre), twenty gold claims and a share in the Ndebele herds. Not surprisingly, hostilities occurred soon afterwards and the six-month war against the Ndebele ended with a company victory in January 1894. After Lobengula's death two weeks later, probably from smallpox, the company took over the chief's lands by right of conquest and Rhodes became virtual ruler of the territory (soon named Rhodesia) stretching north from Bechuanaland to the British Central African Protectorate. 'What were you doing, since last I saw you, Mr Rhodes?', the Queen is supposed to have enquired of her new Privy Councillor. 'I have added two provinces to Your Majesty's Dominions', came the reply. By 1895 Rhodes had reached the apogee of his political career, a career which was shortly to be smashed by the ill-conceived Jameson Raid on the Transvaal in December 1895 in which the British Colonial Secretary, Joseph Chamberlain, was said to be implicated. Indeed, Chamberlain's eight years of office, the clash at Fashoda, the scramble for leases in China and the eruption of the Boer War were to see the final climax of imperialism and to witness the end of an era.

[36] The Popularity of Expansion

By 1895 empire was becoming a popular panacea for the troubles of the times, both economic and political. Imperial expansion was held to be in the interests of employment, markets, civilisation, security and future greatness. The Queen's Diamond Jubilee celebration in June 1897 was turned into a great imperial pageant to bring home to the growing electorate the pomp, power and splendour of Britannia's heritage. 'Imperialism in the air — all classes drunk with sightseeing and hysterical loyalty' noted Beatrice Webb in her diary. The British

people began to take a new pride in their empire — allegedly the most
secure, extensive and beneficent empire the world had ever seen. To
the ideas of Anglo-Saxon kinship and the imperial bond of brotherhood
was added the betterment of subject races and the education of black
savages. It was for their good that the white man had a duty to conquer
and control 'the dark peoples of the world' and to extend safety,
personal freedom and new economic and intellectual opportunity. The
old idea of trusteeship gained a new popular appeal. Rudyard Kipling
portrayed exactly the feelings of these years in his poem, published in
1899, urging the Americans to take up *The White Man's Burden*:

> Take up the White Man's burden —
> Send forth the best ye breed —
> Go bind your sons to exile
> To serve your captives' need;
> To wait in heavy harness,
> On fluttered folk and wild —
> Your new-caught, sullen peoples,
> Half-devil and half-child.

In Kipling's verse the sense of moral obligation was strong.

Empire sentiment reached its zenith in the years 1898–9. It was
respectable, popular and mirrored the moral sentiments and philosophy
of history of the late Victorians. It also reflected, at least on the surface,
the arrogance and smugness of the age. *The Times*, the *Pall Mall Gazette*
and the new popular press, most notably the halfpenny *Daily Mail*,
heightened the public pulse.

> The *Daily Mail* stands for the power, supremacy and greatness of the
> British Empire. . . . The *Daily Mail* is the embodiment and mouth-
> piece of the imperial idea

announced the newspaper magnate Alfred Harmsworth (later Lord
Northcliffe). A similar spirit was expressed in the poetry and popular
literature of the time. The patriotic Tennyson had been succeeded as
Poet Laureate by the more crudely jingoistic Alfred Austin. His counterpart among the novelists was G. A. Henty who produced some ninety
volumes (hardly part of the British literary heritage) with titles like
The Dash for Khartoum, *With Roberts to Pretoria*, and *Through the Afghan
Passes*. His style was rather flat, the plots transparent and his heroes
colourless. Nevertheless his stories of British 'pluck', 'dash', 'good-
fellowship' and 'character', all playing the game in the best public-
school tradition, had considerable influence on generations of British
schoolboys. From these works, and the writings of Rider Haggard,

Conan Doyle, John Buchan, W. E. Henly, Robert Louis Stevenson and Joseph Conrad, the British public learned to identify themselves with the empire and its 'heroes'; the pro-consul was idealised and the British tommy, the private soldier, was glorified. It all added to the heightened atmosphere of the age.

In politics Lord Rosebery, the leader of the Liberal Imperialist band which included Asquith, Grey and Haldane, was foremost in rousing the country to the new imperial ideal. He wanted to give direction and purpose to the idealism and civilising zeal associated with the British empire: 'the greatest secular agency for good the world has seen'. In a speech before the Royal Colonial Institute in March 1893, he declared:

> It is said that our empire is already large enough, and does not need extension. That would be true enough if the world were elastic, but unfortunately, it is not elastic, and we are engaged at the present moment in the language of mining in 'pegging out claims' for the future. We have to consider that countries must be developed either by ourselves or some other nation, and we have to remember that it is part of our heritage to take care that the world as far as it can be moulded by us, shall receive an English-speaking complexion, and not that of other nations.

By shelving Irish Home Rule in 1894, Rosebery hoped to reunite the Liberal Unionists under the banner of Liberal Imperialism. The declaration of a protectorate over Uganda in 1894 symbolised, to the dismay of the remnant of Gladstonian survivors, the acceptance of empire-building by the majority of the Liberal party. Curzon (a Tory) paid tribute to Rosebery before leaving to take up his Viceroyalty in 1898:

> From his lips we have all of us, on many occasions, imbibed the lessons of an Imperialism, exalted but not arrogant, fearless but not rash, an Imperialism which is every day becoming less and less the creed of a party and more and more the faith of a nation.

The great Lord Salisbury never subscribed to such an imperial creed. He was more of a diplomatist than an empire-builder, responding only reluctantly to the cries for imperial expansion. In 1898 he divided the nations of the world into 'living' and 'dying' states. The weak were becoming weaker and the strong becoming stronger:

> For one reason or another — from the necessities of politics or under the pretence of philanthropy, the living nations will gradually encroach on the territory of the dying, and the seeds and causes of conflict among civilised nations will speedily appear.

Salisbury regarded it as his job to dampen down the sources of such conflicts and to keep British foreign policy on an even keel. It was this cautious statesman (who became Prime Minister for the third time in 1895) who was to preside over the climax of imperialism.

[37] Joseph Chamberlain at the Colonial Office

One of Salisbury's most significant appointments in the new government was that of Joseph Chamberlain as Colonial Secretary (1895–1903). Chamberlain was a relative late-comer to politics, not entering Parliament till the age of forty. Prior to this he had been a wealthy and successful businessman in a firm of Birmingham screw manufacturers who had devoted his talents to municipal improvement. On entering the Commons he joined the Liberal ranks as one of the most outspoken critics of Disraeli's foreign policy. The Afghan war, in particular, seemed to him 'the natural consequence of jingoism, Imperialism, "British interests", and all the other phrasing of the mountebank government'. When the Disraeli government fell in 1880, he was rewarded with the office of President of the Board of Trade.

It was during Gladstone's second ministry that Chamberlain became interested in colonial policy and eventually came to favour a positive and expansive attitude in imperial affairs. His patriotism was aroused by German and French colonial expansion in Africa and the Pacific and by Russian 'aggression' in central Asia. These events, together with doubts about Britain's rigid adherence to free trade in a world of tariff barriers and rising competition, stimulated him to ponder the desirability of closer imperial union. Ireland proved to be the test case. Chamberlain broke with Gladstone in 1886 over his Irish Home Rule policy and left the Liberal party. A year later he departed on a tour of North America where he became imbued with ideas of the greatness of the Anglo-Saxon destiny. From this time on he dreamed of a great imperial partnership with an imperial defence system and an imperial customs union protecting British goods. It was a vision of a united empire in which Great Britain developed the backward portions and the empire assisted Great Britain in meeting industrial competition overseas and erasing poverty at home. It was with these ideas in mind that he accepted the seals of the Colonial Office in 1895.

The advent of the new Colonial Secretary was soon felt, most notably in West Africa and South Africa where Chamberlain played a major role in the polemics that led to the Boer War. He also tried to accelerate the pace of imperial expansion and of development in the tropics. He wished to assist the 'undeveloped estates' which were ripe for investment. The British West Indies provided a suitable field for exertion. Economic assistance for impoverished Crown colonies was a new departure for Whitehall. Nevertheless in 1898 Chamberlain announced a five-year plan for West Indian reconstruction and also the provision of a loan to alleviate local distress, improve communications and establish new industries. In addition the Department of Tropical Agriculture and two schools of tropical medicine were established to provide the necessary research. While the economies of the West Indian islands were not restored overnight, some improvement was immediately apparent. A less tenacious and less influential Colonial Secretary could never have achieved this much. Even Chamberlain could not repeat the exercise. Parliament was not accustomed to throwing its money about in the back-waters of the empire.

But Chamberlain's business-like instincts and desire for an imperial federation were not the sole components of his imperialist outlook. Like Rosebery, he had a visionary conception of the 'White Man's Burden'. 'You cannot', he explained to the Royal Colonial Institute in March 1897, 'make omelettes without breaking eggs; you cannot destroy the practices of barbarism, of slavery, or superstition . . . without the use of force'. But he went on:

> We feel that our rule over these territories can only be justified if we can show that it adds to the happiness and prosperity of the people, and I maintain that our rule does, and has, brought security and peace and comparative prosperity to countries that never knew their blessings before. In carrying out this work of civilisation we are fulfilling what I believe to be our national mission.

Here was an exposition of the virtues of empire at a time when the imperial idea had reached its zenith.

By the end of the century, as Salisbury's powers declined, Chamberlain was one of the most influential men in the Cabinet, even conducting his own private foreign policy aimed at securing an alliance with Germany. He did not, however, achieve his most cherished ambitions. He could not persuade the self-governing colonies to join an imperial federation or customs union; he did not arrange an alliance with Germany. In 1903 he finally resigned from the Balfour administration and broke with the Conservative leadership in order to conduct another campaign, this time for tariff reform. This rent the Conservative party in two and the administration met its Waterloo in 1905. Chamberlain, who might have been prime minister of either political party, ended by splitting both. He then wore himself out in his crusade for imperial preference, suffered a stroke in July 1906 and remained stricken till his death in 1914. It was a sad end to a promising career. Nevertheless Chamberlain had made an indelible mark on the map of Africa.

[38] West Africa, 1895–1902

Before 1895 the British government had not seemed to pay much attention to the British West African colonies. In themselves the small, struggling colonies were worth little. Since the Berlin Conference France had extended her power deep into the Western Sudan and Salisbury was content to see the frontiers of French Senegambia and Guinea drawn tight round the Gambia and Sierra Leone by the agreements of 1889 and 1891. The trade of these two colonies was so small that the staking out of additional claims was not thought worthwhile. The doctrines of private enterprise and informal influence still held the day.

The Gold Coast also received little help; its hinterlands looked like going the same way. The French were driving forward into the Upper Volta regions to the north of Ashanti and the British administrators were told that any claims they wished to assert would have to be met by local resources — a task made formidable by the prior need to pacify Ashanti. The story was much the same at Lagos. The colony lacked the means to extend its authority inland and the Ibadan–Ilorin war in the interior crippled its trade. Salisbury showed little concern for the hinterlands of Lagos and the Gold Coast in the arrangements of 1889 and 1891.

Salisbury's main area of activity was the Niger. Here, at least, the river provided some access to the heavily populated interior, trade prospects seemed promising, and Sir George Goldie's company had managed to push through the rain-forests into the Sudan beyond. In 1890 a paper protection for the company's sphere was provided in the Anglo-French agreement of that date. The western boundary, however, was left undecided and as disputes flared up over the Nile the French loosed countless expeditions into the Gold Coast hinterlands and the Niger bend.

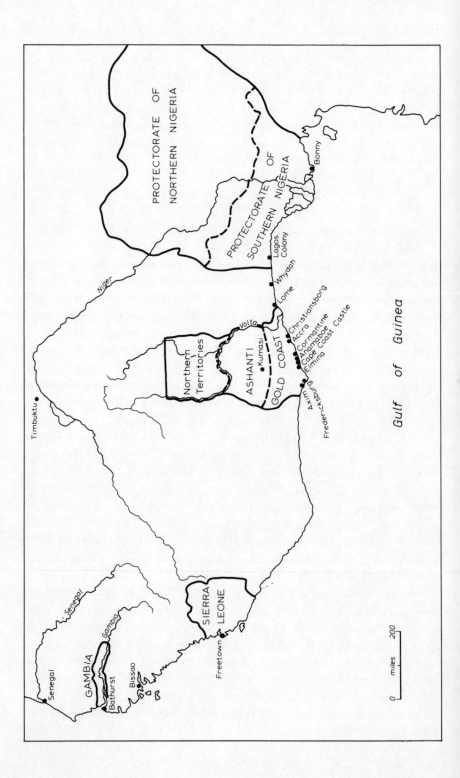

Salisbury's interest in the Niger may not have been unconnected with his Nile strategy. He was concerned lest the French reached the Nile via the Upper Niger and the Congo, thus attempting to link their possessions in the east and west. The company's commercial claims and the skirmishings on the northern boundary of the British Niger sphere were also of some importance, therefore, to the British position in Egypt. And as the chance of agreement over Egypt and the Nile receded, French rivalry on the Niger became more fierce as pawns were sought for a bigger game.

Chamberlain backed wholeheartedly the tentative British expansionist developments in the Niger area. He prized West Africa for its own sake. Once again he got much of his own way. Inland railways were started, an expedition against Ashanti was authorised and attempts at closer and more efficient administration were supported. The result was foreseeable: in 1899 the British government reluctantly had to rush through an emergency measure guaranteeing loans of £3,500,000 to cover his West African and West Indian ventures. Nevertheless the beginnings of tropical administration had been made. Chamberlain clearly did not expect local revenues to bear the total cost of development, nor did he expect immediate returns on British government loans. For a British Colonial Secretary to hold such views was new indeed. Chamberlain looked even further afield: he was prepared to invest men as well as money in expeditions to occupy and pacify inland regions. Salisbury suspected that Chamberlain rather enjoyed breaking eggs to make omelettes.

Northern Nigeria, with its reputed wealth and dense population, provided the obvious example of an 'undeveloped estate'. Chamberlain decided to bring it under imperial control. For Chamberlain the Royal Niger Company was merely a caretaker to be dismissed when the superior resources of the state could be brought to bear upon the region. Salisbury, however, not wishing to paint the world red, viewed things differently. It was not so much that he disagreed with the colonial secretary's aims (he was equally determined not to concede anything his country could establish an undisputable claim to), but he objected to the tactics Chamberlain proposed to adopt. While things were going well in Egypt it seemed pointless to antagonise the French. Chamberlain wanted to resist by force the French thrust into the Lower Niger. In order to keep him in the Cabinet, Salisbury compromised. He allowed Chamberlain a free hand in West Africa while he continued his own conciliatory policy in Paris. The outcome was the

organisation of the West African Frontier Force under Colonel Lugard
with orders to enter the Lagos hinterland and to 'occupy the country
which is already occupied by the French . . . to cut off their communications, to prove to the natives that we are as good or better than
they, and to show them that their policy of effective occupation is
futile'. The confrontation worked. The British forces came face to face
with the French army, and the French government, realising that
British interests could not be bartered in West Africa, began to negotiate.
Chamberlain opposed concessions all the way along the line and
eventually secured most of what he wanted by the Niger Convention
of June 1898 — three months before Fashoda. The hinterlands of the
Gold Coast and the British Niger sphere had been safeguarded.

The end of the story is well known. In 1899 the charter of the Royal
Niger Company was revoked and in 1900 Sir Frederick Lugard took
over the administration of the Protectorate of Northern Nigeria. In
the same year the Colonial Office accepted responsibility for the
Protectorate of Southern Nigeria (an extension of the original Oil
Rivers Protectorate of 1885). With the colony of Lagos the foundations
of modern Nigeria had been laid. Similarly, by the end of Salisbury's
administration the area which comprises present-day Ghana had fallen
under British control. The Ashantis accepted a British protectorate and
a British Resident when the Asantehene submitted to a British expeditionary force without a fight in 1896; a protectorate was extended over
the country to the north of Ashanti (the Northern Territories) in 1897.
Ashanti was finally annexed in 1901 after a nine-month war caused by
the British governor's demanding possession of the symbolic golden
stool (the 'soul of the nation') of the exiled Asantehene. Although the
country extended 400 miles inland and contained over 2,000,000 people
it was nowhere near as large as Nigeria. That these two countries
should have had such extensive hinterlands at all, however, was largely
due to the work (and faith) of one man — Joseph Chamberlain —
which is still reflected in the map of Africa today.

[39] The Fashoda Confrontation

The West African events were little more than a side-show compared
with the more momentous developments in north-east Africa which
brought France and Great Britain to the verge of war. Here Salisbury

retained control of affairs firmly within his own grasp. The situation was far too delicate to allow Chamberlain and his friends in the Cabinet to influence developments by turning the open confrontation into a full-scale war. To such an old-style diplomatist as Salisbury, resounding diplomatic successes and the deliberate humiliation of rivals were things best avoided.

When Salisbury became Prime Minister he had little thought of reconquering the Sudan, and Sir Evelyn Baring (Lord Cromer) was too concerned with Egyptian finances to look favourably on new ventures southwards. While the dervishes remained in control of the Sudan there was little threat to the headwaters of the Nile. But the crushing defeat of the Italians by an Abyssinian army at the battle of Adowa in March 1896 altered all that. Emperor Menelik's army had been assisted by French rifles and Russian artillery advisers. The possibility of the French replacing the Italians in Abyssinia and the possibility of Menelik allying with the Mahdists transformed the situation. Twelve days after Adowa, in an effort to demonstrate solidarity with the Triple Alliance by some act intended to relieve the pressure on the Italians at Kassala, Salisbury authorised Sir Herbert Kitchener to advance to Dongola in the eastern Sudan. Predictably, the French retaliated by attempting to clinch their alliance with Menelik and by equipping further expeditions to advance on the Nile.

All these developments were most distasteful to Salisbury. Since 1895 he had tended to drift away from cooperation with the Triple Alliance and wanted to improve relations with France. The collapse of British influence in Constantinople; the spectre of France, Russia and Germany acting in concert against the Japanese in the Far East; and the Kaiser's behaviour in sending a congratulatory telegram to President Kruger of the Transvaal on the rebuff of the Jameson Raid, convinced Salisbury that much could be gained by finding some accommodation with France. Hence his policy of conciliation in West Africa which Chamberlain so abruptly reversed.

However, now that French expeditions were advancing from both east and west towards the Nile, Salisbury pressed on with the building of the Mombasa railroad to forestall the French dash for Fashoda with a British expedition from the south. And so four expeditions were being planned from different directions across tremendous distances and through hostile country with the aim of laying claim to Fashoda.

Fashoda (modern Kodok) was chosen for an obvious reason: in January 1895 the British had laid claim on behalf of Egypt to the

territory as far south as Khartoum and for themselves to the sources of
the Nile as far north as Fashoda. The French reasoned that the intervening area of the Sudan was open to all-comers and intended to
establish their own claims by occupation. A physical presence would at
least, they felt, give them a better bargaining position at any conference
concerning a general settlement of the Egyptian disputes. As Kitchener
advanced south to Dongola, a French engineer, Captain Marchand,
left for Brazzaville to establish the French claims to Fashoda.

Knowledge of this long-planned expedition and the fact that the
British expedition from the south had not even set out led Salisbury to
send Kitchener orders to capture Khartoum. Kitchener fought his way
slowly and methodically down the Nile until he faced the massed forces
of the Khalifa (the Mahdi's successor) at Omdurman on 2 September
1898. A five-hour massacre ensued. The ill-armed but heroic dervishes,
in wave after wave, threw themselves at the British rifles and machine
guns until some 11,000 of them lay dead on the battlefield. The carnage
was terrible. Gordon's death had been finally and bloodily revenged.
Khartoum was occupied, the Mahdi's tomb desecrated and the Sirdar
of the Egyptian Army, the callous Kitchener, apparently toyed with
the idea of using the Mahdi's skull as an ink-stand or goblet. Instead
the British troops obligingly used it as a football. It was even rumoured
that they had looted and murdered wounded dervishes. These reports
cast a dark shadow over British jubilation at the news of the victory.
The desecration of the Mahdi's tomb caused anger and horror in
Great Britain. Queen Victoria admonished Kitchener: 'the destruction
of the poor body of a man who, whether he was very bad and cruel,
after all was a *man* of a *certain* importance — savours . . . too much of
the Middle Ages'. The British government even felt it necessary to
issue a Blue Book to refute charges of inhumanity.

But Kitchener's work was still not complete. He had already learned
of Captain Marchand's arrival at Fashoda, 300 miles to the south,
on 10 July. He now followed his instructions to the letter and led a
flotilla of gunboats southwards in search of the French. He arrived at
Fashoda on 19 September and, as Salisbury had instructed, treated the
seven Frenchmen with courtesy, avoiding any outright confrontation.
Both commanders congratulated each other on their recent exploits.
Kitchener pointed out that Fashoda belonged jointly to the British
and Egyptian governments and handed the Frenchman a written
protest against occupation of any part of the Nile Valley by France.
Marchand declined to retire without orders from home. He did not

object, however, to Kitchener, diplomatically dressed in his Egyptian uniform, raising the Egyptian flag some yards away from the tricolour. After enjoying a glass of sweet champagne the two men parted on amicable terms. It was all very much an anti-climax in Africa but it saw the climax of imperialism in Europe.

The Fashoda incident brought war in sight for the next two months in Europe. The British demanded evacuation while the French argued for delay. But their position was untenable. The British held all the cards. They had an army on the spot at Khartoum, a strong and determined government, united support from the British people and naval superiority in the Mediterranean. The French were forced to climb down. Their government was tottering and the country was torn in two by the Dreyfus affair. In March 1899 a comprehensive agreement was concluded. The rights of Great Britain over the whole Nile basin from source to mouth and a joint Anglo-Egyptian condominium over the Sudan were acknowledged. In return France was confirmed in possession of her West African empire and received the central Sudan from Darfur in the east to Lake Chad in the west. The final lines were drawn and the scramble for tropical Africa was over. In Great Britain Salisbury was at the height of his popularity in 1899. But in the Cabinet his control of foreign policy and the very principles according to which he worked had already been challenged. His cool attitude towards developments in the Far East caused concern when the scramble for Africa was succeeded by the 'scramble for China'.

[40] The Scramble for Leases in China

The scramble for Africa and the so-called scramble for China had little in common. In China the scramble was more for economic advantage than for territorial gain. No European power was strong enough to absorb China into its imperial system. The contest was for trading concessions to be wrung from the hapless Chinese. Thus when Great Britain's virtual monopoly of China's foreign trade was challenged during the last two decades of the nineteenth century she had little to gain and much to lose.

The problem Salisbury had to face was whether to continue the long-standing policy of maintaining the integrity of the Chinese empire or to protect British interests by outright annexation. Salisbury refused to recognise that a crisis existed and refused to make a decision. This inaction infuriated Chamberlain, who was obsessed by the *potential* market of 400 million Chinese. It seemed to Chamberlain, in particular, that Salisbury was prepared to conciliate France in West Africa and was just as ready to make concessions to Russia in China. If Salisbury had his way not only China but the whole of the British empire might disintegrate.

The trouble had begun after the Sino-Japanese war of 1894–5 when Germany, France and Russia combined to force Japan to disgorge some of her gains under the Treaty of Shimonoseki, principally the lease of Port Arthur. After this, greater Russian and French pressure was brought to bear on Peking in return for loans to pay off the Japanese indemnity. Russia was extremely active in northern China and Salisbury hoped to counteract this influence by diplomacy. He realised that Russia had as much to lose as Great Britain by any seizure of territory which might spark off a general scramble. He hoped, therefore, to come to some understanding by recognising separate 'spheres of preponderance'. Since the possibility of raising an alliance against Russia in the Far East was negligible and since Great Britain was heavily involved in disputes with France on the Niger and the Nile, to Salisbury the only sensible course seemed to be to continue pressing the Chinese government to make concessions to British merchants and to continue the attempts to settle all problems with France and Russia by diplomatic means. Accordingly he welcomed Russian attempts to penetrate China commercially, provided always that the 'open door' was maintained. This soft line towards Russia, however, was not good enough for Chamberlain and certain other members of the Cabinet.

The crisis occurred when the Kaiser seized Kiochow in November 1897. The Tsar replied by occupying Port Arthur in the following month. What were the British to do? Were they to condone the German and Russian 'leases' by insisting on territorial compensation of their own, or were they to risk war by insisting that Russia should withdraw? The Cabinet was left to decide: Salisbury had fallen ill and Balfour was in charge of the Foreign Office. After several confused discussions it was decided that a makeweight had to be found and Wei-hai-wei was leased in April 1898. The scramble for leases had begun. By 1900, Great Britain, Germany, Russia, France, Japan and Italy had all staked their claims; only the United States took nothing. The rest had their ninety-nine-year leases, 'treaty ports', spheres of influence and exemption from

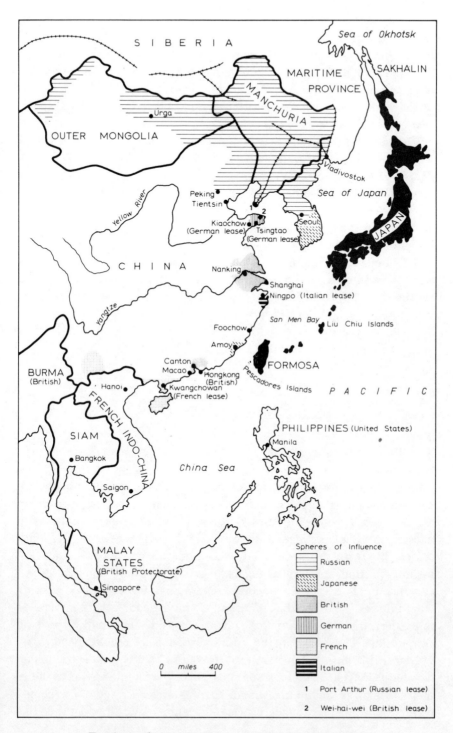

Foreign spheres of influence in China about 1900

Chinese courts of law. The partition went no further. The powers were too jealous of each other and combined instead to pillage China. But they had sown dragon's teeth and reaped the harvest in the Boxer Rising of 1900, the most notorious reaction to the imperialism of the European at the end of the century. Salisbury had correctly assessed that the real crisis still lay in the future.

The events of March 1898 and the staking out of claims in China were, however, seen at the time as a defeat for British policy. The British were not accustomed to being beaten. Salisbury's policy was attacked in Parliament and the press and it was suggested that the rapidly ageing Prime Minister was losing his touch. Most significant of all, it began the movement in the Cabinet to ease Salisbury out of the Foreign Office. Lansdowne began to look for an ally in the Far East and Chamberlain began his quest for a German alliance. Salisbury's reputation was restored to some extent after Fashoda but he never fully regained his hold over his colleagues. The end of the century, however, was to see a far greater calamity for the British than the Boxer Rising. The closing years of Victoria's reign were dominated by the climax of events in another continent — in the south of Africa.

[41] The Anglo–Boer War

The discovery of a major gold reef in the South African Republic (the Transvaal) in 1886 changed a small, stagnant, pastoral economy into one of the most prosperous states in Africa. This transformation affected the whole balance of power in South Africa. The dwindling fortunes of the Transvaal were dramatically reversed and the new-found wealth caused old Paul Kruger to dream of a Dutch hegemony in South Africa. But with the Rand gold strike came an influx of thousands of fortune-hunting immigrants (*uitlanders*) most of whom claimed British citizenship. These posed a complex problem for the Boer farming communities. To allow the *uitlanders* — some 44,000 of them in 1896 — full citizenship would turn the Transvaal over to the English-speaking community. This was something Kruger could not countenance.

In Great Britain the phenomenal rise of the Boer Republic to such an economically dominant position was viewed with dismay. The long-desired union of the South African colonies and Boer republics seemed further off than ever. In fact, instead of becoming another dominion like

Canada, there was now a very strong possibility that an independent 'United States of South Africa' might emerge under the leadership of the Transvaal. British paramountcy in South Africa and the very security of the all-important Cape route to India seemed to be at stake. In this situation the British government lent an attentive ear to the views of Cecil Rhodes, the Prime Minister of the Cape, and watched the position of the *uitlanders* with close concern. The immigrants paid substantial taxes and could be conscripted but were not allowed to vote and did not possess any seats in the Volksrad. While these British citizens continued to have grievances, the British government could claim an interest in the Transvaal beyond that based on vague claims to suzerainty. The situation was ominous.

In 1895 Rhodes aimed at overthrowing Kruger's republic by force. Arms were smuggled into the Republic and a rising of *uitlanders* was planned for the end of December. This was to be supported by a small force of the British South Africa Company which would intervene ostensibly to protect British women and children supposedly threatened by the Boers. The plan was well-known in Cape Town and London. Chamberlain apparently connived actively with the plotters. This was all done under cover, however, as the British government could not openly endorse such blatant interference in the internal affairs of the Republic.

The rising never occurred. How sincere the mine-owners and capitalists were in wishing to overthrow the Kruger regime has never been established. But Dr Leander Starr Jameson, the British South Africa Company's administrator in Rhodesia and the commander of the support force, decided to go ahead with the planned invasion on 29 December 1895. The result was a fiasco. Four days later the column of 600 mounted troopers surrendered ignominiously to Kruger's troops.

Although Chamberlain immediately condemned the invasion and denied all prior knowledge of the event, the Jameson Raid had unfortunate repercussions. The result was an undoubted reverse for Rhodes. He was forced to resign the premiership of the Cape, the alliance with the Afrikaner Bond under J. H. Hofmeyr was at an end and there was a wave of anti-British feeling throughout South Africa which did much to consolidate Afrikanerdom. The Orange Free State was forced into the arms of its northern neighbour and, in the Transvaal, the diminishing prestige of the elderly Kruger rapidly revived. After the raid the Republic began to import arms from Europe. There was also an international repercussion: the Kaiser sent a congratulatory telegram to Kruger which infuriated British public opinion.

In Great Britain liberal opinion was horrified at the turn of events and Rhodes and Chamberlain had to appear before the notorious 'Commission of no-Inquiry' conducted by the House of Commons. The affair had the appearance of a whitewashing exercise. Rhodes's activities were condemned but Chamberlain was held to be blameless. There was a definite lack of incriminating documentary evidence. Even today Chamberlain's role in the events prior to the Jameson Raid is difficult to assess. Chamberlain has been acquitted of complicity in the plot by his biographer, J. L. Garvin, and by Lady Pakenham in her *Jameson's Raid* (1960). The researches of J. van der Poel, *The Jameson Raid* (1951), J. S. Marais, *The Fall of Kruger's Republic* (1961), and J. A. S. Grenville, *Lord Salisbury and Foreign Policy* (1964), point in the opposite direction. It would appear that Chamberlain did have a much greater knowledge of the affair than he cared to reveal. Nevertheless he got off scot-free, and even the unfortunate Jameson, who received a' light sentence, became something of a popular hero with the imperialist masses of the late 1890s. The British ended by being more determined than ever to reassert their paramountcy in South Africa. For the Boers the atmosphere had become even more poisoned and the problem of the *uitlanders* remained unresolved.

British policy in South Africa now had to be reconstructed. To fulfil this mission Chamberlain in 1897 appointed Sir Alfred Milner as Governor of the Cape Colony and British High Commissioner. This was a most unfortunate appointment. Milner, a brilliant Oxford scholar who had a great reputation as a civil servant in both England and Egypt, was the last man to negotiate an understanding with the Boer President. Blinded by his almost mystical belief in British imperialism and by his race-conscious patriotism, he believed that the whole future of the British empire and of Great Britain's position as a great power was at stake. Compromise, therefore, was impossible. Chamberlain saw the matter in a similar light: 'there is a greater issue than the franchise or the grievances of the Uitlanders at stake . . . our supremacy in South Africa and our existence as a great Power in the world is involved'.

Both Chamberlain and Salisbury, however, wanted a peaceful solution. While relations with the United States were strained and Great Britain faced France on the Nile and Russia in Asia, the time was far from ripe for a conflict with the Boers. Indeed, the British Cabinet was not without some sympathy for this unfortunate people.

Arthur Balfour thought the *uitlanders* 'rather unreasonable' and argued
that 'were I a Boer . . . nothing but necessity would induce me to adopt
a constitution which would turn my country into an English Republic,
or a system of education that would reduce my language to the 'patois'
of a small and helpless minority'. The British government were certainly
not intent on provoking a war in 1898.

But Lord Milner was of a different opinion. Force, or the threat of
force at least, seemed to be the only possible way of making Kruger
concede the British position. Chamberlain did not improve matters by
reasserting British 'suzerainty' over the Transvaal. A violent press
campaign whipped up discontent among the *uitlanders* and in March
1899 more than 21,000 persons signed a petition about vastly exaggerated grievances which was forwarded to the Colonial Office.
Chamberlain became convinced that some show of strength was
essential. On 10 May he wrote:

> The spectacle of thousands of British subjects kept permanently in the
> position of helots, constantly chafing under undoubted grievances, and
> calling vainly to Her Majesty's Government for redress does steadily
> undermine the influence and reputation of Great Britain and the
> respect for the British government within its own dominions. . . . The
> best proof of its power and its justice would be to obtain for the
> Uitlanders of the Transvaal a fair share in the government of a country
> which owes everything to their exertions.

Events were rapidly building up to a crisis. And now that the Fashoda
crisis was past, the Sudan campaign over and, above all, now that
Great Britain and Germany had come to an agreement over the
division of the Portuguese colonies should that empire collapse (an
agreement which removed German interest in the Transvaal), Great
Britain was far readier to adopt a strong line.

In May 1899 Kruger and Milner had a face-to-face confrontation
at Bloemfontein. Milner demanded that all *uitlanders* should have full
political equality after five years: Kruger insisted on a seven-year
residence qualification and requested that the 1884 Convention should
be examined by impartial arbitrators. Milner refused and the conference broke up with Kruger crying, 'It is our country that you want'.
Two months later, however, the Volksrad granted the vote to seven-
year residents and, in August 1899, offered to lower the period to five
years. Chamberlain was delighted. But Milner was firmly against
accepting such concessions — especially when Kruger demanded, as a
condition, the ending of British suzerainty. Thus even though the

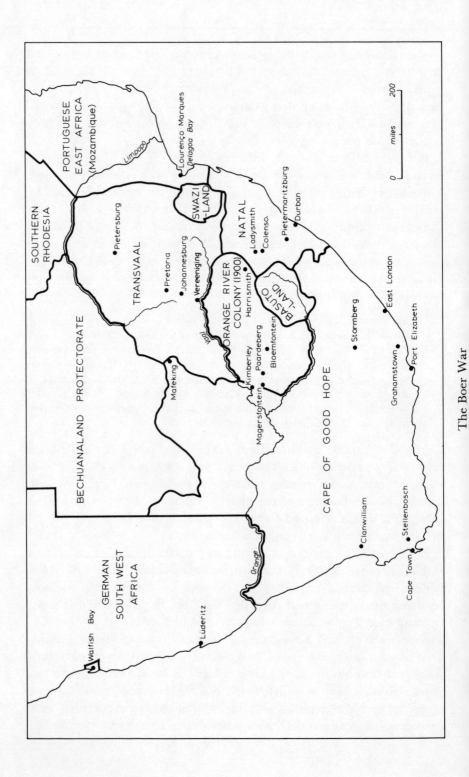

The Boer War

peace party was strong in the Transvaal, in the Cape and in Britain, in the end Milner's obstruction and Kruger's suspicions wrecked all hope of compromise. A dispirited Chamberlain and an unhappy Cabinet convinced themselves that war was inevitable. Reinforcements were rushed to South Africa. With British forces beginning to mass on the Republic's frontiers, Kruger demanded, on 9 October 1899, their withdrawal within forty-eight hours and the submission of all outstanding questions to arbitration. When no answer came, Great Britain and the two republics were at war. In the last resort Milner and not Chamberlain dictated British policy.

And so the South African war, which cast ever-lengthening shadows over the dying years of Victoria's reign, had begun. It was to provide a bizarre spectacle for three bitter years. The British empire, with its huge resources, unlimited manpower and mighty navy, was at war with (and apparently unable to defeat) two republics whose population, as Lloyd George so vividly put it, 'did not exceed that of Flintshire and Denbighshire'. In the end the British had nearly 450,000 men in the field, including detachments from Canada, Australia, New Zealand and India. The Boers numbered no more than 50–60,000 — an amateurish army of largely untrained farmers, lacking in equipment, ammunition, heavy firing power, field hospitals and all the paraphernalia of modern warfare. These bands of mounted men were highly mobile, however, and proved excellent marksmen and a formidable enemy. They had to be smothered by sheer weight of numbers and supplies. The final victory was neither glorious nor cheap.

Early expectations of a short campaign soon proved mistaken. The war began with a series of bitter blows to British prestige. The Boers invaded the Cape and Natal and besieged the garrisons of the strategically significant towns of Kimberley, Mafeking and Ladysmith. During 'Black Week', December 1899, substantial British relieving forces suffered a series of reverses at Stormberg, Magersfontein and Colenso. Not until February 1900 did British fortunes begin to revive. The British sent out the illustrious Lord Roberts of Kandahar as commander-in-chief with Lord Kitchener as chief of staff. Then the British troops, employing new outflanking tactics, swept forward. Kimberley, Ladysmith and Mafeking were relieved to the accompaniment of hysterical rejoicing in London. By June 1900 Johannesburg and Pretoria had been occupied and the Transvaal government departed by railway to Delagoa Bay. Kruger left to preach the Boer cause in

continental Europe. The war appeared to have been won and both
republics were annexed as British Crown colonies. Roberts returned
to the victory parades in London and Kitchener was left to mop up the
remaining Boer resistance. In Great Britain, the Conservative government held its 'Khaki' election in October hoping to cash in on the
victory. The Conservatives were returned with an increased majority
with Joseph Chamberlain, the subject of bitter attacks, still at the
Colonial Office.

But the war was far from over: it lasted another eighteen months.
The Boers, expertly led by such great generals as Botha and Smuts, and
by such brilliant tacticians as De Wet and De la Rey, with no more
than 20,000 men still left in the field, resorted to highly successful
guerrilla tactics. By early 1901 the British grasp on the new colonies
had not been consolidated and the Boers even took the offensive by
invading Cape territory. Realising he could not defeat the commandos
in the field, Kitchener adopted a drastic new scorched-earth policy.
Farmsteads and crops were burned, cattle captured and women and
children herded into internment camps. Conditions in these camps were
appalling. By the end of the war, through deficiencies in diet and
sanitation and epidemics of highly contagious diseases, some 26,000 of
the 118,000 inmates had perished. It seemed to the Boers that the
British were trying to exterminate their people. There was a tremendous
outcry in Great Britain and the new Liberal leader, Sir Henry Campbell-
Bannerman, labelled Kitchener's tactics 'methods of barbarism'. The
British government belatedly intervened to ensure an improvement in
camp conditions.

But still the humiliating war dragged on. Great Britain was friendless
in Europe and the hostile press of Europe jeered at the British inability
to defeat an enemy which they outnumbered twenty to one. In South
Africa Kitchener finally hit upon the idea of dividing the countryside
into sections by miles of barbed wire and conducting systematic campaigns against the commandos. Slowly, Boer numbers were whittled
down and Boer resistance was smothered. Finally, the Boer leaders
agreed to lay down their arms at a conference held at Vereeniging on
the Vaal river on 31 May 1902. According to the settlement all
Afrikaners who took the loyal oath were to be released, the Afrikaans
language was to be safeguarded, and civil and then self-government
were to be restored to the new colonies as soon as was practicable.
Voting rights for the Bantu people would not be dealt with before this
had occurred. The British also undertook to contribute towards the

repair of war damage and to grant interest-free loans. It was a magnanimous peace for a heroic and by no means dispirited foe. Temporarily, at least, the British had regained supremacy in South Africa.

But was it worth it? The whole nation had had a traumatic experience. The glorious British empire had been unable to defeat the puny Boer republics for three years. The crude excesses of the jingoistic imperialism of the closing years of the century were followed by a more sober frame of mind and a sense of guilt. Many of the unsavoury episodes of the war had shocked Victorian sensibilities. For once the British people took notice of the hostile criticism coming from Europe and the United States. They also became rather uncomfortably aware of Great Britain's 'splendid isolation'. Great Britain had survived one war but could she, friendless, face the next? The Boer War had severely damaged the British image. Rudyard Kipling, that frequently misunderstood poet of empire, caught the mood exactly:

> Let us admit it fairly, as a business people should.
> We have had no end of a lesson: it will do us no end of good.

The Anglo-Boer War, it has been said, knocked the gilt off the Victorian age.

PRINCIPAL EVENTS, 1880–1902

1880   First Boer War. Canada appoints first High Commissioner in London

1881   Convention of Pretoria. British North Borneo Company chartered. Revolt of the Mahdi in the Sudan

1882   Occupation of Egypt

1883   Cromer appointed British agent and Consul General in Egypt. Dispute begins with Bismarck over Angra Pequena

1884   Convention of Pretoria renegotiated. Papua annexed. November. Berlin West Africa Conference begins

1885   Death of General Gordon at Khartoum. Penjdeh crisis. Upper Burma annexed. British protectorates in Bechuanaland and Oil Rivers. London Convention hands Egyptian bâton to Bismarck. Indian National Congress founded

1886   Royal Niger Company chartered. Anglo-German treaties concerning East Africa and the Pacific. Gold discovered in the Transvaal

1887   Queen Victoria's Golden Jubilee. Colonial conference

1888 Imperial British East Africa Company chartered. Zululand annexed. British protectorate in Matabeleland
1889 British South Africa Company chartered. Salisbury announces decision to remain in Egypt for the foreseeable future
1890 British treaties with Germany and France concerning East and West Africa. Rhodes becomes Prime Minister of the Cape. Responsible government in Western Australia
1891 Anglo-Portuguese colonial treaty. British protectorate in Nyasaland
1892 Indian Councils Act
1893 Responsible government in Natal
1894 Uganda Protectorate. Colonial conference at Ottawa
1895 Chamberlain becomes Secretary of State for the Colonies. British East Africa Protectorate. Jameson Raid
1896 Kitchener advances into the Sudan. Ashanti War
1897 Diamond Jubilee. Colonial conference. Royal Commission on the West Indies. Milner appointed High Commissioner for South Africa. Protectorate over Northern Territories
1898 Chamberlain's Five-Year Plan for the West Indies. Niger Convention with France. Wei-hai-wei leased. Fashoda confrontation. Curzon appointed Viceroy of India
1899 Anglo-French agreement concerning Nile valley. Anglo-Boer war begins. British defeats at Magersfontein, Stormberg and Colenso
1900 British victory at Paardeberg. Ladysmith, Kimberley and Mafeking relieved. Boxer Rising in China. Northern Nigerian Protectorate. First Pan-African Congress in London
1901 Death of Queen Victoria. Ashanti annexed. North-West Frontier Province created. Commonwealth of Australia formed
1902 Peace of Vereeniging

Further Reading
E. A. Benians, J. Butler, & C. E. Carrington (eds), *Cambridge History of the British Empire*, Vol III, *The Empire-Commonwealth, 1870–1919.* Cambridge University Press (Cambridge, 1959).
J. Lehmann, *The First Boer War.* Cape (London, 1972).
D. M. Schreuder, *Gladstone and Kruger: the Liberal Government and Colonial 'Home Rule', 1880–85.* Routledge & Kegan Paul (London, 1969).
R. E. Robinson, J. A. Gallagher (with Alice Denny), *Africa and the Victorians: the official mind of imperialism.* Macmillan (London, 1961).

A. Nutting, *Gordon: Martyr and Misfit*. Constable (London, 1966).

C. W. Newbury, 'Victorians, Republicans and the Partition of West Africa', *Journal of African History*, Vol. III, pp. 493–501 (1962).

H. Brunschwig, *French Colonialism, 1871–1914: Myth and Reality*, trans. by W. G. Brown (Pall Mall, London, 1966).

J. Stengers, 'L'Impérialisme colonial de la fin du XIXe siècle: Mythe ou Réalité', *Journal of African History*, Vol. III, pp. 469–91 (1962) trans. in P. J. M. McEwan (ed.), *Readings in African History*, Vol. 2. Oxford University Press (London, 1968).

C. W. Newbury & A. S. Kanya-Forstner, 'French Policy and the Origins of the Scramble for West Africa', *Journal of African History*, Vol. X, pp. 253–76 (1969).

A. J. P. Taylor, *Germany's First Bid for Colonies, 1884-85*. Macmillan (London, 1938).

S. E. Crowe, *The Berlin West Africa Conference, 1884–85*. Negro Universities Press, 2nd ed. (Connecticut, 1970).

P. Gifford & W. R. Louis (eds), *Britain and Germany in Africa: imperial rivalry and colonial rule*. Yale University Press (New Haven, 1967).

P. Gifford & W. R. Louis (eds), *France and Britain in Africa: imperial rivalry and colonial rule*. Yale University Press (New Haven, 1972).

H–U. Wehler, 'Bismarck's Imperialism, 1862–90', *Past and Present*, No. 48, pp. 119–55 (1970).

M. E. Chamberlain, *The Scramble for Africa*. Longmans (London, 1974).

R. O. Collins (ed.), *The Partition of Africa*. Wiley (New York, 1969).

R. E. Robinson & J. A. Gallagher, 'The Partition of Africa' in *New Cambridge Modern History*, Vol. XI. Cambridge University Press (Cambridge, 1962).

J. D. Fage, *A History of West Africa: An Introductory Survey*. Oxford University Press, 4th ed. (Oxford, 1969).

J. E. Flint, *Sir George Goldie and the Making of Nigeria*. Oxford University Press (London, 1960).

A. J. Wills, *An Introduction to the History of Central Africa*. Oxford University Press, 2nd ed. (London, 1966).

P. Mason, *The Birth of a Dilemma: the Conquest and Settlement of Rhodesia*. Oxford University Press (London, 1958).

R. Oliver & G. Mathew (eds), *History of East Africa*, Vol. 1. Oxford University Press (London, 1963).

V. Harlow & E. M. Chilver, *History of East Africa*, Vol. 2. Oxford University Press (London, 1965).

R. Coupland, *The Exploitation of East Africa, 1856–90: the Slave Trade and the Scramble*. Faber, 2nd ed. (London, 1968).

R. Oliver, *Sir Harry Johnston and the Scramble for Africa*. Chatto & Windus (London, 1957).

J. S. Galbraith, *Mackinnon and East Africa, 1878–95*. Cambridge University Press (Cambridge, 1972).

M. Wilson & L. Thompson, *The Oxford History of South Africa*, Vol. II: *South Africa, 1870–1966*. Oxford University Press (London, 1971).

G. N. Sanderson, *England, Europe and the Upper Nile, 1882–99*. Edinburgh University Press (Edinburgh, 1965).

Lady G. Cecil, *Life of Robert, Marquis of Salisbury*. Hodder & Stoughton, 4 vols (London, 1921–32).

C. J. Lowe, *The Reluctant Imperialists: British Foreign Policy, 1878–1902*. Routledge & Kegan Paul (London, 1967).

W. L. Langer, *The Diplomacy of Imperialism, 1890–1902*. Knopf, 2nd ed. (New York, 1965).

W. P. Morrell, *Britain in the Pacific Islands*. Oxford University Press (London, 1960).

J. M. Ward, *British Policy in the South Pacific, 1786–1893*. Australasian Publishing Co. (Sydney, 1948).

M. Edwardes, *The West in Asia, 1850–1914*. Batsford (London, 1967).

B. Williams, *Cecil Rhodes*. Constable (London, 1921).

J. G. Lockhart & C. M. Woodhouse, *Rhodes*. Hodder & Stoughton (London, 1963).

J. L. Garvin & J. Amery, *Life of Joseph Chamberlain*. Macmillan, 6 vols (London, 1936–69).

J. Marlowe, *Cromer in Egypt*. Elek (London, 1970).

A. L. Al-Sayyid, *Egypt and Cromer: A Study in Anglo-Egyptian Relations*. Murray (London, 1968).

J. A. S. Grenville, *Lord Salisbury and Foreign Policy: the Close of the Nineteenth Century*. Athlone Press (London, 1964).

L. Young, *British Policy in China, 1895–1902*. Oxford University Press (London, 1970).

E. Pakenham, *Jameson's Raid*. Weidenfeld and Nicolson (London, 1960).

J. van der Poel, *The Jameson Raid*. Oxford University Press (London, 1951).

J. Marais, *The Fall of Kruger's Republic*. Oxford University Press (London, 1961).

T. C. Caldwell (ed.), *The Anglo-Boer War*. Heath (Boston, 1965).

G. Blainey, 'Lost causes of the Jameson Raid', *Economic History Review*, Vol. XVIII, pp. 350–66 (1965).

J. E. Flint, *Cecil Rhodes*. Hutchinson (London, 1975).

D. Judd, *Radical Joe*. Hamish Hamilton (London, 1977).

E. Belfield, *The Boer War*. Leo Cooper (London, 1975).

Part VI
The Passing of the *Pax Britannica*

[42] The Influence of the Anglo–Boer War

Although by 1901 the British empire had not expanded to its fullest extent (this point was not reached until 1921) the empire had passed its zenith. Never again were imperialism and the empire on which the sun allegedly never set such a popular concern with the general British public. The Anglo-Boer War not only administered a shock to British power, prestige and self-esteem, but in many quarters brought about a revulsion against the apparent motives behind imperialism and the methods used in establishing British rule. Although Great Britain emerged victorious from the war she was by no means unscathed. The South African war rightly left a nasty scar on the British conscience. As British politicians rushed to plug the holes in British defences, both at home and abroad, and tried to re-establish friendly relations with all the leading continental powers, the critics of empire received more respectful attention. Of most immediate concern was their assertion that Great Britain, with her world-wide commitments, had finally exceeded the limits of her power.

An overhaul of the military system was most urgent. It had taken a British army with large colonial contingents three years to overcome opposition in two small republics. The British military establishment and the means by which it was administered were clearly in need of investigation. In the Egyptian campaign of 1882 it had taken Great Britain a month to mobilise a single expeditionary Army Corps. In 1887 it was not even possible to equip fully an Army Corps for a Jubilee parade at Aldershot. While the British military strength might look good on paper, in reality Great Britain could not even field as large an army as Switzerland. How, then, could Britain defend herself, let alone her empire? Such doubts led to the placing of the Committee of Imperial Defence on a permanent footing in 1902. In the war in South Africa the great British lion had shown a dangerously soft under-belly.

The Boer War had an even greater effect on the British public's

attitude towards the empire. Not only had the war been a very distasteful one but the expected results had not been forthcoming. For all
the grand talk of the franchise rights of the *uitlanders* and the need
to break the Transvaal government's monopoly of the supply of
dynamite to the mines, neither of these objectives was secured in 1902.
Had the war been worth it after all? The British Parliament was presented with a bill for £250 million, as well as the continuing costs of
administration. And where were the expected benefits for British
emigrants? The Rand magnates seemed much more intent on obtaining
cheap Chinese coolie labour than on paying high wages for British
workers. Perhaps the war's critics had been right after all: on behalf of
the Rand millionaires a grab had been made for the territory of the Boers
in order to double the dividends on the shares in the gold mines. Such
an interpretation undoubtedly helped to rob the New Imperialism of
much of its moral content. That peculiarly self-confident element in
Victorian expansion finally disappeared.

With this disappearance came a new assessment of imperialism. In
1904 Augustine Birrell, President of the National Liberal Federation,
declared that a vote for the Conservatives at the next election would be
a vote for 'a future of Imperialism, of Caesarism, of Empire, of expansion abroad in places where no white man can live, of military con-
scription at home, of false ideals of national greatness and of national
honour'. The Anglo-Boer War had certainly made imperialism a
popular term of abuse in Europe. Having begun its career as a description of the policies of Napoleon III, by 1900 it had become a word
signifying an arrogant and bullying form of British nationalism. The
Pax Britannica, it was said, smothered rather than liberated the peoples
who fell under its sway. What, then, was the position of the British
empire when the Victorian age came to an end?

[43] Resistance, Pacification and Administration

Although at the end of the century the huge area painted red on the
map looked impressive, it was a matter for debate how much of this
territory Great Britain actually ruled. At one end of the scale were the
self-governing colonies, shortly to be officially termed 'Dominions',
where the British government had little say except in foreign policy and
defence matters; at the other end were small uninhabited islands in the

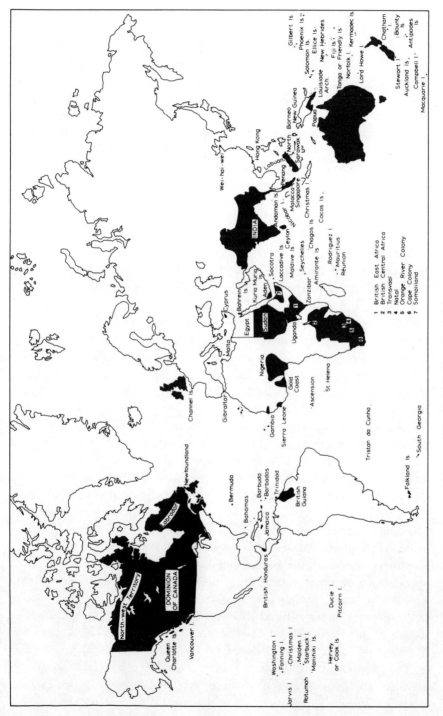

The British Empire in 1901

1 British East Africa
2 British Central Africa
3 Transvaal
4 Natal
5 Orange River Colony
6 Cape Colony
7 Somaliland

South Pacific, vast areas of India where a British administrator had never been seen and, in the African empire, huge, unexplored lands where British rule was not even acknowledged by the indigenous peoples. Indeed, in many parts of Africa British rule was not installed without a fight. Africans were never passive objects that Europeans could use as they wished.

The problem of resistance by indigenous societies to the imposition of alien rule has only comparatively recently been investigated by historians. Previously it was generally held that the alternatives of collaboration or resistance were clear-cut and the results (detrimental to the resisters and favourable to the collaborators) evident. Consequently, those who chose the apparently hopeless course of resistance have sometimes been seen as reactionaries or, as in the writings of Robinson and Gallagher, as 'proto-nationalists', who jeopardised the integrity of their societies. The collaborators, on the other hand, have been viewed as progressives, realists who perceived the futility of resistance and consequently by cooperation enhanced their own authority and increased the prosperity of their people.

Such a simple and one-sided interpretation will no longer suffice. Indigenous response was usually based on rational calculations of self-interest and the manner and results of resistance affected future European administration and future relationships with the colonial rulers, frequently to the advantage of the resisters. Sometimes collaborators and resisters were the same men acting in changed circumstances. The stance adopted depended on what could be gained from collaboration, what the white man threatened and whether a 'balance of power' could be struck. The strength of some indigenous societies and the extent to which European encroachment was resisted has sometimes been underestimated. Some African societies appeared so formidable that the Europeans were careful not to challenge them. In such circumstances it was the Africans who exploited the needs and weaknesses of the newcomer and the distinction between collaborator and resister tended to become increasingly blurred. The significance of this confused relationship has been explored by Professor R. E. Robinson in an important paper entitled 'Non-European Foundations of European Imperialism: A Sketch for a Theory of Collaboration' in R. Owen & R. Sutcliffe (eds), *Studies in the Theory of Imperialism* (1972).

The establishment of British rule, therefore, followed no simple pattern. In some areas the imperial power superseded a pre-existing political authority; in other areas the pre-existing political authority continued to exist under the dominance of the new imperial power; and in some places the imperial power actually had to create a distinctly political authority in what had previously been stateless societies. But in all three cases the imperial power was quick to assert a legal and rational basis for its position.

In an essay entitled 'Lion Rampant' in the *Journal of Commonwealth Political Studies* for 1964, Professor D. A. Low argued that an important element in the establishment of British imperial authority in the early years stemmed from the desire to incorporate traditionally legitimate political authorities within the imperial system, thus ruling wherever possible through rajas, emirs, nawabs, sultans, chiefs and kings. Rarely, however, did the British reach an understanding with the existing political authorities. Frequently the British came to terms with *parvenus*, newcomers who succeeded to the traditionally legitimate offices because of their alliance with the British. Since the enlistment of foreign aid in internal power struggles was quite acceptable, the fact that these men had not been the rulers before the arrival of the British did not make them any less legitimate in the eyes of their own people. What it did do was to make the rulers more ready to acknowledge the authority of the British who were the best guarantee for their continuing hold on the traditional offices.

Low also suggested that while the British monopoly of coercive powers was an obvious factor of considerable importance, the end to which it was put — the establishment of a *pax* — was equally important. Whatever else the British presence may have led to, the effect of peace was all to the good. In other respects the effects of the imperial presence were limited: very few demands were made in the early stages. Imperial control was generally asserted gradually over a period of years as the administration became stronger. Initially the peoples may have had no concept of an inherent right to independence; a generation soon grew up that knew no order other than European control; and, as time went by, more and more members of the group had a vested interest in the continuance of the existing regime. Rebellion then became a more difficult business, especially once the imperial bureaucracy had begun to establish a strong and effective hold.

This gradual growth of British power on the spot was a more subtle process and entirely separate from the constitutional status as depicted in the language of the lawyers ('spheres of influence', 'paramountcy' and 'protectorate') which frequently had little meaning for the subject peoples. Professor Low ended by suggesting three main stages in the establishment of British rule: *impact* when 'influence' was followed by 'sway'; *domination* when 'ascendancy' turned into 'predominance'; and *control* when 'mastery' became 'dictation'. By abandoning the language of European lawyers, Low constructed a formula of general applicability throughout Africa which is meaningful for both Europeans and Africans.

The gigantic nature of the task, the very speed with which new territory was acquired and the consequent high costs of administration made it more or less inevitable that rule would be established by indirect means. Indeed, the British are chiefly remembered in Africa today for the doctrine of 'indirect rule' developed by Lord Lugard in Nigeria. Lugard believed that earlier attempts at assimilation had been mistaken. Doubtful whether British institutions were capable of being transferred to Africa, he devised a system of government designed to allow the African to adjust to the impact of Western civilisation without losing his identity. Decentralisation and continuity were to be the key features of a unified system of government. The paramount chiefs (with the administrative machinery at their disposal) were to remain as dependent rulers. British residents (district officers) were to advise and cooperate with these chiefs so that the administration developed along its own lines into a system of modern local government. By the utilisation of indigenous institutions and the education of chiefs, continuity with the past would be preserved and the foundations for the future improvement of society laid. It was a neat combination of tradition, Victorian ethics and theory. Lugard publicised his techniques in *Political Memoranda: Revision of Instructions to Political Officers* (1919) and his principles in *The Dual Mandate in British Tropical Africa* (1922). This system, which later became almost a religious dogma, was widely adopted in other parts of British Africa in later years, being revised in the 1930s until it was quietly abandoned in 1947.

From its introduction, 'indirect rule' was a subject for controversy. Lugard and his wife were born propagandists and had the best of the argument in their day. But the system certainly tended to prop up tyrannical, almost feudal, governments; eventually proved unsuitable as a means of administering the social services; and, above all, provided no place for the new educated elite. Such people became not only critics of the system but the agitators for its removal — the centre of a new nationalism. For Africans generally, 'indirect rule' was no more than an imperialist device for prolonging an alien regime. Even Lord Lugard's reputation has recently been blasted. Despite a warmly sympathetic two-volume biography by Dame Margery Perham, evidence for a splendid onslaught on the reasoning behind 'indirect rule', and on the means deployed and the propaganda tactics used by the Lugards to exaggerate its success, has been ably marshalled by I. F. Nicholson in *The Administration of Nigeria 1900–1960: Men, Methods and Myths* (1969). This debate is just beginning.

However, it is quite easy to see that, by the end of Queen Victoria's reign, British administration in Africa, outside the southern part of the continent and the older Crown colonies, was still in its infancy. Pacification had only just begun and resistance still remained to be quelled. Nevertheless the basis of future nationalisms, which were to play such an important part in the eventual decline of the British empire, can already be traced. And this trend is confirmed when we extend the horizon beyond the newly acquired tropical territories to other parts of Africa, to the West Indies and to India.

[44] The New Nationalisms

African nationalism has often been viewed as a phenomenon which emerged after the Second World War. The concept of the 'nation state', it was thought, was entirely alien to the African. Therefore, African nationalism was the product of colonial rule. Consequently most studies of African nationalism tended to concentrate on the development of towns, the spread of education and the growth of westernised elites who were ostracised politically and socially and could not reach the level of employment and salaries that they were qualified to attain. More recently, however, the interplay of modern elements with traditional institutions and customs, which the new indigenous leaders exploited, has been noted. And now that it is gradually becoming accepted that initial African resistance to colonial rule was not always an entirely reactionary and negative matter, it has become possible to see a connection between modern African nationalism and what is usually termed 'primary resistance' and 'secondary opposition' (messianic movements, separatist churches and tribal associations). All these examples of opposition were intended to establish alternative institutions for allegiance, new focal points for rallying the masses and gathering indigenous support against the alien intruders. This link has been argued most effectively in two articles by Professor T. O. Ranger entitled 'Connexions Between "Primary Resistance" Movements and

Modern Mass Nationalism in East and Central Africa' in the *Journal of African History* (1968).

Thus it is not only possible to see that by the turn of the century in many parts of Africa British administration was only making a shaky beginning; it is also possible to trace the seeds of those movements which were to lead to the eventual overthrow of the colonial administration. Sometimes colonial opposition existed continuously from the moment of foreign domination: the frequent deposition of the holders of traditional offices and the taking of sides in civil wars meant that opposition to the new rulers was built in to the system. In other cases colonial nationalism was injected by European ideas and practices or by fundamental changes in society which occurred during the period of occupation. Clearly while a period of colonialism may, in most cases, have been an indispensable pre-condition for African nationalism, its origins can be traced back to traditional institutions as well as new elites.

African nationalism was also influenced by another movement — Pan-Africanism — emanating from the United States and the West Indies. With the benefit of hindsight, it is now possible to see the organisers of this movement as the heralds of a new era, opening up exciting new horizons for ambitious young Africans. One of the earliest pioneers of this idea was Edward Blyden who was born in 1832 in the West Indies. He later moved to Liberia where he became a well-known Islamic scholar and had a varied career as a diplomat. As the first President of the Liberian University, he delivered a foundation address on 'The Idea of an African Personality'. This new emphasis on African individuality, or 'negritude' as it has come to be called, focused attention on the movement for Negro emancipation in the United States.

There had already been limited contact between American blacks and African students attending American Negro colleges. In 1897 John Chilembwe (who in the 1915 rising was to lay the foundations of his place as the folk-hero of modern-day Malawi nationalism) visited the United States and, in the same year, Dr Martin R. Delaney coined the phrase 'Africa for the Africans'. This concept received a gigantic impetus in the early years of the twentieth century from the writings of Dr W. E. B. Du Bois, the first Negro graduate of Harvard, and from the Black Zionist movement of a Jamaican, Marcus Garvey. From the first Pan-African meeting in London in 1900, organised by H. Sylvester Williams, a West Indian barrister, emanated a protest against the treatment of Africans in South Africa and Rhodesia. Little notice was taken. The First Pan-African Congress met in Paris in 1919 in an (unsuccessful) attempt to influence decisions concerning Africa. By the time the Fifth Congress met in Manchester in 1945, attended by Du Bois, George Padmore, Kwame Nkrumah and Jomo Kenyatta among others, African political consciousness had been awakened. A mass movement of Africa for the Africans was under way. The seeds of this movement had been clearly sprouting in 1900; within the next sixty years the harvest was reaped. The formative period of the new national-ism, with its triangular base in Africa, the United States and the West Indies, occurred during the closing years of the nineteenth century and the opening years of the twentieth century. This period also saw the flowering of another national movement of equal importance, this time in the Indian sub-continent.

[45] India from the Mutiny to the Morley–Minto Reforms

By 1900 British rule in India seemed to be firmly entrenched. After the mutiny, the East India Company had been replaced by the pomp, circumstance and arrogance of the British Raj, and the British sense of trusteeship then gave way to the concept of a permanent presence. 'We are all British gentlemen', declared one Viceroy, Lord Mayo, 'engaged in the magnificent work of governing an inferior race.' The brutal episodes in 1857 had led to a bitter hatred between the races and, in the process, the more enlightened ideas about Indian political develop-ment and progress were extinguished.

The structure of the new government had been laid down in the 1858 Government of India Act and the Indian Councils Act of 1861. In Great Britain a Secretary of State for India was appointed to be advised by a quasi-independent Council of fifteen members, most of whom had to have served in India for at least ten years. In India the Governor-General, as representative of the sovereign, assumed the title of Viceroy. He was assisted by a Council of five members each of whom acted as the head of a department of state. The Governor-General-in-Council ruled India. For legislative purposes, however, the Council was expanded in 1861 to include several non-office-holders of whom two were Indians. At the same time legislative functions were restored at provincial level, and so 'Legislative Councils' were created in several provinces. The object seems to have been to associate influential

Indians with the government rather than to obtain a genuine representative element in the legislatures. All real powers remained with the Viceroy's Council. It was, as Sir Charles Wood, the Secretary of State for India (1859–66), described it, 'a despotism controlled from home'.

For the rest of Queen Victoria's reign, the government of India retained this structure, with one addition in 1892. The Indian Councils Act of that year provided for the indirect election of non-official members to the central and provincial Legislative Councils. It was a small political advance but the non-official Indian members always found themselves outnumbered by Europeans. It was hardly a system designed to appeal to the educated Indian elite. Debarred from any effective role in the government, Indians found it equally difficult to enter the civil service. Indian *babus*, especially the despised English-educated Bengalis, were not considered suitable material for what was supposed to be the most talented bureaucracy the world had ever seen. Of course there was open competition but the examinations were held only in London; an Indian candidate would have to raise at least £1,000 to enable him to travel and stay in London; he would have to acquit himself well in Classics and Mathematics; and if he failed the examination there was little likelihood of a second chance as from 1865 the maximum entry age of candidates was twenty-one. The chances of an Indian entering the senior grade of his own civil service were extremely remote. As one Secretary of State for India, the Duke of Argyll, asserted, 'mere intellectual acuteness is no indication of ruling power'. Consequently, it was no accident that only one Indian entered the I.C.S. between 1853 and 1868. By the end of the 1880s there were only a handful of Indians in a service of some 900 ruling a population in excess of 250 million.

Obviously the British Raj depended on the collaboration of the few and on its passive acceptance by the multitude. The first Viceroy, 'Clemency' Canning, sought to buttress British rule with the support of the upper classes of Indian society and attempted to strengthen the loyalty of the Indian princes by giving them an interest in the maintenance of British power. The princes in the 'protected states', which contained a quarter of India's population, could normally be relied upon. At a lower level landlords were given proprietary rights and a few were appointed magistrates. Then there were the small elite of the I.C.S., the minor public officials and professional men who earned their living by serving the new regime — the teachers, doctors, lawyers, journalists, engineers, railway workers, technicians, clerks, and soldiers who owed their position and income to the British. These men had a stake in the Raj and these were the men the British needed to cultivate.

Unfortunately, in the atmosphere of post-1857 India, this was one thing the British were not prepared to do. And so, when Disraeli's Viceroy, Lord Lytton (1876–80), ruled India for the benefit of the rulers — he reduced tariffs on British goods, circumscribed the vernacular press and lowered the maximum age for entry into the I.C.S. to nineteen — and when the imperious Curzon (1898–1905) roused Indian passions and alienated the princes — calling them 'a set of unruly and ignorant and rather undisciplined school-boys' — the British were courting trouble. Only for one short period, when Gladstone returned to power in 1880 and Lord Ripon was Viceroy (1880–4), did the old idea of trusteeship temporarily re-emerge. Gladstone maintained that the British purpose was not to support the feudal classes but to train Indians to govern themselves. Unhappily, Gladstone was too pre-occupied elsewhere to devote much attention to India, and the visionary plans of Ripon came to nothing. Consequently, as the hopes and aspirations of the new elite faded, a sense of frustration arose which eventually touched even those who had made successful careers in the Raj. The British-built railways and the spread of newspapers made possible, for the first time, all-India associations. It was the efforts of these new middle-class associations that led to India's political awakening.

The new elite had been educated in the English language and had imbibed British liberal traditions. These men were aware of the growth of responsible government in the colonies of British settlement and of the existence of representative institutions in other parts of the empire. Naturally such middle-class organisations as the British Indian Association, the London India Society and the East India Association soon demanded 'Representative and Responsible Government for India'.

This movement led to the foundation of the Indian National Congress in 1885. One of its leading spirits was an Englishman, Allan Octavian Hume, son of the Radical MP Joseph Hume, and a former member of the I.C.S. Hume acted as Secretary-General for the first twenty years of Congress's existence, during which time no fewer than four Englishmen served as President. The Congress, an assembly of seventy-two delegates, took the form of an annual conference and seminars. The delegates were well-educated moderates and the tone of their proceedings was dominated by an unswerving loyalty to the British Crown.

The British connection was regarded as a blessing and the demands
were moderate in the extreme: some form of election to the Legislative
Councils; simultaneous examinations for the I.C.S. in London and
India, the maximum age of entrants to be raised to not less than twenty-
three; Indians to be given commissions in the army; and the restoration
of a duty on cotton imports. In fact, the delegates demanded more
employment in the official service, so that better use of their services
could be made. Thus successive Viceroys seemed to regard the Congress
as a suitable 'safety valve' for pent-up grievances. Even in 1895, the
eleventh India National Congress merely appealed to the 'august
mother of free nations' for a gradual transformation of the character
of British rule:

> to liberalize it, to shift its foundations, to adapt it to the newly-developed
> environments of the country and the people, so that, in the fullness of
> time, India may find its place in the great confederacy of free States,
> English in their origin, English in their character, English in their
> institutions, rejoicing in their permanent and indissoluble union with
> England, a glory to the mother-country, and an honour to the human
> race.

By 1900 Curzon considered the tea-party was nearly over:

> My own belief is that the Congress is tottering to its fall, and one of my
> greatest ambitions while in India is to assist it to a peaceful demise.

But Curzon was far from right. Congress was destined to become one of
the largest political mass organisations in the world. And Curzon was
to have a role in pointing Congress towards its manifest destiny.

Curzon, full of boundless energy and reforming zeal, descended on
India in 1898. After a promising career as Parliamentary Under-
Secretary at the Foreign and India Offices and a dazzling marriage to
an American heiress, he was appointed Viceroy at the early age of
thirty-nine. Curzon was born to rule and the Indian sub-continent
seemed to provide a suitable realm for his dominion. In some respects
Curzon was well-qualified for the post. He possessed immense powers of
work and an unswerving dedication to duty; he was high-minded,
impartial and incorruptible; he was filled with missionary idealism and
an enthusiasm to uphold the empire of India — 'the miracle of the
world'. But he was also vain, petty, rude, impatient and overbearing.
He could not delegate responsibility and treated subordinates as though
they were serfs. Indians he chose to ignore. Curzon's viceroyalty was one
of autocratic grandeur aptly symbolised by a remote figure swaying on

the back of a gorgeously bedecked elephant on ceremonial occasions.

Curzon's intentions were good enough. He instigated improvements in education, the railway system and irrigation; he sponsored research into agriculture and arranged better credit facilities for farmers; he also stamped out every abuse in army and administration that he came across. These were notable successes. But he also had his failures. Most prominent of these was the uproar surrounding his decision in the interest of administrative efficiency to partition the largest province, Bengal. Only a man of Curzon's olympian insensitivity could have remained unaware of the dangers of dividing a predominantly Hindu community of 78 million into two separate provinces: West Bengal, with a Hindu population of 47 million in which Bengalis now found themselves a minority amongst Biharis and Oriyas; and East Bengal and Assam, with a mainly Muslim population of 31 million. It led to an immediate Hindu agitation in Bengal and a widespread boycott of British manufactures. The partition provided the Indians with their first truly national grievance.

The reverberations were immediately felt in Congress. The aims and methods of the moderates had already been challenged and a new 'extremist' Hindu party had grown up under the leadership of Bal Gangadhar Tilak who now raised the slogan 'swaraj' (self-rule). Freedom, not partnership, was the new cry. The 'extremists' regarded the alien British presence as an evil and emphasised the glories of their own past, the Hindu scriptures and Indian languages — anything which demonstrated their separateness. They encouraged acts of terrorism. Religion had the greatest direct appeal and revivalist movements aimed at restoring Hinduism to its ancient purity.

This repeated emphasis on the Hindu religion caused the Muslims to establish their own political organisation. Most educated Indians were Hindus; if Congress achieved any constitutional advances the Muslims could not hope to benefit to the same extent. Not only were they less educated in the British ways, but they were a smaller section of the community — 70 per cent being Hindu, 21 per cent Muslim. Therefore leading Muslims met at Dacca in Eastern Bengal in December 1906 and formed the All-India Muslim League. The League aimed at protecting the political rights and interests of the Muslims and showing their loyalty to the British. A resolution was passed supporting the partition of Bengal. There were now two political organisations to be reckoned with.

As unrest grew in India and the acts of terrorism increased, the moderate nationalist leader, Gopal Krishna Gokhale, pleaded in London with the elderly Liberal Secretary of State, John Morley. Administrative reform and increased Indian participation in government were clearly needed to quell the unrest. Morley, who believed that Gokhale's request to treat India 'on the same footing as our self-governing colonies like Canada' was a 'fantastic and ludicrous dream', consulted the Viceroy. The Morley–Minto reforms were the result. Though the opinions of the two men diverged, both agreed that the government of India had to remain autocratic. Their reforms, therefore, merely tinkered with the structure of government: two Indians were admitted to the Council of the Secretary of State in London and one Indian each to the Executive Council of the Governor-General and the Governors. By the Indian Councils Act 1909, the Indian membership of the central Legislative Council was also expanded and for the first time communal electorates were introduced — with separate seats for Muslim representatives. The 'loyal' Muslims received their reward. Similar changes were made at provincial Legislative Council level. Once again a small political advance had been made.

But, as in other parts of the empire, mere tinkering with the constitution was not enough. The British had refused to state an ultimate goal for India. There was no time-table for self-government. Nevertheless, even more than in Africa and the Caribbean, the strength of national sentiment (as well as the divisions within Indian society) had been demonstrated. When Queen Victoria died the Indian empire appeared to be at its most splendid; but the British Raj was not destined to last another half-century. As S. Gopal commented in *British Policy in India 1858–1905* (1965), the viceroyalty of Curzon marked the apogee of British Indian administration, the beginnings of adult Indian nationalism and also the start of the revolution which reached its goal in 1947.

[46] South Africa to the Union

In South Africa the British government was confronted by an equally perplexing situation and equally important decisions were made. Milner and Chamberlain had led Great Britain into the Boer War in order to ensure British supremacy throughout South Africa. But how was military victory to be translated into enduring British supremacy in a country where the British were outnumbered by Afrikaners and the two groups together were outnumbered by Africans? Milner's answer was clear:

> The *ultimate* end is a self-governing white Community, supported by *well-treated* and *justly governed* black labour from Cape Town to Zambesi.

He intended to achieve this aim by massive British immigration to swamp the Boers and by a policy of 'modernisation' in the two new Crown colonies — a liberal educational system, economic development and efficient administration. Self-government could then be granted to the Boers and the various colonies of South Africa could be welded into a new federal Dominion under the safe guidance of a British political majority which would treat the African peoples fairly. The solution was simple but the goal proved unattainable. No mass wave of British immigration was forthcoming and the war, combined with the activities of Milner, gave Afrikaner nationalism a powerful boost which made it stronger than it had ever been before. By the time Milner left South Africa in 1905, his conditions for granting self-government to the Afrikaners had not been achieved and the new Dominion seemed as far off as ever. Milner's term of office ended with about as much success as that of the other great pro-consul of empire — Lord Curzon in India.

However, political advance was not long delayed. In December 1905 Henry Campbell-Bannerman formed a Liberal administration and won a land-slide victory in January 1906. The new government granted responsible government to the former republics after framing a constitution which they hoped would maintain British preponderance. But *Het Volk* won a majority of the seats in the election of February 1907. Thus, within five years of the end of the Boer War, the British handed back the conduct of internal affairs to the Afrikaners. This was all the more remarkable as the new constitutions for the Boer communities provided for an all-white male adult electorate. Never before, not in the 1853 Cape Constitution nor in the Natal Constitution of 1856, had the British consented to make race a criterion for participation in the political system. It is true the Peace of Vereeniging had left the native franchise for consideration after self-government had been granted, but Asians and Coloured peoples were not similarly debarred from receiving the vote. The British, however, had no wish to outrage the Boers. Campbell-Bannerman's Liberal government made no attempt to alter the structure of society or the distribution of political power in the former republics before handing back the reins of government. It was a

precipitate decision crucial for the future: the unforeseen price of un-
intended magnanimity was paid by the African and non-European
peoples of the whole of South Africa.

After the first general elections in 1907, the Afrikaner parties formed
governments in the Transvaal and the Orange River Colony. In
February 1908, John X. Merriman, of English origin, formed a Bond-
supported ministry in the Cape. Three of the self-governing colonies
were now ruled by Afrikaner parties. By this time also, all four governments were receptive to ideas of integration. The Cape and Natal had
been badly hit by a post-war economic recession and events in Natal —
the Zulu uprising in 1906 — convinced most South African whites that
some form of union was essential. And so, finally, eight years to the day
after the Peace of Vereeniging had been signed, the Union of South
Africa was born with Louis Botha as its first Prime Minister. The
constitution of the new Dominion was a unitary one. Significantly the
Cape franchise remained the only franchise knowing no colour bar. It
was the last great retreat of the British in South Africa.

The interests of the native Africans had been sacrificed as the price of
unity and conciliation. A new state had indeed been born. But it was a
state with a caste-like society. Thus, within a few years of Queen
Victoria's death, the aim of many late Victorian policy makers had
been achieved — but the new Dominion lacked a sense of 'British
nationality' and was the fulfilment of Afrikaner unity. The Boers
rejoiced in their new-found freedom.

[47] Dominion Status

In the Victorian empire, annexation and devolution occurred side by
side. As British rule and influence expanded in the new Crown colonies
and protectorates of the late Victorian era, so British power and
influence contracted in the colonies of British settlement. The rise of the
'new nationalisms', especially among Indians and Boers, had been
preceded by a strong sense of separate development in the self-governing
colonies — Canada, Australia and New Zealand. The 'quiet revolution'
of responsible government in the early and mid-Victorian decades had
proved to be a transitory phase and colonial provincialism was replaced
by a growing nationalism.

The responsibly governed colonies began to demand greater local
initiative. The British government accepted a Canadian protective

tariff in 1859. A South Australian constitutional crisis resulted in the Colonial Laws Validity Act of 1865 which permitted colonial parliaments to amend their own constitutions within the limits of the 'colonial law for the time being in force in the said colony' and confirmed that only colonial laws which conflicted with British Acts of Parliament or Orders-in-Council would in future be disallowed. In 1871 Sir John Macdonald, the Canadian Prime Minister, became one of the signatories to the Treaty of Washington. In 1880 Canada appointed the first High Commissioner in London. In 1883 the Canadians sent their first independent envoy to a conference on submarine cables in Paris. And so, although the Foreign Office continued to conduct foreign affairs for the empire as a whole, the Canadians were consulted whenever their interests were at stake and even acted as British delegates in minor diplomatic matters. Sole British control of the empire's foreign policy had been breached and the other self-governing colonies began, as soon as they were able, to demand similar privileges.

In the matter of imperial defence, however, it was the mother country which took the lead. In 1887 Lord Salisbury invited to a colonial conference several public men from the colonies who were in London for Queen Victoria's Golden Jubilee celebrations. Once the conference assembled, Salisbury disclosed its purpose as he dwelt on that one peculiarity which distinguished the British empire from others: 'a want of continuity; it is separated into parts by large stretches of ocean; and what we are here for today is to see how far we must acquiesce in the conditions which that separation causes, how far we can obliterate them by agreement and organisation'. The colonists were not impressed. Federation was dismissed out of hand and the only support the government received for imperial defence was an offer from Australia and New Zealand to subsidise an auxiliary naval squadron in Australasian waters.

In 1897, during Queen Victoria's Diamond Jubilee celebrations, another colonial conference was convened. Once again the question of federation was raised and once again it was given short shrift. This time, however, the Colonial Secretary, Joseph Chamberlain, pressed the colonial premiers more urgently about imperial defence. But, once again, the response was disappointing: Cape Colony offered an unconditional contribution to the Royal Navy and the Australian colonies increased their earlier contribution.

More encouraging, however, was the colonial response at a time of real need. During the Boer War contingents came to British assistance from Australia, New Zealand and, on a voluntary basis, from Canada. The self-governing colonies supported Great Britain in a war in which they had little direct interest. Reinforced by these events, Joseph Chamberlain made a further appeal for defence contributions at another colonial conference assembled in 1902 on the occasion of Edward VII's coronation. This time he suggested an Imperial Council and an Imperial Reserve. Neither suggestion was acceptable. Sir Wilfrid Laurier arrived from Canada determined to oppose 'a school in England and Canada . . . which wants to bring Canada into the vortex of militarism which is now the curse and blight of Europe'. The Imperial Reserve was rejected and only small additional financial contributions for the Royal Navy were forthcoming from the Cape Colony, Natal, New Zealand, Newfoundland and Australia. Imperial federation was not even discussed. The only important outcome was the decision to continue the conferences at four-yearly intervals.

Clearly, in view of the growth of colonial nationalism some new definition of the relationship between mother country and self-governing colony was necessary. The very word 'colony' implied an inferiority which was intensely disliked. Sir Wilfrid Laurier, the most forthright champion of colonial independence, announced in 1900:

> I claim for Canada this, that in future, Canada shall be at liberty to act or not act, to interfere or not interfere, to do just as she pleases, and that she shall reserve to herself the right to judge whether or not there is cause for her to act.

No one denied that Canada had such a right. In 1900 the empire was at war, but the contribution made by the self-governing colonies was for local decision. Even Milner, the great imperial pro-consul in South Africa, could describe the empire in the year of Queen Victoria's death as 'a group of sister nations spread throughout the world, united and not divided by the ocean, each independent in its own concerns, all indissolubly allied for a common purpose, all free and willing subjects of the most ancient and august Monarchy in the world'. The self-governing colonies were naturally eager to receive official acknowledgement of this status.

This was achieved at the first of the new quadrennial conferences organised in 1907. The designation 'Dominion' was adopted to distinguish the self-governing colonies from the rest of the empire. The establishment of an 'Imperial Council' was also finally rejected. Instead the conference was renamed an 'Imperial Conference' with the Prime

Minister of the United Kingdom as president and the Prime Ministers of the Dominions as *ex officio* members along with the Secretary of State for the Colonies. A permanent secretariat was to be created inside the Colonial Office. Thus the conferences became institutionalised with fixed membership and regular meetings, all matters to be decided on the basis of 'one government, one vote'. These conferences were the forerunners of the later Commonwealth heads of government meetings and 1907 marked the first official administrative recognition in London of the gradual transformation of Empire into Commonwealth. Within a few years of Queen Victoria's death, decisions had been made which became landmarks in the future development of India, South Africa and the Commonwealth as a whole.

[48] The Tariff Reform Movement

If there were certain stresses evident within the British empire at the turn of the century — in the Crown colonies and protectorates, in India and in the self-governing colonies — the stresses coming from outside the empire were of even greater importance in the passing of the *Pax Britannica*. After 1870 the mid-Victorian boom began to fade. In the last quarter of the nineteenth century, as the 'Great Depression' descended, Great Britain began to experience large fluctuations in her economy, a contraction of her export industries and bouts of serious unemployment. Most alarming of all was the new challenge from competitors who had grown up behind the protective walls of foreign tariff barriers. The golden age of British manufacturing and trade was over.

What remedy was there? The Birmingham Chamber of Commerce thought they had the answer. Their delegates, reporting in 1885 to a Commission of Inquiry into the causes of the decline of British commerce, complained:

> We are being ruined. We work as hard now as ever but without profit. . . . Protective tariffs have closed the civilized markets to us. . . . Under the shelter of tariffs, Germany and America have developed their factories, and making their profit out of home sales, the Germans throw the surplus on our markets at absurdly low prices. Time was when the Asiatic and Oceanian East purchased our nails. Today German nails actually compete here in our own market of Birmingham. Buttons,

which we used to sell to the whole of Europe, now come to us from
Germany instead. German iron wire is now sold in our Birmingham
shops. . . .

The remedy proposed by the Chamber of Commerce was simple:

Commercial union with our Colonies, A Customs Union comparable
to the German Zollverein should be established between them and the
home country.

The solution appealed to one leading politician — Joseph Chamberlain.

The suggestion appeared to make sound sense. In 1900, trade with
the empire constituted only one-third of British overseas trade. The
possibilities of development seemed tremendous. If only the empire
could be welded into a commercial whole, foreign goods could be
excluded, British industries protected, a safe market secured in the
colonies, colonial raw materials and food could be admitted cheaply
and Great Britain's status as a world power would be ensured in the
twentieth century. So evolved Chamberlain's visionary scheme of an
imperial customs union improving British trade prospects, permitting
social reform at home and the development of the backward portions
of the British empire.

Chamberlain launched his campaign for tariff reform on 15 May
1903. He resigned office in September 1903 to take the campaign into
the country. Balfour's Cabinet was split over the issue; the Unionist
party was in disarray; the Liberal party, for once, was triumphantly
united. Not surprisingly, in view of the increasing unpopularity of
Balfour's administration, the Conservatives lost the election of January
1906 and the Liberals returned to power.

Even if the 'fetish of free trade' had not secured the defeat of tariff
reform, it is extremely unlikely whether the self-governing colonies
would have been prepared to cooperate. Chamberlain's suggestion of
an imperial common market had no appeal in the Dominions. They
wished to continue protecting their infant industries and had no wish
to join a free trade area with one of the world's most industrially
advanced countries. In many cases tariffs also provided a source of
national revenue — and fiscal autonomy would not be foregone for the
sake of the empire. What the colonies wanted was imperial preference
in the form of differential duties. Preference was compatible with
protection at home and special trading relations with members of the
empire overseas. Canada, during the years 1897–1900, had given
33⅓ per cent preference to British manufactures. But it evoked no

British response. Instead the Dominions tried to arrange a preferential system among themselves.

Thus with this divergence of interest, the trade policy of the empire could not be centralised. Great Britain continued to be an essentially free-trading nation for another thirty years. When challenged by foreign competitors, she retreated into her satellite world of formal and informal colonies. The cotton industry, for example, turned from Europe and North America to Asia and Africa; iron and steel also came to rely on the empire and underdeveloped world. This shift of markets was an easier, cheaper and more convenient alternative to modernisation. Thus, between 1860 and 1890, the world's leading and most dynamic industrial economy degenerated into one of the more sluggish and conservative. By 1900, Great Britain no longer possessed a competitive economy but was, instead, living off the remains of her former world monopoly and her past accumulation of wealth. By the end of the century one of the nineteenth-century bases of Britain's greatness — the lead given by early industrialisation — had gone for ever. The end of the *Pax Britannica* was near.

[49] New Trends in British Foreign Policy

The *Pax Britannica* had always been something of a mirage. In the nineteenth century Great Britain never tried to act as the world's policeman. She intervened only where her immediate interests were at stake and normally only where naval intervention was likely to be effective. In the late nineteenth century the growing British pre-occupation with imperial federation, an imperial customs union, an Imperial Reserve and colonial contributions to the Royal Navy, was the product of an increasing sense of insecurity. In the competitive climate of the 1890s Great Britain greatly enlarged her imperial commitments and responsibilities — at a time when her ability to defend an empire which extended as far east as Wei-hai-wei was falling into question. Joseph Chamberlain earnestly instructed the Dominion Prime Ministers at the colonial conference of 1902:

> We do require your assistance in the administration of the vast Empire which is yours as well as ours. The weary Titan staggers under the too vast orb of its fate. We have borne the burden for many years. We think it is time that our children should assist us to support it. . . .

His fear that Great Britain may at last have overreached herself was a very real one.

By 1902 British defence capabilities seemed to be stretched to the limit. In Africa, Great Britain, immediately after two striking military and diplomatic successes at Omdurman and Fashoda, had endured the humiliation of the Boer War. In South America, Great Britain had bowed before the American assertion of the Monroe Doctrine, settled her differences over Venezuela by arbitration and reluctantly agreed to the building of the Panama Canal on American terms in the Hay–Pauncefote Treaty. In the Near East, Great Britain, no longer being able to force the Straits, had ceased to play a leading role in the Eastern Question. On the borders of India, the empire continued to be threatened by Russian activities in or near Persia, Afghanistan and Tibet. And in the Far East, the continued Russian presence in Manchuria after the Boxer Rising had been crushed provided Great Britain with the greatest threat she had yet had to face in this part of the world. In extent, British commitments and responsibilities were global. It was questionable whether Great Britain could continue to stand alone and still defend these world-wide interests. Not all members of the Cabinet possessed Salisbury's confidence. A policy of 'splendid isolation', it was urged at the time, was becoming outdated.

This much over-worked cliché, apparently coined in the Canadian Parliament in 1896, was adopted by Chamberlain to stigmatise the Prime Minister's policy. The difficult times the British people were experiencing made its use popular. However, the phrase was never associated with Salisbury personally by his contemporaries. It referred to the age-old policy of not making peace-time alliances, especially those containing a *casus belli*. Ever since 1815, Great Britain had tried to cooperate with those powers who wished to preserve European peace. Salisbury merely continued this trend. In a characteristic speech in Caernarvon in April 1888 he declared:

> We belong to a great community of nations, and we have no right to shrink from the duties which the interests of the community impose upon us. There is all the difference in the world between good-natured, good-humoured effort to keep well with your neighbours, and that spirit of haughty and sullen isolation which has been dignified by the name 'non-intervention'. We are part of the community of Europe, and we must do our duty as such.

But the Prime Minister's obviously declining grip on political matters and the growing difficulties in the world made others doubt the efficacy of a policy of acting without allies in the future. In 1900 the rapidly ageing Salisbury was eased out of the Foreign Office.

One general cause of concern was the gradual undermining of British naval supremacy. Ambitious naval construction programmes embarked upon by Japan, Germany and the United States at the end of the century seemed likely to put the 1889 Two-Power Standard — a British fleet equal to that of the two strongest naval powers in any part of the globe — beyond British reach. Of more immediate concern was Russian penetration into northern China. Previously naval supremacy had determined the balance of power in the Far East. The British fleet could not, however, forestall Russian penetration overland. The need to contain the Russian advance caused Joseph Chamberlain to campaign for an alliance with Germany. What the British had to offer that would make it worthwhile for Germany to take on Russia or France for British imperial interests, however, was never considered. Thus the approaches came to nothing: objections to the German conditions for an alliance were, declared Lord Lansdowne, the new Foreign Secretary, 'virtually insuperable'. But he also insisted:

> We may push too far the argument that, because we have in the past survived in spite of our isolation, we need have no misgivings as to the effect of that isolation in the future.

When direct approaches to Russia were unproductive, therefore, he looked with favour on the possibility of an alliance with Japan.

Japan's interests coincided with Great Britain's in the need to stem the Russian advance into China. Japan also possessed the means and the will to oppose that advance. Neither Salisbury, Chamberlain nor Lansdowne liked the Japanese conditions, which included British recognition of Korea as a Japanese sphere of influence and British agreement to maintain a naval force in Pacific waters equal to that of any other power in the Far East. Fear that Japan might come to terms with Russia, however, overrode these doubts. The alliance was signed on 30 January 1902.

The Anglo-Japanese alliance has frequently been regarded as a turning-point in British foreign policy: a turning away from 'splendid isolation' to the policy of understandings, limited commitments and increasing involvement in continental politics which characterised British policy in the decade before 1914. Salisbury certainly agreed that it marked the end of the policy of cooperation without alliances, and Lansdowne, in presenting the alliance to Parliament, urged the

Lords to forget musty formulas and 'old-fashioned superstitions' about the desirability of isolation. However, it is misleading to confuse this alliance with the British position in Europe. The Japanese agreement was a purely regional pact to cope with the situation in Asia. If anything, it made a European alliance less necessary. Once she had obtained support in the crucial area where she was most vulnerable, Great Britain had a growing confidence in her world position. No other obligation to go to war was entered into before the First World War. The Anglo-Japanese alliance was to be the exception, not the rule.

By the Anglo-Japanese alliance Great Britain regained her free hand. She possessed an ally in the front line against Russia in the Far East and now felt strong enough to resist Russia in Persia and India. But the most significant repercussions probably concerned Japanese preparations for war against Russia. Alarmed by the prospect of a Russo-Japanese war in which the allies of the two combatants might become involved, the French Foreign Minister, Theophile Delcassé, set about restoring good relations with Great Britain. The French already had enough problems of their own, especially in Morocco where the government of the Sultan collapsed towards the end of 1902. Accordingly, when Lansdowne proposed a general *détente*, an amicable settlement was quickly arranged: Great Britain could remain in Egypt; France could take Morocco. Thus the Egyptian question, which had bedevilled British foreign policy since 1882, was finally removed from Anglo-French relations. Outstanding colonial disputes from Newfoundland to Siam and from West Africa to the New Hebrides were also settled and the Entente Cordiale came into operation in April 1904.

Was this another new departure in British foreign policy? On the contrary, Salisbury's son informed Balfour in 1905:

> In truth the French agreement was in its inception not a departure from our previous foreign policy, but strictly in accordance with it. For the last twenty years we have been engaged with different Powers, notably with Germany and with France, in adjusting conflicting claims, and in bargaining so as to get rid of causes of friction . . .

Great Britain's subsequent *détente* with Russia in 1907, in an attempt to sort out disputes over Persia, Afghanistan and Tibet, was the logical culmination of the policy which Salisbury had begun in 1895–6.

Thus the years 1895–1907 witnessed an important new trend in Great Britain's relations with other states. It is not satisfactory, however, to describe this process simply as the end of isolation. Great Britain certainly felt 'isolated' at the end of the century in the sense that she had no continental allies. But this was to be true of the future as it had been true of the past since the time of the Crimean War. The change is better described as the adoption of different practical arrangements for looking after British interests. The vital decisions were taken in a piecemeal fashion and did not form part of an articulate plan. The reorientation began with the decision in 1889 to remain in Egypt, a decision which removed the need to support Turkish territorial integrity. This decision inaugurated a drift away from co-operation with the central powers, a tendency that was never anti-German in origin and was only gradually realised. Only through the consequences of a 'new course', developed piecemeal and almost blindly, did Great Britain and Germany begin to drift apart. In fact it was the attempts Germany made to break the *ententes* and the bullying policy of blackmail she adopted, especially in the two Moroccan crises, which forced Great Britain and France closer together. Hitherto the arrangements Great Britain had made to protect her world-wide interests had been dictated by the simple facts of geography. After the first Moroccan crisis British eyes were concentrated not on the peripheries of their empire, but on the balance of power in Europe.

[50] The End of an Era

Queen Victoria lived on for three weeks into the twentieth century. She died on 22 January 1901. It was appropriate that the Victorian age should come to an end as the twentieth century dawned. In 1897 the British empire had reached its zenith. The Diamond Jubilee celebrations witnessed scenes of imperial splendour and pageantry presided over by a frail and ageing Queen who, being scarcely able to walk, sat in her carriage for the Service of Thanksgiving outside St Paul's Cathedral. It was a moment of tremendous pride in empire. It was the time of jingoism in the music halls with hearty renderings of 'Rule Britannia!' and 'Soldiers of the Queen'. It was the time of literary excesses by admirers of the empire and of the cheap popular press feeding the imaginations of millions with stories of imperial greatness. Great Britain was both the land of hope and the land of glory.

The years 1897–1900 saw the 'Climax of Imperialism'. Imperialism had become a sanctified philosophy. For some, like Milner, it possessed 'all the depth and comprehensiveness of a religious faith'. Curzon declared:

> In Empire we have found not merely the key to glory and wealth, but the call to duty, and the means of service to mankind.

The British empire was a proud nation's gift to humanity. Never before and never again was the empire to be such a popular symbol of British power, achievement and future hopes. In the last burst of imperial pride and blustering patriotism the Unionist government appealed to the electorate and achieved a resounding victory in the 'Khaki Election' of 1900.

The Boer War, however, marked the end of the British sense of invulnerability. Great Britain was seen to be detested in many quarters of the globe. There were ominous clouds forming over Europe and Asia which threatened British imperial interests. Within the empire itself, the self-governing colonies were demanding further recognition of their autonomy, India was sitting uneasily under the rule of Curzon and the problems of pacification and administration in the new Crown colonies and protectorates had yet to be grappled with. In 1902 a more solemn air of reality descended on the British people. The death of Queen Victoria was accompanied by a decline in Victorian ideals and aspirations and by the end of Victorian optimism and sense of superiority.

This mood of presentiment was evident in 1897. It was most notably captured in Kipling's 'Recessional':

> If, drunk with sight of power, we loose
> > Wild tongues that have not Thee in awe,
> Such boastings as the Gentiles use
> > Or lesser breeds without the Law —
> Lord God of Hosts, be with us yet,
> Lest we forget — lest we forget!
>
> For heathen heart that puts her trust
> > In reeking tube and iron shard,
> All valiant dust that builds on dust,
> > And guarding, call not Thee to guard,
> For frantic boast and foolish word —
> Thy mercy on Thy People, Lord!

As the national mood of self-praise and congratulations engulfed the British public, Kipling warned that sterner virtues would be required if

Great Britain were to retain her place in the world. Kipling returned to this theme in 'The Islanders', published in 1902, in which he poured scorn on 'the flannelled fools at the wicket' and 'the muddied oafs at the goals'. By then the Boer War had pointed the moral.

In fact, the wild rejoicing which accompanied the relief of Mafeking and the end of the Boer War was the reaction of an uncertain people. In January 1902 Joseph Chamberlain admitted:

> We are people of a great empire. . . . We are the most hated nation of the world and also the best loved. . . . We have the feeling, unfortunately, that we have to count upon ourselves alone, and I say, therefore, it is the duty of British statesmen and it is the duty of the British people to count upon themselves alone, as their ancestors did. I say alone, yes in splendid isolation, surrounded by our kinsfolk.

At the turn of the century British fears and uncertainties were masked by an upsurge of arrogance and near-hysteria.

By the end of Victoria's reign a huge area of the globe had been painted red. The British ruled an empire which embraced a quarter of mankind and covered a quarter of the earth's surface. Then, it hardly seemed conceivable that Britannia's heritage was not destined to last for much more than fifty years. Yet in 1897 Kipling had been filled with a sense of foreboding:

> The tumult and the shouting dies;
> > The Captains and the Kings depart:
> Still stands Thine ancient sacrifice,
> > An humble and a contrite heart.
> Lord God of Hosts, be with us yet,
> Lest we forget — lest we forget!
>
> Far-called, our navies melt away;
> > On dune and headland sinks the fire:
> Lo, all our pomp of yesterday
> > Is one with Nineveh and Tyre!
> Judge of the Nations, spare us yet,
> Lest we forget — lest we forget!

In January 1901 the death of Queen Victoria marked the passing of the golden age of the British empire.

PRINCIPAL EVENTS, 1902–10

1902   Anglo-Japanese alliance. Colonial conference

1903   Chamberlain resigns and campaigns in the country for Tariff Reform. Durbar at Delhi

242 THE PASSING OF THE PAX BRITANNICA

1904   Anglo-French *entente*
1905   Alberta and Saskatchewan created. Bengal partitioned. Balfour government resigns in December
1906   Liberal landslide victory at General Election. Responsible government established in the Transvaal. All-India Muslim League founded
1907   Anglo-Russian *entente*. Responsible government in Orange River Colony. Imperial conference
1909   Morley–Minto Reforms. Indian Councils Act
1910   Union of South Africa

Further Reading

A. P. Thornton, *The Imperial Idea and its Enemies: A Study in British Power*. Macmillan (London, 1959).
R. Price, *An Imperial War and the British Working Class*. Routledge & Kegan Paul (London, 1972).
R. E. Robinson, 'Non-European Foundation of European Imperialism: A Sketch for a Theory of Collaboration' in R. Owen & R. Sutcliffe, *Studies in the Theory of Imperialism*. Longmans (London, 1972).
D. A. Low, *Lion Rampant: essays in the study of British imperialism*. Cass (London, 1973).
M. Perham, *Lugard: the Life of Frederick Dealtry Lugard*. Collins, 2 vols (London, 1956 & 1960).
I. F. Nicholson, *The Administration of Nigeria, 1900 to 1906: Men, Methods and Myths*. Oxford University Press (London, 1969).
T. O. Ranger, 'Connexions between "Primary Resistance" and Modern Mass Nationalism in East and Central Africa', *Journal of African History*, Vol. IX, pp. 440–53 & 631–41 (1968).
R. O. Collins, *Problems in the History of Colonial Africa, 1860–1960*. Prentice Hall (Englewood Cliffs, N.J., 1970).
S. Gopal, *British Policy in India, 1858–1905*. Cambridge University Press (Cambridge. 1965).
P. Woodruff, *The Men who Ruled India*, Vol. II: *The Guardians*. Cape (London, 1954).
R. J. Moore, *Liberalism and Indian Politics, 1872–1922*. Arnold (London, 1966).
B. N. Pandey, *The Break-Up of British India*. Macmillan (London, 1969).
A. Seal, *The Emergence of Indian Nationalism*. Cambridge University Press (Cambridge, 1968).
D. Dilks, *Curzon in India*. Hart-Davis, 2 vols (London, 1969–70).
G. H. Le May, *British Supremacy in South Africa, 1899–1907*. Oxford University Press (London, 1965).
L. M. Thompson, *The Unification of South Africa, 1902–10*. Oxford University Press (London, 1960).

D. C. Gordon, *The Dominion Partnership in Imperial Defence, 1870–1914.* Johns Hopkins (Baltimore, 1965).

J. E. Kendle, *The Colonial and Imperial Conferences, 1887–1911.* Longmans (London, 1967).

D. M. L. Farr, *The Colonial Office and Canada, 1867–87.* Toronto University Press (Toronto, 1955).

B. H. Brown, *The Tariff Reform Movement in Great Britain, 1881–95.* Columbia University Press (New York, 1943).

B. Semmel, *Imperialism and Social Reform.* Allen & Unwin (London, 1960).

C. H. D. Howard, *Splendid Isolation. A Study of ideas concerning Britain's international position and foreign policy during the later years of the third Marquis of Salisbury.* Macmillan (London, 1967).

I. Nish, *The Anglo-Japanese Alliance: The Diplomacy of Two Island Empires, 1894–1907.* Athlone Press (London, 1966).

G. Monger, *The End of Isolation: British Foreign Policy, 1900–07.* Nelson (London, 1963).

C. J. Lowe & M. L. Dockrill, *The Mirage of Power: British Foreign Policy, 1902–14.* Routledge & Kegan Paul (London, 1972).

M. Beloff, *Imperial Sunset: Britain's Liberal Empire, 1897–1921.* Methuen (London, 1969).

B. Porter, *Critics of Empire: British radical attitudes to colonialism in Africa, 1895–1914.* Macmillan (London, 1969).

J. Morris, *Pax Britannica: The Climax of an Empire.* Faber (London, 1968).

General Index

Index of historians and economists referred to in the text